# Manual

of

# Patrology.

By The Rev. Bernard Schmid, o. s. b.

With the Approbation of the Archbishop of Freiburg.

Freely Translated from the Fifth German Edition by
a Benedictine.

Revised, with notes and additions for English readers,
by the

## Right Rev. Mgr. V. J. Schobel, D.D.

With a Preface by the Right Rev. J. H. Hedley, O. S. B.,
Bishop of Newport.

St. Louis, Mo., 1899.
Published by B. Herder,
17 South Broadway.

NIHIL OBSTAT
STI. LUDOVICI, DIE 3. DECEMBRIS 1898.
F. G. HOLWECK,
CENSOR LIBRORUM.

IMPRIMATUR
ST. LOUIS, MO., DEC. 7TH, 1898.
JOHN J. KAIN,
ARCHBISHOP OF ST. LOUIS.

BECKTOLD
PRINTING AND BOOK MFG. CO.,
ST. LOUIS, MO.

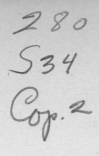
# PREFACE.

This little book, by a German Benedictine Father, is intended as nothing more than an " introduction " to the knowledge of the Fathers of the Church. It might be called a " handy-book " to the great collection of writers whose works appear in the " *Cursus Patrologiæ*." No student has any chance of thoroughly mastering the whole of the three or four hundred volumes of Migne's edition. But, on the other hand, no one can pretend to a scientific knowledge of divinity, unless he has read the Fathers to some purpose. Students, therefore, whether those who are passing through their course in a seminary, or those who, in more mature years, are following up some portion of the Church's great doctrinal inheritance, will always find a use for a small and well arranged guide to the epochs, the authors, and the subjects of patristic literature.

An acquaintance with the writings of the Fathers of the Church is useful to students of theology on many heads.

First, to be tolerably well read in the Fathers is to know theology in its historical aspect. No man ever possesses a true knowledge of things that have grown, unless, to a certain extent, he can trace the process of their growth. To understand, in all its circumstances and surroundings, the development of any one dogma, is a splendid training in scientific theology. To appre-

(3)

ciate what it was in the past, and in the actual circumstances that made St. Augustine defend with such
amplitude and determination his views of grace and
predestination, which, nevertheless, as he said, had
always been held by the Church of God; to see
with your own eyes in the pages of Athanasius and
Hilary, how the terminology of the doctrine of the
Blessed Trinity becomes distinct and clear-cut; to feel
the tremulous and indignant emphasis which Leo puts
in his oft-repeated formula of the Word made flesh;
to follow Cyril of Alexandria through the thicket of
his earnest speech, and recognize at every turn the
traces of an adversary who is intent on denying to
Jesus Christ his eternity and his divinity — this kind
of study is a very different thing from learning formularies by heart, or getting up patristic texts in com-
pendiums.

Moreover, it is from the study of the Fathers that
modern theology derives what I may call its elasticity.　This is an age of manuals, abstracts, catechisms,
and other apparatus for accomplishing the process
which is known as "cramming."　Education con-
ducted on principles of this kind can never become
part of one's mental and spiritual life.　The knowledge thus gained lies in the receptive power like a
stone on the surface of a field; whatever crop the
field grows, the stone has no share in fertilizing it.
The Fathers did not write abstracts.　They searched
the Scriptures, compared testimonies, examined traditions and expostulated with false teachings.　Most of
them launched out from time to time into literary exposition, into rhetoric, or into poetry.　A modern
catechism read without the light of patristic illustration is both inadequate and misleading.　When faith is

described as being "to believe without doubting whatever God has revealed," the patristic student thinks of the long centuries, full of intellectual activity, during which that august word has been invoked, written about, defined, divided, lifted up, trampled upon and fought over — and he is the less likely to fancy that this definition tells him all about it. When he reads that God is the Supreme Spirit, Who exists of Himself, "he will remember, if he has read Athanasius, Hilary, and John Damascene, how the Greek and Latin intellect have striven to put into philosophic language the revelation of God's Name, I am Who am." The formularies say with easy consciousness that man was "made to God's image and likeness;" the Fathers have discussed from a hundred points of view what this divine revelation means. The formularies lay down the Church's faith in the dogma of the creation of the world, and that of the generation of the Second Person of the Blessed Trinity; and the great folios of the Fathers contain hundreds of pages on the Scriptural proofs of the difference in origination between the visible creation and the Eternal Word. The catechism says, "There are seven sacraments." The patristic student looks for them in the Fathers, and he finds no lists, no Tridentine definitions, but, instead, scattered testimonies, appeals to Scripture and to Roman tradition, fervent exhortations, implicit assertions, from which, finally, he gathers the unvarying teaching of the Catholic Church, as a man fills his basket with fruit, not from the shop-windows, but from the trees of the wide luxuriant forest. It is this kind of reading that makes theology elastic. By this word it is not meant that the study of the Fathers can or ought to make any

student question the absolute truth of dogmatic definitions, or of any portion of the Church's magisterium.
If this were so, the Fathers would have discussed to
no purpose, and written their great treatises in vain.
But dogmatic formularies can be viewed in two aspects.
They are definitions of Catholic truth, and they are
also summaries of history — monuments of the
Church's living activity. They cannot be reformed
or diminished. But they have a living and stimulating power of their own. They are far from being
dead forms. They touch and affect every faculty that
man possesses — the imagination, the heart, the feel-
ings, the memory, the sense of affection, of Christian
pride and joy. Moreover, just as existing definitions
have arisen out of legitimate development, so they, in
their turn, afford starting points for further investigation and devout speculation. This twofold quality of
dogma, its stimulating power and its capacity of
growth, is what I have called its elasticity.

Dogma, to a cultured and truly Catholic intelligence, is not a prison, but a spacious and fertile
garden with unexplored distances and delights. It is
in this spirit that it is treated by the great Fathers of
the Church. They give you its philosophy, its sense,
its relation to human nature. They read its glories
in the oracles of God, in the history of God's dealings
with His chosen people. They use it for devotion, for
prayer, for the promotion of justice and brotherly
love. They make religious truth, not the narrow
catch-word of the chapel or the school catechism, but
what it really is — the strong creative principle of the
widest and most essential science upon which man's
intelligence can employ itself. It is this kind of
largeness that one learns from the Fathers. Their

expositions may sometimes seem antiquated, tedious, or fanciful. They wrote for their times, which are not our times. The form in which we have their works does not always do justice to their own presentment of their thoughts. But, on the whole, the spirit is there — the spirit of breadth and of actuality — and it is a spirit we can only learn in their school.

The mere personality of each of the great Fathers of the Church, almost apart from his writings — although it is impossible to separate him from them — is of the greatest interest to the student of theology. Such men as Clement of Alexandria, Origen, Gregory of Nazianzen, Basil, Chrysostom, Augustine, Leo, Gregory the Great, Ambrose, Jerome, have each of them in their life-story a stimulation, an educative power, such as belong only to the world's foremost names. The right way to make their acquaintance, is to read their lives and their works together, so that one may illuminate the other. The best key to the comprehension of a writer is his own individuality, his character, his personal relations, and his surroundings. Whatever may be said about the style of the Fathers, it is certain that the greater part of them write a genuine literary language, a language of great clearness, strength, delicacy, and beauty. Many of them have marked individuality of style. It would be difficult to mistake Nazianzen or Chrysostom, or any of the great Latin Doctors.

To read through the Fathers as a whole, is not within the power of a student. But even a student can do two things. First of all, he can learn to appreciate that "historical" method of teaching theology, which is more followed now than it used to be. The way with "manuals" has too often been to fling iso-

lated patristic texts at the learner, without comment
or explanation. But Passaglia and Franzelin have
brought back into the schools the custom of reading
a Father's words by the light of his period and surroundings; of putting into clear relief the apodictic
terms; of accumulating testimonies, and showing how
they converged to a common point. Even if one cannot go through the whole of Petavius, one can learn
the significance of patristic terms and phrases, and
one can follow up the texts that come in one's course.
But there are students who go through their course
without distinguishing Origen from Damascene,
Irenæus from Gregory the Great, or even Clement
of Alexandria from Leo. As for St. Augustine, there
are too many who finish their studies with the conviction that he can be quoted for both " yea " and
" nay " in nearly every disputed point of grace and
predestination. A little attention and the use of a
handy-book would enable a student to deal with patristic names in a spirit of discernment; and such
discernment adds immeasurably to the interest and
profit of theological study.

Next, there is no student who could not, under
guidance, read at least a few portions of the more important Fathers. There are some he would read for
their exposition of Scripture, some for dogmatic
argument, some for moral exhortation, or for history,
personal traits, eloquence, or invective. No ecclesiastical education seems to be complete unless one has
read a chapter or two of Origen against Celsus, an
oration of Gregory Nazianzen, some letters of Chrysostom, with the whole of his work on the priesthood,
the homilies of Leo, the letters of Jerome, the Confessions of St. Augustine, with some of his City of God,

and liberal excerpts from the pastoral writings of Gregory the Great.   Even so much as this would enable us to guess the richness of an unexplored world, and tempt us to do more when the opportunity offered. And that opportunity would not be wanting.   There are large tracts of patristic writing that are comparatively out of date, crabbed, dry, and dull.   But there is abundance that is living, actual, bright, and impressive — far more, indeed, than any reader is likely to exhaust.   For our study of dogma, all through life, we can always find new views in the Fathers; for our exhortation, pregnant phrases that carry whole sermons in their bosom; for our devotion and spiritual life, the ideas and principles of men who did not copy other men, but lived face to face with eternal truth, and very close to Jesus Christ.

† JOHN CUTHBERT HEDLEY, O. S. B.,<br/>Bishop of Newport.

Feast of St. Lawrence,
Aug. 10, 1898.

# INDEX OF CONTENTS.

## PART II.

*PATROLOGY PROPER.*

CHAPTER I.

*Greek and Oriental Fathers and Writers.*

CHAPTER II.

*Latin Fathers and Writers.*

# INTRODUCTION.

## § 1. *Meaning and Object of Patrology.*

By Patrology is meant a systematic treatment and exposition of such preliminary subjects and questions as are necessary to acquire a proper knowledge of the writings of the Fathers, and to make proper use of them in theology. Patrology, therefore, differs from the knowledge of the Fathers, or what is called patristical science, the special object of which is to arrange systematically, according to definite principles, all that can be gathered from the works of the Fathers concerning matters of faith, morals, and ecclesiastical discipline. Nor is it the same as the history of ancient Christian literature, because the latter includes the literary works not only of the Fathers, but also of other ancient ecclesiastical writers, and confines itself to the consideration of the historical development of Christian literature, as such.

The object, therefore, of Patrology, in this narrow sense, is, in the first place, to lay down and establish the rules and principles which help to determine the authority of the Fathers, and the authenticity, right use, and application of their works in theology. In the next place, its object is to give some account of the life, education, mental training, literary and pastoral work of each of the Fathers, also to determine their precise position in the Church, with their relative merits in ecclesiastical science. A further

(19)

duty of Patrology is to explain the substance, scope, and number of their writings, the peculiarity of their views, their style of writing, and, finally, to indicate the best editions of their works. In its wider and less proper sense, however, it also takes into consideration those ecclesiastical authors who, though not Fathers, have yet exercised more or less influence upon the development of Christian life and knowledge.

## § 2. *Importance of Patrology.*

1. Patrology is of the highest importance for every student of theology. Theology is the science of revealed truth; but the two main sources of revealed truth are Scripture and tradition. Now the Fathers of the Church are the best expounders of the Holy Scripture, and they are also the chief witnesses and representatives of tradition. Hence it is plain that the study of the Fathers is absolutely necessary for the student of theology. Again, if he desires to know something of the history of the Church from her very beginning, and of the long, unbroken chain of those who ever witness to her nature and constitution, her teaching and worship, or of her great and world-subduing power, he must needs go back to the times of Christian antiquity and search its memorable records; he must try and enter into the very spirit of the Fathers, and feel their living faith and burning love for Christ and His Church. No wonder, then, that the greatest theologians have ever applied themselves with the utmost diligence to the study of the holy Fathers.

*Cf. Möhler*, Patrologie, pp. 1–15. (German ed.)

## § 3. *History of Patrology.*

It was only in the last century that Patrology was raised to the dignity of a theological science, properly so called. The Fathers of the Church, however, had laid the first stone of the building, as, for instance, *Eusebius* of Cæsarea, by the many and most valuable notices bequeathed to us in his Church History, regarding the life and writings of the early Fathers of the Church; and St. *Jerome*, by his book, " De viris illustribus, sive catalogus de scriptoribus ecclesiasticis," which, beginning with the Apostolic and ending with his own age, contains an account, in 135 chapters, of the life and writings of the same number of authors. The work was taken up and continued in a similar manner by the priest *Gennadius* of Marseilles (d. 496), St. *Isidore of Seville* (d. 636), Bishop *Ildephonsus of Toledo* (d. 667), and some later writers.

Amongst the Greeks, the Patriarch *Photius* (d. 891), composed, under the title " Photii bibliotheca,"* a similar work of comprehensive learning and great acuteness, containing also some abridgments from heathen authors.

In the West, little or nothing more was done in this respect, until the Abbot *Trithemius* (d. 1516), and the Cathedral-Dean *Myräus* (d. 1640), took up the work in a very laudable manner. These were followed by Cardinal *R. Bellarmine* (d. 1621), who aroused an increased interest in ancient ecclesiastical literature, and brought its scientific cultivation to an unprecedented point of excellence by his elab-

---

* The Greek title is Μυριοβίβλιον ἢ βιβλιοθήκη.

orate work, " Liber de scriptoribus ecclesiasticis,"
written in accordance with the rules of historical
criticism.

A century later came the Benedictines (Maurists),
and the Oratorians of France, who labored with the
greatest zeal and wrought marvels in this department.
*Nicolas le Nourry*, O. S. B. (d. 1724), collected the
results of their minute and comprehensive researches
in his valuable "Apparatus ad bibliothecam max. vett.
Patrum " (2 vols., Paris 1703-1715), containing most
learned dissertations.  *Elie Dupin* (d. 1719), Doctor
of the Sorbonne, brought out his " Nouvelle bibliothèque des auteurs ecclésiastiques " (19 tom. 4°.
Amsterdam 1693-1715), splendidly written, but not
free from Gallican prejudices and other questionable
views.  It extends as far as the seventeenth century,
and includes biographies of ecclesiastical authors, a
catalogue and criticism of their writings, as well as an
examination of their doctrine and style.   The Benedictine *Remy Ceillier* composed on the same plan his
" Histoire générale des auteurs sacrés et eccl." (23
tom. 4°.  Paris 1729-1763; 15 vols. 4°.  Paris 1858-
1865), reaching to the middle of the 13th century;
*Tillemont* his valuable  " Mémoires pour servir de
guide dans les premiers six siècles de l'histoire ecclé-
siastique " (20 tom.  4°.  Paris 1693), and the priest
*Tricalet* his " Bibliothèque portative des Pères " (9
tom.  8°.  Paris 1757-1762).

In Germany, little in comparison was done for the
advancement of patrological studies.  The names of
the most noteworthy men who devoted themselves to
this work are the following:  *Dom. Schramm*,  O. S.
B. (d. 1797), "Analysis Operum SS. Patrum " (18
tom. 8ᵛᵒ.  Aug. Vind. 1780); *Lumper*, O. S. B. (d.

1800), "Historia theologica-critica de vita, scriptis atque doctrina SS. Patrum trium primorum sæculorum" (13 tcm. 8ᵛᵒ. Aug. Vind. 1799); *Möhler*, "Patrologie, oder christliche Literärgeschichte" (Regensburg 1840 — unfortunately incomplete); *Permaneder*, "Bibliotheca patristica" (Landish. 1841); *Fessler*, "Institutiones Patrologiæ" (2 tom. Œniponte 1850-1851), de novo editæ a *B. Jungmann* (Œnip. et Ratisbonæ 1890-1896); *Alzog*, "Handbuch der Patrologie" (4ᵗʰ edition. Freiburg 1888). Finally, we have two recent works in German which unite in themselves all the merits of the above-named works, without their deficiencies, namely the exemplary Abridgment of Patrology and Patristic Science, by *Dr. Jos. Nirschl* (3 vols., Mainz 1881-1885), and the Handbook of Patrology, by *Dr. Otto Bardenhewer* (Freiburg 1894).

Amongst Protestants, who, in consequence of their peculiar rule of faith, are generally less concerned with patrological studies, the following deserve mention: the apostate Premonstratensian *Casimir Oudin*, "Comment. de script. eccl." (2 fol. Lips. 1722) — also *William Cave* (d. 1713), "Scriptorum eccl. historia liter." (2 fol. Lond. 1689, continued by Wharton and Cerens), and particularly *J. Alb. Fabricius*, for his very learned "Bibliotheca patristica" (graeca 14 tom. 4°. Hamb. 1718 — latina 2 tom. 4°. Venet. 1728.) In recent times, however, Protestant historians display a most exemplary zeal in the study of Christian antiquity, although their labors are directed towards particular points of investigation, rather than towards a general presentation of the writings of the Fathers, while their method is generally that of negative criticism.

Practical directions for the study of the Fathers as well as the principles for determining their authority and the authenticity of their works, and other similar questions, had been given earlier by the Carthusian *Nat. Bonav. d'Argonne* in "De optima methodo legendorum Ecclesiæ Patrum" (Aug. Vind. 1756); by *Honoratus a Sancta Maria* in "Animadversiones in regulas et usum critices" (Venet. 1751); by the Cistercian and University Professor *Steph. Wiest* in "Institut. Patrologiæ" (Ingolst. 1795), and, in later times, by *Permaneder* and *Fessler* in the above mentioned works.

## § 4. *Division of Patrology.*

Patrology may be divided into two main parts, namely, a general and a special part.

The *general* part is of an introductory and propædeutical character. It considers, in the first place, the definition of the term "Fathers of the Church," proceeding next to explain the principles which determine their authority, and, finally, supplying the means necessary to a proper understanding and use of their works in theology.

The *special* part embraces the more immediate subjects of Patrology, namely a brief description of the life and education of the several Fathers or ecclesiastical writers; an account of the number and value of their works, of their doctrine and characteristic peculiarities; and, lastly, an indication of the best editions, as well as the literature bearing on the subject.

# PART I.

## GENERAL, INTRODUCTORY, OR PROPÆDEU-TICAL.

### § 5. *Meaning and Importance of this Part.*

Propædeutic is the name which the learned generally give to any theoretical introduction to a particular
branch of science. The purpose of such an introduction is to determine the meaning and object of that
particular science, as well as to point out the means
necessary for pursuing it with fruit and profit.
Accordingly, this part of Patrology, forming, as it
does, the introduction and ground work to the knowledge of the Fathers of the Church, has first to determine what is meant by an *Ecclesiastical Writer, Father*,
and *Doctor* of the Church, and what is the respective
authority of each in theology. In the next place, it
has to explain the rules and principles by which
authentic works are distinguished from unauthentic.
Lastly, it must show us how to understand the works
of the Fathers rightly, and how to use them profitably.
This part, therefore, will not only be useful, inasmuch
as it helps to facilitate the study of early theology,
but also necessary, inasmuch as it will direct the
student aright in his investigations, preserving him
from possible excesses, or narrow and onesided views.

# CHAPTER I.

## NOTION AND DEFINITION OF THE TERMS " ECCLESIASTICAL WRITER, FATHER, DOCTOR."

### § 6. *Ecclesiastical Writers.*\*

In a general sense, the name of *ecclesiastical writer*, as distinguished from inspired writer, may be given to all those who, ever since the days of the Apostles, have written in explanation or defense of the Christian doctrine.  But in the narrower or specific sense, ecclesiastical writers differ from those who are called Fathers or Doctors of the Church.  The difference derives from the character of their lives and writings. Ecclesiastical writers are called those men who, though living in the communion of the Church, have yet not always in their lives and writings expressed her pure and genuine traditional doctrine, as, for instance, Clement of Alexandria, Origen, Tertullian, Lactantius, Eusebius, Rufinus, Cassian, Theodoret of Cyrus, and others.  If St. Irenæus, in spite of his Chiliastic opinions, and St. Gregory of Nyssa, in spite of his Origenistic ideas, are counted among the Fathers, it is because they did not propound their opinions apodictically as the teaching of the Church.  Those Christians who have left behind writings on matters of faith, but did not live in the communion of the

---

\* It has been considered expedient to omit in the English translation  the opening sentence of  this paragraph in the author, and to introduce  some  other  slight  alterations  of the text.  (R.)

Church, as, for instance, Novatian, are called Christian writers (scriptores christiani).

Cf. *Fessler-Jungmann*, Institut. Patrol. §§ 5-9.


### § 7. *Fathers of the Church.*

By *Fathers of the Church* are understood those ecclesiastical writers of old, who, on account of their learning and holiness of life, have been recognized as such by the Church. (Recte credentium Ecclesiæ filiorum genitores.)

Four conditions are necessary for a Father of the Church:—

(1.) *Antiquity* (*competens antiquitas*).

(2.) *Ecclesiastical learning and orthodox doctrine* (*doctrina orthodoxa*).

(3.) *Holiness of life* (*sanctitas vitæ*).

(4.) *Approbation of the Church* (*approbatio Ecclesiæ*).

1. *Antiquity* (*Antiquitas*). Patrologists are not all agreed as to this condition. Some close the patristic period with the fourth, others with the sixth, others with the fourteenth century; whilst others, again, entirely object to any limitation of time; for, as Möhler says, "There must be Fathers of the Church as long as the Church herself lasts." But according to the more common opinion, the patristic age is most appropriately closed with the end of the Græco-Roman period, so that Isidore of Seville (d. 636), may be considered as the last Father of the West, and John Damascene (d. 754), the last of the East.

2. *Ecclesiastical learning* (*orthodoxa doctrina.*) By this condition are excluded not only anti-Christian and heterodox, but also those Christian writers who

have held and propounded erroneous views, or distinguished themselves in profane, rather than in ecclesiastical knowledge.   As regards the extent and measure of the knowledge required, it is not so much the
depth or comprehensiveness of learning that is to be
considered, as rather the fact that the writings of a
Father are of great importance for some point or other
of ecclesiastical science.

3. *Holiness of life* (*sanctitas vitæ*).   This condition
is absolutely required in a Father of the Church.   For
there exists an internal connection between true ecclesiastical learning and personal sanctity, and only those
can be considered as Fathers who have helped to produce and to fashion the spiritual life of the Church,
not merely by their writings, but also by their
example.

4. *Approbation by the Church* (*Approbatio Ecclesiæ*).   This approbation may be formal or explicit, as,
for instance, by a general council, or by the Pope as
supreme teacher of the Church; or only tacit and
implicit, i. e., by the mere consent of the Church dis-
persed throughout the world.   This condition is no
less necessary than the other three, for the doctrine
taught by the Fathers can only claim authority inasmuch as the Church herself considers their writings,
so to speak, as her classics, and the Fathers themselves as her own witnesses to the divine tradition.
Nevertheless, this approbation by the Church does not
imply freedom from every error; it only testifies to
the fact that those men whom she recognizes as
Fathers, have lived to the end of their lives in constant
communion with her, have distinguished themselves by
piety and orthodox doctrine, and are, in consequence,
perfectly trustworthy witnesses to her belief and

teaching. The Fathers may be divided (1.) according to language, into Greek and Latin; (2.) according to authority, into Greater or Lesser; (3.) according to age, into (a.) Apostolic, as Clement of Rome, Polycarp, Ignatius, and others, bringing us up to about the year 150; (b.) Ancient or Early, as Justin, Irenæus, Cyprian, Gregorius Thaumaturgus, and others, till the end of the third century; and (c.) Later Fathers, as Gregory Nazianzen, Epiphanius, Hilary of Poitiers, Paulinus of Nola, Cæsarius of Arles, and all others from the fourth to the eighth century.*

Cf. *Fessler-Jungmann* l. c. §§ 10–12.

### § 8. *Doctors of the Church.*

By *Doctors of the Church* we mean those ecclesiastical writers who, on account of their learning and holiness, have been expressly honored with this title by the Church.

Therefore in a Doctor of the Church are required:

(1.) Eminent ecclesiastical learning (doctrina orthodoxa eminens).

(2.) Remarkable holiness of life (insignis sanctitas vitæ).

(3.) Express approbation on the part of the Church (approbatio expressa).

The condition of antiquity is not necessary, as the Church can at all times distinguish with this honorable title men eminent for piety and orthodox learning. The Greek Church has her Doctors as well as

---

* Usage seems to vary considerably in this respect. Some authors speak of Apostolic and Post-Apostolic Fathers, subdividing the latter class again into Ante-Nicene and Post-Nicene. (R.)

the Latin. Amongst the Greeks are Athanasius
(d. 373), who, however, is not entered as a "great
œcumenical Doctor" in the Greek liturgy; Basil (d.
379), Gregory of Nazianzen (d. 389), and Chrysos-
tom (d. 407). Amongst the Latins, Ambrose (d.
397), Jerome (d. 420), Augustine (d. 430), and
Gregory the Great (d. 604), are specially styled the
Great (magni, egregii) Doctors of the Church.
Later on were added to them — by Pius V., Leo the
Great (d. 461) and Thomas Aquinas (d. 1274); — by
Pope Sixtus V., Bonaventure (d. 1274); — by Pope
Pius VIII., Bernard of Clairvaux (d. 1153); — by Pius
IX., Hilary of Poitiers (d. 368), Alphonsus of
Liguori (d. 1787), and Francis of Sales (d. 1622);
and by Pope Leo XIII., Cyril of Jerusalem (d. 386),
Cyril of Alexandria (d. 444), and John Damascene
(d. 754). Others, also, like Isidore of Seville (d.
636), Anselm of Canterbury (d. 1109), Peter Chryso-
logus (d. 450), Peter Damian (d. 1071), are honored
by the Church as Doctors in her liturgy, inasmuch
as they have the antiphon proper to Doctors, and
Credo in the mass of their feasts.

Cf. *Fessler-Jungmann* l. c. § 13.

---

# CHAPTER II.

## AUTHORITY OF THE FATHERS OF THE CHURCH.

### § 9. *Authority of the Fathers in General.*

By authority, as attributed to writers, is meant their
power and right to command intellectual assent
(auctoritas movens vel obligans). It is a moral

power, affecting the mind and will of the reader, determining his judgment, and obliging him to assent to the words or statements of the writer. This authority varies in degrees. It may be greater or less, and even absolute, according as it is calculated to produce in the mind a more or less probable, or a certain assent.

The authority of the Fathers has been very differently estimated at different times. Some few, after the example of the Abbot Fredegis, in the ninth century, placed their authority on a level with that of the prophets and Apostles ; while others, on the contrary, especially Protestants, beheld in the writings of the Fathers mere literary testimonials of no paramount importance in matters of faith. But the greater number of theologians have determined the authority of the Fathers by the following rules : —

(1.) In matters of natural science, the words of one, or many, or of all the Fathers together, have only as much weight as the reasons on which they are based. Tantum valent, quantum probant ; i. e., their authority extends no farther than their proofs.

(2.) Even in matters appertaining to faith or morals, the testimony of one or two Fathers of the Church does not suffice to produce certainty, but only probability. The same holds good of the authority of many Fathers, in cases where other Fathers contradict, or hold a different opinion.

(3.) But the agreement of all the Fathers of the Church together (consensus Patrum), in matters of faith and morals, begets complete certainty and commands assent, because they, as a body, bear witness to the teaching and belief of the infallible Church, representing the Church herself. The consensus, however, need not be absolute; a moral agreement suffices, as, for instance, when some of the greatest Fathers testify to a doctrine of the Church, and the rest, though quite aware of it, do not positively oppose it. Whatever, therefore, the holy Fathers unanimously teach as the divinely revealed tradition of the Church, must be accepted and believed as such. "He who departs from the unanimous consent of the Fathers, departs from the Church." "Qui ab unanimi Patrum consensu discedit, ab universa Ecclesia recedit." "He who rejects the holy Fathers, confesses that he rejects the whole Church." "Qui sanctos Patres reiicit, fatetur se universam Ecclesiam reiicere."* "The things that are drawn from the unanimous mind of the Fathers, possess a firm and invincible force against adversaries." "Quæ ex consensu spirituali Patrum depromuntur, firmam habent et inexpugnabilem contra adversarios vim."†

This binding authority of the "consensus Patrum in rebus fidei et morum" rests both upon a natural and supernatural basis.

(1.) *Natural or historical basis.* As men of great ecclesiastical learning, they are able to know and testify to that which the Church believed and taught in their times. As honest and holy men, they were willing to bear witness to the truth, and, finally, their agreement with each other is a guarantee for the truth of their testimony. This may be called their natural and historical authority.

(2.) *Supernatural basis.* The Fathers give their testimony as the expression of their own faith, in due subordination to the supernatural power and author-

---

* S. Aug. c. Julian. II, 37.      † St. Martin, P.

ity of the teaching Church, and under her constant supernatural supervision. The Church, moreover, approves, confirms, and authenticates their testimony, inasmuch as she acknowledges them as orthodox teachers, and appeals herself to this unanimous testimony as proof incontestable of her doctrine. This may be called their supernatural authority. Although the supernatural authority of the consensus Patrum rests ultimately upon the infallibility of the Church, nevertheless their testimony may, without fear of a vicious circle, be invoked also in favor of doctrines for which there exists no authoritative pronouncement by the Church. For, in the first place, their consentient teaching is in itself an equivalent of the authoritative teaching of the Church, and, in the second place, their authority, as competent historical witnesses of belief and tradition, is independent of the Church, and is derived from the natural principle of philosophy, that the unanimous testimony of men capable of knowing the truth, and willing to tell it, is trustworthy and deserving of credence.

*Editions and Literature.* — *Melch. Canus*, Loci theol., lib. VII, c. 3. — *Permaneder*, Patrol. gener., pars II, c. 3. — *Fessler-Jungmann* l. c. § 14 — *Al. Schmid*, Untersuchungen über den letzten Gewissheitsgrund des Offenbarungsglaubens. München 1879. — *Franzelin*, De div. trad., II. c. I–II.

## § 10. *Authority of Single Fathers.*

The authority of single Fathers in matters of faith or morals is not in itself supreme or absolute, as if their " dicta " were infallible ; but to reject it, except for very grave reasons, would hardly be justifiable, particularly if a Father represents a doctrine not merely as his own private opinion, but as the teaching of the Church. The latter is the case when the Fathers expound and defend their opinions as undoubted truths of faith; or denounce as heretics those of an opposite opinion, or make use of such words as are equivalent to a profession of faith, viz. : we believe (credimus); we have been taught (edocti sumus); Christ has said (Christus dixit); the Apostles have handed down (Apostoli tradiderunt); the Church believes or holds (Ecclesia credit vel tenet); and such like. For the rest, the individual Fathers are not all of equal authority. The various degrees of authority may be determined by the following rules : —

(1.) The greater the holiness and learning of a Father, and the greater the honor in which he is held by the Church, the greater is his authority.

(2.) Those Fathers who were in close connection with a great number of bishops, or who lived near to the times of the Apostles, have greater authority than others less favorably placed. Again, those surpass others in authority who, by their special treatises, have successfully defended any assailed dogma of the Church, and brilliantly explained its meaning, such as SS. Athanasius, Augustine, and Hilary.

(3.) Of pre-eminent authority are those Fathers who were at the head of churches founded by the Apostles themselves, as SS. Clement of Rome, Ignatius, Polycarp; or who were successors of St. Peter, as St. Leo the Great and St. Gregory the Great; or who were preferred by the holy Fathers themselves before others. Those, again, rank higher in authority who received especial praise from the Church, or whose virtues were especially recommended by other devout and learned bishops, or whose works have been publicly read and approved by general councils.

Cf. *Wiest*, Instit. patr., §§ 354–357. — *Fessler-Jungmann* l. c. § 14, 6.

## § 11. *Authority of the Fathers on Questions of Faith and Morals.*

The Fathers, in their unanimous consent, are the venerable organs and the fully competent witnesses[*] of the revealed doctrine of Jesus Christ, deposited in the Church and handed on by her from generation to generation. "For," as St. Augustine says, "they held to what they found in the Church; they taught what they had learnt; what they had received from the Fathers, they transmitted to the children." "Quod invenerunt in Ecclesia, tenuerunt; quod didicerunt, docuerunt; quod a patribus acceperunt, hoc filiis tradiderunt." [†]

As the revealed doctrine of Jesus Christ embraces principally those things which we must believe and practice in order to obtain eternal life, so also does the authority of the Fathers extend to whatever we have to believe and to practice in the work of our salvation. And as the binding authority of the teaching Church

---

[*] So far as the Fathers of a certain period are all, or mostly, bishops, their consentient testimony in matters of faith or morals, is not only indirectly, but directly and in itself infallible, because they are the divinely appointed witnesses (testes praeordinati), and the divinely instituted organ and channel of tradition. (R.)

[†] S. Aug. c. Julian., II. 9.

has reference to things of faith and morals (res fidei et morum), so also is the decisive authority of the consensus Patrum likewise restricted within the same limits, outside of which no words of theirs require an unconditional assent.

Whence it follows that the authority of the Fathers is binding only when they all agree upon a question of faith and morals, or when the doctrine of an individual Father is explicitly and definitely recognized or declared as a rule of faith by the universal Church.

In all other cases their authority is greater or less according to the arguments alleged in support of their opinion, and should never be lightly rejected. These restrictions will suffice, on the one hand, to prevent all subjective arbitrary use of the Fathers in theology, and, on the other, to give as free and wide a scope as possible to scientific theology.

Cf. § 9.— See *Franzelin*, de trad. div., Thes. 14–15.

### § 12. *Authority of the Fathers in Expounding Holy Scripture.*

As the consent of the holy Fathers represents the mind of the universal Church (sensus universalis Ecclesiæ), which was infused into her by the Apostles, and which is identical with that intended by the Holy Ghost, it follows that the unanimous explanation of Holy Scripture given by the Fathers, is of the same authority as that of the Church herself. It is therefore unlawful to depart or differ from it. St. Leo says, "It is not lawful to understand Scripture otherwise than the blessed Apostles and our Fathers have learnt or taught." "Non licet aliter de Scripturis divinis sapere, quam beati Apostoli et *Patres* nostri didice-

runt atque docuerunt." * Again, the Council of
Trent gives the following warning: "Let no one,
trusting to his own wisdom, in matters appertaining to
faith or morals, and the building up of Christian
doctrine, dare, by twisting the Sacred Scriptures to
his own sense, to interpret them against the unanimous consent of the Fathers." "Nemo suæ
prudentiæ innixus in rebus fidei et morum, ad ædificationem doctrinæ Christianæ pertinentium, S. Scripturam ad suos sensus contra unanimem consensum
Patrum interpretari audeat." † And the Vatican
Council not only renewed this Tridentine decree, but
also explained thus its full sense and bearing: "In
matters of faith and morals appertaining to the building up of Christian doctrine, that is to be held as the
true sense of Scripture which holy Mother Church
has held and holds, whose office it is to judge of the
true sense and interpretation of the Holy Scriptures;
and, therefore, no one is allowed to interpret that
same Sacred Scripture against this sense, or against
the unanimous consent of the Fathers." "Ut in rebus
fidei et morum, ad ædificationem doctrinæ Christianæ
pertinentium, is pro vero sensu sacræ Scripturæ
habendus sit, quem tenuit et tenet S. mater Ecclesia,
cujus est judicare de vero sensu et interpretatione
Scripturarum sanctarum, atque ideo nemini licere,
contra hunc sensum, aut *contra unanimem consensum
Patrum* ipsam Scripturam sanctam interpretari." ‡

From these decrees of the Church we may deduce
the following principles: —

(1.) If the Fathers, in expounding a passage, do

---

* Leo M., Ep. 8, c. 1.
† Concil. Trid., Sess. IV., Decret. de usu ss. libror.
‡ Concil. Vat., Sess. III., cap. 2., De revelatione.

not agree, it is lawful to explain it according to one's own well-grounded opinion.

(2.) The concordant explanation of Scripture by the holy Fathers is binding only in subjects of faith and morals, but not in other scientific questions. (Cfr. § 11.)

(3.) The degree of authority to be given to a Father in the explanation of Holy Scripture, is in proportion to his learning, sanctity, and the honor or approbation accorded to him by the Church. (Cf. § 10.)

To St. Jerome belongs very special distinction and authority, for the Church speaks of him as her greatest teacher in the exposition of Holy Scripture: "In exponendis sacris Scripturis Doctorem maximum."

' *Editions and Literature.* — *Nat. B. Argon.*, De optima methodo legendorum Eccles. Patrum, P. 3, c. 4. — *Fessler-Jungmann* l. c. § 15. — *Reithmayr*, Biblische Hermeneutik. Kempten 1874. §§ 31–33.

§ 13. *Authority of the Fathers in Ascetic or Pastoral Theology.*

In order to determine their authority in these two branches of theology, we have to consider, in the first place, whether the principles laid down, and the means pointed out by them for the guidance of souls, are such as to have been either formally or explicitly, or at least implicitly, revealed by God. If that be the case, the holy Fathers enjoy the like authority in ascetic and pastoral theology, as in questions of faith or morals (Cf. § 11). But when the principles and means set forth are merely based upon conclusions drawn from revealed truths (conclusiones virtualiter et implicite revelatæ), or founded upon psychological principles, or depending upon external

circumstances, then the authority of the Fathers varies.
In the first instance, it is very great indeed, for they
were able to draw their conclusions from revealed
truths with an assurance proportionate to their comprehension of the sacred truths.  In the second instance, the authority is less, but still sufficiently grave,
inasmuch as the writers had much experience, if not
in theoretical, at least in practical psychology.  In
the third instance, much will depend upon whether the
circumstances under which they lived and wrote are
the same or similar to those of our own times.  If so,
the principles and practical rules laid down by them
still hold good.  In the contrary case, the spirit,
rather than the letter of their words, is to be studied
and followed.

Cf. *Fessler-Jungmann* l. c. § 15.


§ 14. *Relation of the Fathers to Holy Scripture and
the Church.*

1. As regards the relation of the writings of the
holy Fathers to the Sacred Scriptures, we may say,
that though both have the same object, namely, to
explain revealed truths, and though both are acknowledged by the Church as trustworthy interpreters and
witnesses of revelation, nevertheless there is a great
and material difference between them.  The sacred
writers are one and all inspired, and each of their
dicta represents infallible truth, which is not the case
with the Fathers or their dicta.*  So far, the Sacred

---

* The author here is not quite explicit enough, but there
is no doubt that he means to deny to the Fathers both the
gift of inspiration and the gift of infallibility in each particular statement.  (R.)

Scriptures are immeasurably superior to the works of the Fathers. On the other hand, the Fathers, as the organs of tradition, treat of many things appertaining to faith which are not found in Holy Writ. Moreover, they unfold the contents of Holy Scripture in all their parts and show clearly how particular truths of faith are contained in the written Word of God.

2. Concerning the relations of the Fathers and of Scripture to the Church, it may be said that both stand on the same level. For as the Church bears infallible witness to the fact of inspiration and to the number of divinely inspired books, and unerringly explains their sense, so, in like manner, does she witness to and interpret with the same absolute infallibility the divine and Apostolic tradition contained in the patristic writings. From this twofold source, the Church, under the guidance of the Holy Ghost, ever draws forth the truth, and proposes it to the faithful as God's own word, to be accepted and held with absolute certainty.*

Cf. *Vinc. Lirin.*, Commonit., c. 23.

---

# CHAPTER III.

## CRITICISM IN PATROLOGY.

### § 15. *Notion of Criticism.*

1. Criticism in general may be defined as that science which teaches us how to distinguish truth from error. As applied to literary works, criticism means

---

* The final sentence of this paragraph in the German original has been omitted as irrelevant to the subject. (R.)

the knowledge and application of those rules by which we can distinguish the genuine and authentic from the spurious and substituted works of an author. Patrological criticism, therefore, has to set forth the principles which enable us to discern with certainty the genuine patristic works from the spurious, the certain from the doubtful, the complete from the curtailed and mutilated. This criticism is of paramount importance, owing to the existence of a great number of spurious and interpolated works of the Fathers.

2. According to *authorship*, a work is called genuine * (opus genuinum), if it has really been composed by the author whose name it bears ; spurious, or supposititious (spurium, suppositum), if it has been ascribed to, or bears the name of, one who is not the author ; doubtful (dubium), when the author is uncertain, and the reasons alleged for or against its genuineness are evenly balanced.

3. According to its *contents*, a work is called genuine, when it contains neither more nor less than the original (opus sincerum) ; it is called not genuine, or false (adulteratum), either when it contains anything that has been inserted by a strange hand (opus interpolatum), or when any part of it has been curtailed, suppressed, or omitted (opus mutilatum) ; it is styled entire or integral (opus integrum), if no essential portion has been abstracted. The name of fragments

---

* The author does not use the word authentic, which is strangely absent from a treatise like this, and would be particularly so in English, where the word seems to be now commonly used as synonymous with genuine, though there are those, I believe, who carefully distinguish between a genuine ($\gamma\nu\acute{\eta}\sigma\iota o\varsigma$) and an authentic ($a\dot{v}\vartheta\acute{\epsilon}\nu\tau\eta\varsigma$) work. (R.)

(fragmenta), is given to parts of a work. Such writings as have been certainly written by some definite author, but have not been handed down to our own times, are called lost (deperdita).

4. With regard to *form*, the works of the Fathers are either autographs (autographa), that is, written by their own hand, or originals (originalia), when only dictated by them. The transcriptions of the original works are called copies (copiæ, manuscripta), and their value will depend upon their age and accurate correspondence to the original. They may exist in manuscript (codices manuscripti), or in print; in the latter case, if simply printed, they are called " codices impressi; " but if printed from a selection and comparison of a number of the best codices, they are called " codices editi; " those that have been printed first being termed " codices principes."

Cf. *Nat. B. Argon. l. c.*, P. II, c. 16. — *Wiest* l. c. §§ 15-19. — *Fessler-Jungmann* l. c. §§ 17-18.

## § 16. *Causes of Substitution, Interpolation and Loss of Patristic Works.*

1. One of the most frequent causes of substitution is to be found in the unscrupulous conduct of heretics, who, in order to impart weight and authority to their false doctrines, or to obtain easy currency for them, published books under the names of celebrated Fathers.

As a second cause, we may name the blind and false piety of certain members of the Church, who thought they would render a service to her cause, and refute heresies more effectively, by composing orthodox works, and passing them under the name of a

Father, or again, by giving to a modern production the weight and name of an old and renowned writer.

A third cause of substitution was often the ignorance, fraud, and covetousness of copyists, who, when they found in one volume or collection various writings, together with those of a Father, would not hesitate to ascribe them all to him; or again, confused authors of the same name, or even deliberately affixed to their own copies the more celebrated name of a Father, in order to enhance their authority, reputation, and value.

It has even happened that works were substituted for the mere pleasure of deceiving others. Sometimes, by a mere blunder, the persons introduced as chief actors or speakers in a work have been mistaken for its authors, especially in cases where the book bears the name of the principal actor, as in the "Octavius" by Minucius Felix.

2. The interpolation of works may be due, first, to the malice of heretics, who have fraudulently introduced into them heretical sentences, or excluded those that were orthodox; secondly, to the temerity of critics, who have arbitrarily altered what did not suit their own ideas; thirdly, to the heedlessness of copyists, who often omit a line, or copy entire passages incorrectly; finally, also, to time, which has been a fruitful source of alteration in the manuscripts, during the long lapse of years.

3. The loss of so many patristic writings is chiefly due to the evil influence of particular epochs of barbarism, to the accidents of war, devastations and fire, and, especially in the case of the earlier writings, to the Christian persecutions.

Cf. *Wiest* l. c. § 6–14. — *Fessler-Jungmann* l. c. § 19.

### § 17. *Criteria, or Marks of Genuineness and Spuriousness.*

Those marks or criteria which enable us to judge of the genuineness or authenticity of a work, are called the positive principles of criticism; and those by which we discover its spuriousness, the negative. Both, again, are divided into internal and external marks, according as they are contained in the work itself, or are drawn from other sources.*

1. Among the external marks of genuineness, we may number, in the first place, the agreement of the various codices as to the author. If a number of codices, especially the more ancient ones, indicate one and the same author, and if there be no special reason for attributing the work to a writer other than the one recorded on the title page, then the work must be considered as genuine. Exceptions to this rule may not be presumed, but have to be proved.

A further external mark of authenticity is to be sought in the testimony of the author himself, or in that of any other contemporary writer, as for instance, a friend of his early days, or a pupil who is free from any suspicion of fraud. Such testimony is still more valuable if confirmed by subsequent trustworthy writers.

The internal criterium for the genuineness of a work consists in the similarity of method and style, in the

---

* The author's definition of internal and external marks is not very clear and distinct, but, from the explanation which follows, we gather that the internal marks are drawn only from the character, style, and contents of the works, while all other signs, even when found in the work itself, are ranked as external.  (R.)

agreement of the contents, or subject-matter, with the condition of the times when the book is supposed to have been written, and also with the temper, genius, character, and life of the author to whom it is attributed. This criterium, however, is not of itself absolutely decisive, but affords only a greater or less probability, as the case may be. But if supported by external testimony, it is a safe and certain test of genuineness.

2. The chief mark of spuriousness is to be found in the fact, that a work does not harmonize with the style, character, and times of the supposed author. Thus, works in which mention is made of persons, events, religious rites, and such like, which clearly belong to later times, are to be considered as spurious, or, at least, interpolated; and such is also the case if the style of composition differs strikingly from that of the Father to whom the work is ascribed, or from that of the period to which it is supposed to belong.

Smaller variations of style, however, are not unusual in one and the same author.

A further sign of spuriousness lies in the total absence of witnesses, i. e., documents and ancient writers. Thus, if a work bears the name of a certain author, while all existing manuscripts and codices mention another, it must be regarded as spurious. But if some codices mention one and some another, then the genuineness of the work is doubtful. And the same must be said of a work ascribed to a distinguished Father, of which, in spite of many occasions, no mention is made for several centuries by any ancient writer. It must be observed, however, that this argument drawn from silence (argumentum ex silentio), must always be employed with great prudence.

*Editions and Literature.* — *Wiest* 1. c. § 12. — *Dupin*, Nouv. biblioth., partie seconde de la Préface, pp. 9–18. — *Hefele*, in the Tübinger Quartalschrift (Jahrg. 1842), pp. 438–442. — *Fessler-Jungmann* 1. c. §§ 20, 21. — *De Smedt*, Principes de la critique historique. Liege 1883. — *Nirschl*, Propædeutik der Kirchengesch. Mainz 1888. §§ 15–20.

### § 18. *Rules for the Application of Criticism.*

In order to apply correctly the principles laid down above and more surely to discern the real author of a work, the following rules must be observed: —

1. In the first place, we must carefully observe the name of the author given by the codices or manuscripts, and then proceed to consider their antiquity, number, condition, and agreement.

2. In the next place, we have to see whether the contents of the work are in accordance with the mind and style of the author and with the time of composition. If any want of harmony be apparent, then the matter will require thorough examination.

3. Finally, the testimony of ancient writers is to be brought to bear upon the subject.

If these rules be observed and if they all point to one and the same conclusion, we are able to form a reliable and decisive judgment as to the author of a work.

In order to carry out this examination in a proper manner, the Patrologist should observe the following conditions: —

1. Having collected and classed all the testimonies

bearing on the point, he must accurately and impartially weigh and balance the reasons and arguments on both sides.

2. He must be intimately acquainted with the subject-matter upon which he is to pronounce; that is to say, he must be thoroughly cognizant of the codices, and their conditions and peculiarities, of the history of the times, as well as of the language in which the documents are written.

3. In passing judgment upon any work, he must be animated with the purest love of truth, uninfluenced by personal preference or prejudice.

Cfr. *Mabillon*, Traité des études monastiques, P. II. chap. XIII. — *Fessler-Jungmann* l. c. § 22.

---

## CHAPTER IV.

### USE OF THE FATHERS.

### § 19. *Use of the Fathers in General.*

The use of the Holy Fathers may be either public or private, according as they are used either by an assembled council of the Church, and by the Pope when speaking ex cathedra, in his capacity of teacher of all the faithful (omnium Christianorum Pastoris et Doctoris munere fungens), or merely by individual theologians. Their public use is generally restricted to matters of faith, morals, and Church discipline, and mainly serves to prove with absolute certainty the truth, when assailed or called in question, of the dogmas of the Church. Such an appeal to the Fathers necessarily supposes, as we have seen, their unanimity (cfr.

§ 9). But private use of the Fathers may be made for diverse ends and purposes: either to acquire a clearer knowledge of some dogmatic truth, and to prove and explain it more forcibly; or to obtain suitable moral precepts for various circumstances of life, or to find out the meaning of passages and portions of Holy Scripture. Thus, according to a fourfold purpose, we may distinguish the private use of the Fathers as dogmatical, moral, ascetical or exegetical.

Cfr. *Mabillon* 1. c. Part II. chapters III. IV. — *Fessler-Jungmann* 1. c. § 28.

## § 20. *Use in Matters of Dogma.*

In matters of dogma the holy Fathers may be studied for the following purposes: —

1. In order to draw from their works doctrinal truths, which, though not yet defined as articles of faith, could, nevertheless, not be denied or impugned without temerity.

2. In order to confirm and strengthen our faith by the testimony of Christian antiquity, and to guard against doctrinal innovations.

3. In order to understand thoroughly the fundamental dogmas of our salvation, such as the Blessed Trinity, the Incarnation, the Divinity of Christ and the Holy Ghost, and so forth, which have been treated with particular skill by certain Fathers.

4. In order to render ourselves familiar with the arguments employed by the holy Fathers, to prove the articles of faith, and to defend them against heretics.

5. And lastly, in order to consider how the arguments by which heretics have impugned the various

Catholic truths, may be refuted both by authority and reason.

Cfr. *Wiest* 1. c. §§ 239–245, 280.

## § 21. *Use in Morals and Ascetics.*

In morals, also, a rich harvest may be gathered from the works of the Fathers, for they are replete with moral precepts, and suggest motives for conduct and action. Some of the Fathers, too, have written entire treatises on particular virtues, and laid special stress in their Biblical commentaries upon the moral sense of Scripture passages. Nor are they of less service in the departments of ascetical, pastoral, and homiletical theology. For those Fathers who were conspicuous for their piety, have left us most vivid and beautiful explanations in their writings, and especially in their letters, not only as to how each individual soul may direct itself, but also how others may be led, kept, and advanced in the way of Christian perfection. Again, from their homilies and sermons we may learn how the truths of the faith can be explained and proved, and practically applied to the every-day life of the Christian. As, however, many of the remarks of the Fathers are applicable only to the circumstances of the times in which they lived, their homilies must be judiciously chosen, and as far as possible, applied to the wants and moral conditions of our own time.

Cfr. *Wiest* 1. c. §§ 246–255, 281. — *Fessler-Jungmann* 1. c. § 29.

### § 22. *Use in Biblical Exegesis.*

1. It is usual to distinguish a twofold sense in Scripture, the literal and the figurative or typical, and accordingly, also, two kinds of interpretations, viz. : —

(*a.*) The literal or grammatical-historical interpretation, which considers the contents of Holy Writ according to the proper meaning of the words,* in the light of the context and of the historical facts narrated, (in sensu grammatico, logico, historico).

(*b.*) The figurative, or typical, or allegorical-mystical interpretation, which considers the contents of Holy Writ as signs, i. e., types and figures of the grace, doctrine, and Church of Christ, and of the future life.

The Fathers have not neglected or disregarded either of these two methods of explanation, but have cultivated them both. Some preferred one to the other, while others, more or less, combined the two. The Fathers of the School of Antioch specially cultivated the literal, or historical interpretation; those of the Alexandrian School, the mystical. Others, like St. Chrysostom, St. Augustine, St. Gregory the Great, united both methods.

2. The exegetical labors of the Fathers are seen more particularly in their commentaries on Holy Scripture; also in their homilies, in which they explain to the people certain portions of Scripture, or dwell upon some Scripture character; again, in their scholia,

---

* It would be more accurate to say " according to the literal meaning of the words, whether proper or metaphorical." The proper meaning is generally opposed to the metaphorical, but the author does not take the word "proper " in this strict sense. (R.)

which were short explanations of difficult passages; or again, in prefaces and summaries to different books, or in answers and treatises about special portions or passages.

3. Special mention should be made of what are called " Catenæ Patrum," which are exegetical works, containing a running explanation of single passages of Holy Scripture, extracted from various Fathers. But as the quotations are not always authentic, it is necessary to consult and compare the better editions. The most celebrated of these works is the " Golden Chain," a treatise on the four Gospels by St. Thomas Aquinas (Catena aurea in quattuor evangelia), consisting of selections from more than eighty Greek and Latin Fathers.

Cfr. *Fessler-Jungmann* 1. c. § 30. — *Permaneder* 1. c. § 90.—Wetzer and Welte's Kirchenlexicon, art. " Catenen." Vol. II. 2. ed.

## § 23. *Selection of Fathers.*

1. The works of the Fathers being too numerous to be mastered by any single individual during his lifetime, a selection of the best and most suitable is therefore requisite. As a rule, we ought to read first those works of Fathers in which the doctrines of faith or morals are treated with great brevity and conciseness; or again, those that have been written for special states of life, and which may be read and understood without a great amount of theological or archæological knowledge; as, for instance, the Commonitorium of St. Vincent of Lerins, the Confessions of St. Augustine, the book De Sacerdotio of St. Chrysostom, and the like.

Those who are occupied or interested in the defense of Christian doctrines against the attacks of heathen and Jewish writers, should choose the inestimable treatise of Origen against Celsus ("Contra Celsum"), the "Præparatio et demonstratio Evangelica" of St. Eusebius, the Apologetic ("Apologeticum") of Tertullian, the "Institutiones" of Lactantius, and the writings of the Apologists: Justin, Minucius Felix, Cyprian, and Arnobius.

2. The following rank foremost as controversialists against heretics: Irenæus against the Gnostics; Hippolytus and Tertullian against the Anti-Trinitarians; Jerome against Jovinian, Vigilantius and Helvidius; John Damascene against the Iconoclasts.

3. The student of dogma will find the most minute and acute disputations on

(a.) The Trinity, in the writings of Athanasius, Basil, Augustine, Hilary, and others.

(b.) The Creation, in the writings of Irenæus, Gregory of Nyssa, Augustine, Basil, and Ambrose.

(c.) The Incarnation, in Athanasius and Leo the Great.

(d.) Grace, in Augustine, (Doctor gratiæ), Prosper, and Fulgentius.

(e.) The Sacraments, and especially the Holy Eucharist, in Ambrose, Augustine, and Chrysostom (the Doctor of the Eucharist).

(f). The Church, in Cyprian and Augustine.

4. The subject of morals is treated by St. Basil and St. Gregory the Great in their books on Morals, by St. Ambrose in his book "De officiis," by St. Augustine in his letters. Then again, there are treatises on particular virtues, such as patience or charity, by single Fathers, as St. Cyprian, St. Augus-

tine, St. Basil, St. Chrysostom ; or on particular vices, as envy (De invidia), or on particular states, as virginity, the priesthood (De virginibus, De sacerdotio). On monastic asceticism, we have the works of Cassian, Basil, Macarius the Great, and John Climacus.

5. For purposes of exegesis, the best principles of hermeneutics are contained in the Prefaces of St. Jerome, and in his "Epistola ad Paulinum," as well as in the books of St. Augustine, "De doctrina christiana."

6. Upon Church discipline, valuable explanations are given in the writings of the disciples of the Apostles, the letters of St. Cyprian, St. Augustine, St. Jerome, St. Gregory the Great, etc.

7. In homiletic subjects, the finest specimens are afforded by St. Chrysostom, St. Gregory of Nazianzen, St. Gregory of Nyssa, St. Leo the Great, St. Peter Chrysologus.

Cf. *Wiest* l. c. §§ 157–188. — *Nirschl* l. c. § 14.


§ 24. *Preliminary Conditions to Profitable Use.*

Although the works of the Fathers, speaking generally, do not present such grave difficulties as the Holy Scriptures, yet a certain standard of moral and intellectual culture is requisite for the full and complete understanding of them. In order to read the Fathers with profit, it is necessary not only to hold them and their doctrines in the highest esteem, but also to have an intense love of truth, and a deep attachment to Catholic principles, especially the rule of faith. For since the end and object of all study is to know the truth, there is no safer guide to direct our scientific pursuits, than steadfast adherence to

the principles and rule of faith. Moreover, as the
Fathers almost continually speak the language of
Holy Scripture, the reader of their works must acquire
an intimate knowledge of the Sacred Books, and also
strive more and more to bring his mind into con-
formity with that of the Fathers. He must, finally,
implore the light of the Holy Spirit, that what has
been written by His divine assistance, may also be
rightly comprehended by the aid of His illumination
(James I. 5).

Cf. *Wiest* l. c. § 302–303. — *Permaneder* l. c. §
232–233.

### § 25. *Manner and Way of Using the Fathers.*

To derive profit from the perusal of the holy Fathers,
the following rules should be observed : —

I. Confine yourself to one work at a time, but read
it carefully and repeatedly, until you have grasped
the main subject and method of treatment, and are
able at least to define the outlines, or principal head-
ings of both.

II. Endeavor to carefully impress upon your memory the leading points of the subject of the book.
In this you will be greatly assisted by the practice of
noting down the words of the author himself, his purpose and aim, his train of thought, and the course of
his arguments or proofs.

III. Make a list of the most important passages
(spicilegium repertorium), either in alphabetical
order, or in any other order that commends itself to
you.

IV. Pay great attention to the meaning of each
word, and to the sense of entire passages or treatises.

As regards the *meaning* of words, it is to be noticed that the Fathers make use of words both in the popular and in the philosophical sense of the times. Again, occasionally they do not employ words in the usual and proper sense, but in the sense given to them by heretics; thus it may happen that they use one and the same word in quite different meanings. Furthermore, the literal and proper expressions are to be well distinguished from the figurative or metaphorical.

In order to rightly apprehend the *sense* of a patristic word, or a particular passage, the following rules will be of help: —

(1) Consider well the aim and purpose of the work. Very often the true sense of a difficult passage may be gathered from the aim and object of the entire work.

(2) See for whom, or against whom, the work is written, under what circumstances, and upon what occasion.

(3) Take also into consideration at what part or period of his life a Father composed this or that work.

(4) Try to explain obscure and doubtful passages by those which are clear and explicit occurring elsewhere in the writings of the same Father, or in the works of contemporary Fathers. Incorrect or inaccurate passages of a Father have to be interpreted in the light of the correct and accurate ones, and should be brought into harmony with the writer's general doctrine and orthodoxy of faith. But if it is impossible to harmonize them with the doctrine of the Church, then they must be set aside with all due respect to the author.

(5) We must discover whether a Father is merely

putting forth an opinion, a conjecture, an objection, or whether he is making a dogmatic statement.

Cf. *Nat. B. Argon.* l. c. P. II, c. 2, 10; P. III, c. 13. — *Wiest* l. c. §§ 283–301.

---

# CHAPTER V.

## Means Necessary for Understanding the Fathers.

### § 26. *Causes of Difficulties.*

The difficulties which meet us in reading the Fathers arise partly from the subject-matter discussed, which is at times so lofty that it can scarcely be grasped by the human mind, or expressed in words; as for instance, the doctrine on the Blessed Trinity, free will and grace, predestination. In part, also, these difficulties arise from the form of the patristic works themselves, inasmuch as they may be written in a dead or unfamiliar language, with peculiar phraseology and construction, peculiar method and manner of argument. Obscurity, too, will often arise from the fact that the reader is entirely ignorant of the external circumstances under which the Fathers have written.

It is impossible fully to comprehend the letters and writings of the Fathers when one is ignorant of the occasion which gave rise to them, of their date, of the true author, or of the person to whom, or against whom, they are directed.

Cf. *Fessler-Jungmann* l. c. § 23.

## § 27. *Scientific Means.*

1. In order to derive real spiritual profit from the perusal of the patristic works, it is above all necessary to have a sound knowledge of Latin and Greek, because most of these works are written in one or the other of these two languages. Again, all the Fathers did not write in the elegant and pure style of the Greek and Latin classics; on the contrary, they frequently employed the expressions of the Greek and Latin translations of the Scriptures, and were often compelled to coin new words to express Christian truths and practices. Hence it follows that a knowledge of the non-classical form of these languages is likewise necessary. The knowledge of Syriac and Hebrew, too, is highly desirable, the former for understanding the writings of Syrian authors, the latter for some works of St. Jerome. Valuable helps are afforded by glossaries and good translations.

2. An acquaintance with the ancient systems of philosophy, ancient profane history, and Greek and Roman mythology is likewise requisite, as many ecclesiastical writers, even after their conversion to Christianity, did not at once divest themselves of all the ideas and views of heathen philosophy, but have left numerous traces of them in their compositions. Again, in their apologies, they often refer to contemporary events, or to mythological fables, for the purpose of exposing the absurdity of pagan worship.

3. The chief means, however, is solid theological training, that is, a thorough knowledge of dogmatical and moral theology, without which the patristic writings cannot be properly understood, nor even safely read. Moreover, as the Fathers made the most ex-

tensive and varied use of Holy Scripture, a sound
knowledge of the Bible and of Biblical exegesis is a
great help to the Patrologist.

4. Lastly, a knowledge of Church history is of
necessity. This will bring home to our minds the
events to which the Fathers often allude, the circumstances under which they wrote, the heresies which
they combated, the lawful councils which they defended, and the unlawful which they rejected, as well
as the internal and external conditions and surroundings of their own lives.

Cf. *Wiest* l. c. §§ 304–310. — *Fessler-Jungmann*
l. c. §§ 24–25.

## § 28. *Literary Means.*

Among these we reckon in the first place the choice
of the best special editions of the Fathers, and the
various collections of patristic works, such as " Bibliotheca," " Monumenta," " Spicilegia Patrum ; "
or again, " Analecta Vetera," " Collectanea Veterum
Monumentorum."

1. By editions of the Fathers are to be understood
those literary and critical labors in which the genuineness of the work is carefully examined and
proved, and difficulties as they occur fairly met, and
where the original text is restored as correctly as possible, and explanatory notes are introduced. The
editions may be divided into three classes, according
to the period to which they belong : —

I. First or Oldest Editions, i. e., those before
A. D. 1500.

II. Intermediate Editions, i. e., those from A.
D. 1500–1600.

III. Recent or Modern Editions, from A. D.
1600 downward.

The First (editiones principes, incunabula) are certainly not remarkable for elegance, but are, nevertheless, very valuable and desirable. Amongst the Intermediate Editions, those issued by the learned book-seller Robert Stephen (d. 1559), and Henry Stephen (d. 1594), of Paris, hold a high rank, on account of the pleasant and correct types, as well as the improved text; likewise, though in a lesser degree, those issued by Froben (d. 1527), and Erasmus of Rotterdam (d. 1536), at Basle. Among the Modern Editions, those by the Maurists (French Benedictine Congregation of St. Maurus), the Oratorians, and the Jesuits, are not only conspicuous for beauty of type and excellence of paper, but hold also the first place on account of the newly discovered manuscripts which they have utilized. These Editions contain: (1) lengthy biographies of the holy Fathers; (2) sketches of their genuine works, excluding all unauthentic ones; (3) Latin translations of the Greek texts; (4) expositions of their doctrine; (5) explanations of difficult passages, and (6) carefully executed catalogues of subjects and names. The Paris editions are better than those of Venice.

Speaking generally, the Modern Editions are preferable to the more ancient for obvious reasons. In the first place, they contain certain writings that have only recently been discovered. In the next place, the rules of criticism are more thoroughly applied with regard to the questions of genuineness and authenticity. Lastly, they give a better Latin version of the Greek text, and are provided with explanatory notes, chronological tables, etc.

2. As regards the collections of works of the Fathers, they are of diverse kinds. Some are general,

some special, some Greek and Latin, some only
Latin; some are dogmatical and polemical, others
ascetical and homiletical. Among these collections
the following deserve to be especially noticed: —

(a.) Maxima Bibliotheca Veterum Patrum, 27 Tom.
Fol. Lugd. 1677.

(b.) Bibliotheca Veterum Patrum, 14 Tom. Fol.
Venet. 1765, by the Oratorian Gallandi.

(c.) Bibliotheca Orientalis Clementino-Vaticana, 4
Tom. Fol. Romæ 1719, by the Marionite Joseph
Simon Assemani, containing Syriac, Arabic, Persian,
Turkish, Hebrew, and Armenian writings.

(d.) Collectio Nova Patrum, 2 Tom. Fol. Paris
1706, by Bernard de Montfaucon, O. S. B.

(e.) Spicilegium Veterum Aliquot Scriptorum, 3
Tom. Fol. Paris 1783, by d'Achery, O. S. B.

(f.) Vetera Analecta, 4 Tom. 4°, Paris 1675–1685;
Edit. Nova Fol. Paris 1723, by Mabillon, O. S. B.

(g.) Epistolæ Rom. Pontificum, edited by Peter
Coustant, O. S. B. Paris 1721, and continued till
A. D. 523 by Thiel, Lipsiæ 1867.

(h.) Collectio Selecta SS. Ecclesiæ Patrum Com-
plectens Exquisitissima Opera, cura Caillau et Guillon,
133 Tom. 8ᵛᵒ. Paris 1829 sqq.

(i.) Nova Collectio Scriptorum Veterum, 10 Tom. 4°.
Romæ 1825. Also, Spicilegium Rom., 10 Tom. 8ᵛᵒ.
Romæ 1839, and Nova Patrum Collectio, 7 Tom. 4°.
Romæ 1852, all by the Vatican Librarian, Cardinal
Angelo Mai.

(j.) Spicilegium Solesmense, 4 Tom. 4°. Paris
1852 sqq.; Analecta Sacra Spicilegio Solesmensi Parata,
6 Tom. 4°. Paris 1876–1888, and Analecta Novissima
(containing chiefly mediæval documents), 2 Tom. 4°.
Paris 1885–1888, all by Cardinal Pitra, O. S. B.

All these collections, however, are surpassed in magnitude and completeness by the Cursus Completus Patrologiæ, of the Abbé Migne (d. 1875).

This monumental work, most valuable, in spite of many typographical deficiencies, is a collection of Latin Fathers and ecclesiastical authors from Tertullian to Innocent III., in 217 vols. 4°, besides a copious index in 4 vols., and of Greek authors from the time of the Apostolic Fathers to the Council of Florence, in 162 vols. 4°, together with a Latin translation, and many valuable treatises and learned discussions, but without an index.

Among the manual editions of works of the Fathers published in recent times, the following two deserve special mention : —

(1) SS. Patrum Opuscula Selecta ad usum præsertim Studiosorum Theologiæ, edidit et commentariis auxit H. Hurter, S. J. Œnip., Libraria Wagner. 48 vols. 16ᵐᵒ. Series II. is in 8ᵛᵒ.*

(2) (For those who read German.) Bibliothek der Kirchenväter, in 80 vols. 12ᵐᵒ, besides 2 vols. of general index, published at Kempten in Bavaria, the German translation and edition being by Reithmayr and Thalhofer. This work is approved and recommended by the whole German episcopate.

Most valuable also are the critical editions of the

---

* The " Opuscula Patrum," by *H. Hurter*, S. J., deserve to be specially recommended to all students of divinity. From long practical experience, I can testify to their eminent usefulness. Not only have the texts been aptly chosen by the author for the student's special purposes, but are also provided with learned introductions, notes, and dissertations, the perusal of which will serve the student as a constant repetition of his theology. (R.)

Latin text of ecclesiastical writers, published at the expense of the Royal Imperial Academy of Sciences in Vienna, under the title " Corpus Scriptorum Ecclesiasticorum Latinorum. Vindobonæ, 26 vols. 8°. 1866. sqq.*

For the practical study of theology, or for homiletical purposes, the most valuable collections are the so-called Anthologiæ, or Chrestomathiæ, in which a number of patristic principles, maxims, and dicta, bearing upon particular points, are gathered together.

Among the most noteworthy we may mention : —

*Cigheri*,  " Veterum  Patrum  theologia  universa," 13 tom. 4°. Florentiæ 1791.

*Thomasius*, " Instit. theolog. antiquorum Patrum," 4 tom. 4°. Romæ 1709; and  *Caillau et Guillon*, " Thesaurus Patrum, floresque doctorum ecclesiæ," 8 tom. Paris 1823.

---

\* It is noteworthy, too, that the Prussian government has recently instituted a commission of learned men for the purpose of editing the works of the Fathers and other ancient writers.  (R.)

# PART II.

## PATROLOGY PROPER.

### § 29. *Division.*

The second or special part of this book, comprising Patrology proper, may be divided into four epochs, more or less representing the course of development of Christian literature:

Epoch I. Rise of Christian literature, till the year 150.
" II. Development " " from 150–325.
" III. Full Growth " " " 325–461.
" IV. Decline " " " 461–700.

## FIRST EPOCH.

### RISE OF PATRISTIC LITERATURE.
### AGE OF THE APOSTOLIC FATHERS.

### § 30. *The Apostolic Fathers.*

1. The name of Apostolic Fathers is given to those writers who were disciples of the Apostles, and who, in writing, have handed down to posterity the Apostolic doctrine pure and genuine. Such are the author of the Didache, or Doctrine of the Twelve Apostles, Barnabas, Clement of Rome, Hermas, Ignatius, Polycarp, the unknown author of the Epistle to Diognetus, and Papias.

2. The Apostolic Fathers have left us but few writings, and these almost exclusively in the shape of

( 63 )

letters. The reason of this is to be sought in the fact that the Christian religion did not present itself to them as the result of human investigation, but as a divine revelation, attested by miracles, and so fully satisfying the spiritual needs of the believers, as to obviate the necessity of proofs derived from scientific demonstration.

3. Nevertheless, even in those scanty literary monuments, we are able to trace already the groundwork of the different forms of future theology. In Clement we discover the first germs of Canon Law; in Barnabas the first attempt at dogmatic theology; in Ignatius and in the Epistle to Diognetus the outlines of apologetics; in the Interpretations (Ἐξηγήσεις, Enarrationes) of Papias, the beginnings of Biblical exegesis; and in the Shepherd of Hermas, the rudiments of ascetical and moral theology. It is noteworthy, too, that Clement, in his expositions of the moral law, follows in the footsteps of St. Paul, Ignatius in those of St. John, and Hermas in those of St. Peter.

Though small in extent and in number, still, as the earliest monuments of Christian antiquity and first fruits of Christian thought, these works of the Apostolic Fathers, written in Greek, are of immense value. They treat principally of the religious condition of Christian communities, of grace and truth as manifested in Christ, of faith, of brotherly love, of obedience to ecclesiastical superiors, and of the evil of sin and heresy.

*Editions and Literature.* — *Cotelerius*, SS. Patrum Apost. opp. omnia. 2 tom. fol. Paris 1672. — *Dressel*, Patrum Apost. opp. ed. II. Lipsiæ 1863. — *Gebhardt-Harnack-Zahn*, Patrum Apost. opp. ed. III.

Lipsiæ 1877. — *Funk*, Opera Patrum Apost. editio post Hefelianam quartam sexta. Tubingæ 1887. — *G. Jacobson*, S. Clem. Rom., S. Ignatii, S. Polycarpi, PP. Apostolicorum quæ sup. etc. 2 vols. 8ᵛᵒ. Oxonii 1838. ed. 4. 1863. — *Bp. Lightfoot*, The Apostolic Fathers, comprising the Epistles (genuine and spurious) of Clement of Rome; the Epistles of St. Ignatius, of St. Polycarp, the Teaching of the Apostles, etc. Revised texts with short introductions and English translations. Edited and completed by *J. R. Harmer*. London 1891. 8ᵛᵒ. — *A. Roberts* and *J. Donaldson*, Ante-Nicene Christian Library. The Apostolic Fathers. Vol. I. T. and T. Clark, Edinburgh.

### § 31. *Doctrine of the Twelve Apostles.*

1. The author of the Doctrine of the Twelve Apostles (Διδαχὴ τῶν δώδεκα Ἀποστόλων), a work well known to ancient authors, holds the first place amongst the Christian writings of the Apostolic age. Express mention is made of this work both by Greek and Latin authors, such as Eusebius,[*] St. Athanasius,[†] the author of the Latin work on the dice-players,[‡] St. Jerome,[||] and Rufinus.[¶] Many quotations, also, from the "Doctrine of the Apostles" are to be found in the second part of the Epistle of Barnabas, in the Pseudo-Clementine Apostolic Constitutions (book VII), and very clear traces of the work are apparent in the compositions of Justin, Tatian, Clement of Alexandria, Theophilus of Antioch, Origen, Irenæus, Lactantius, and John Climacus. But from the 12th cen-

---

[*] Hist. Eccl. III. 25.     [||] De vir. ill. c. 1.

[†] Ep. Pasch. 39.     [¶] Exp. Symb. App. c. 38,

[‡] De aleatoribus, c. 4.

tury downwards the "Didache" disappeared, and was
believed to be utterly lost, until 1873, when Philotheus
Bryennius, at that time Professor and, since 1877,
Metropolitan of Nicomedia, discovered in a monastic
library at Constantinople a codex, written by Leo the
Notary in the year 1056, which contained, besides the
Epistle of Barnabas and two Epistles of St. Clement
to the Corinthians and some other writings, the
Διδαχὴ τῶν δώδεχα Ἀποστόλων.

2. According to its contents, the work consists of
two parts; the first, from chapter I–VI, treats of the
two ways of life and death, that is, of the general
duties of a Christian and of whatever is opposed to
them; and from chap. VII–X, of particular duties,
especially the administration of baptism, fasting, and
the reception of the Holy Eucharist. The second
part gives instructions for the admission of brethren,
for discerning true and false prophets, for showing hospitality to Christian pilgrims and strangers,
for the maintenance of teachers (apostles), for the
choice of "bishops" (priests) and deacons, and for
fraternal correction. Chapter XVI closes with an
admonition to watchfulness, a description of the
doings of the Antichrist (χοσμοπλάνος), and the coming
of Our Lord.

Concerning the time and place of origin of the work,
opinions differ very considerably. While some place
it as early as between 50 and 70, others assign it to
the middle, or towards the end of the second century.
The majority, however, of the learned assume the
last quarter of the first century to be the time of its
composition, on the ground that the work itself contains nothing which would point to a later origin, while
its author speaks of prophets and Apostles in a way

that was possible only for a writer of the first century. On other grounds, also, the hypothesis of a later period is untenable.

3. In spite of its small dimensions, the work possesses great merits. It is written with admirable simplicity of style, and its subject-matter is of the highest importance to the Catholic theologian; for it places in his hand an excellent weapon wherewith to defend the traditional doctrine of the Church on the obligation and merit of good works (chp's. VII, VIII, XIII, XV), the necessity of baptism, confession of sins,* the Holy Eucharist, both as sacrament and sacrifice (IV, VII, IX, XIV). It likewise furnishes proof of the lawfulness of baptism per infusionem, "Pour water on the head thrice in the name" . . . . ; †  the duty of submission to ecclesiastical superiors, as well as of the divine institution, authority, and visibility of the Church herself (IV, XI, XIII, XV).

---

* "In the church thou shalt confess thy sins," — Ἐν ἐκκλησίᾳ ἐξομολογήσῃ τὰ παραπτώματά σου, etc., which *Funk* translates: "In ecclesia confiteberis peccata tua, neque accedes ad orationem tuam in conscientia mala," and *Bp. Lightfoot:* "In Church thou shalt confess thy transgressions and shalt not betake thyself to prayer with an evil conscience." It is noteworthy that with the confession of sins ends the way of life (hæc est via vitæ), chap. IV, sentence 12th, and further on, in chap. 14th, first sentence, he says (*B. Lightf. tr.*), "and on the Lord's own day, gather yourselves together and break bread, first confessing your transgressions" (*Funk* translates the Aorist with " postquam delicta vestra confessi estis")—"that your sacrifice may be pure." (R.)

† Ἔκχεον εἰς τὴν κεφαλὴν τρὶς ὕδωρ εἰς τὸ ὄνομα, etc. (cap. 7).

*Editions and Literature.* — Amongst the numerous editions, that by *F. X. Funk* of Tübingen is deserving of the highest praise, especially on account of the Prologomena, written in Latin, and containing the most minute researches on different points. — *Lightfoot-Harmer*, as above. — The publication of the Didache by *Bryennius* has called forth many separate editions, besides a voluminous literature, both in England and abroad. To quote only one or two: J. *Heron*, The Church of the Sub-Apostolic Age: its life, worship, and organization, in the light of the " Teaching of the Twelve Apostles," London 1888. — *J. M. Minasi* gives a most excellent commentary in his learned work: La dottrina del Signore pei dodici Apostoli, etc., Roma 1891.

## § 32. *St. Barnabas, Apostle.*

1. We learn from the Acts of the Apostles,* that *Barnabas* was a native of Cyprus, that his original name was Joses, or Joseph, that he belonged to the tribe of Levi, and was one of the first Christians who, after the death of Our Lord, sold their possessions and laid the price at the feet of the Apostles. Being a man full of the Holy Ghost and of faith,† he was called by the Apostles to the ministry of the Gospel, in which he labored for a long time at Antioch. Here he was joined by St. Paul, whom he had introduced to the Apostles at Jerusalem, and with whom he continued to labor in Syria and the North of Asia Minor, extending Christianity and successfully combating the Judaizing zealots of the law, who, with characteristic

---

* Acts, IV. 36, 37.                          † Acts, XI. 24.

narrowness of mind and utter disregard of the true
spirit of the Gospel, thought it necessary to lay the
yoke of the Mosaic Law even upon the Gentile converts. At the Apostolic Council of Jerusalem, both
he and St. Paul upheld the decision that the Gentile
converts were free from the trammels of the cere-
monial law. After they had " continued at Antioch,
teaching and preaching with many others " * the joyful tidings of the Gospel, they separated from each
other, and Barnabas repaired with Mark to Cyprus.†
How long he labored in his native land, where and
in what manner he ended his life, is unknown. It is
probable that he died in the year 76 ; in any case, not
before the destruction of Jerusalem, which event he
mentions in the sixteenth chapter of his Epistle.

2. A letter which Origen calls " Catholic Epistle " ‡
(ἐπιστολὴ καϑολική) has been handed down under the
name of St. Barnabas, and to him it is ascribed
by the most eminent Christian writers of the first
centuries, as Clement of Alexandria,§ Eusebius,‖
Jerome,¶ and by the Codex Sinaiticus, belonging to
the fourth century, and discovered by Tischendorf
in a monastery on Mount Sinai. This opinion was
adopted and held by such learned writers as Dupin,
le Nourry, Pagi, Möhler, Freppel, Nirschl, Jungmann,
and others. But in more recent times, critics, chiefly
Protestant, but also some Catholic, like Natalis
Alexander, Ceillier, Tillemont, Hefele, Kayser, Funk,
Braunsberger, Bardenhewer, and others, hold that it
is not the work of the Apostle Barnabas, but of some

---

* Acts, XV. 35.                § Strom. II. 6, 7.
† Acts, XV. 39.                ‖ Hist. Eccl. III. c. 25.
‡ Contra Celsum, I. 63.        ¶ De vir. illust. c. 6.

Alexandrian Jewish convert of the same name. Their arguments against the authenticity of the letter are mostly too trifling to be of any weight, and the author's antipathy to Judaism and his depreciation of the Mosaic Law lose much of their force as proofs against genuineness, on a closer examination of the scope of the Epistle, so that it may be said that the arguments are chiefly in favor of its authenticity.*

3. This "Catholic Epistle," which possibly was intended for converts from Judaism, but indirectly also for those from paganism, and for the still unconverted Jews, consists of two parts, one dogmatic-didactic (c. 1–17); the other moral (hortatory or parainetical, c. 18–21). In the first part (c. 1–17), the author, after greeting "his sons and daughters," and after a word of praise for their faith and love, proceeds to show that the Old Covenant was of a merely typical character, and of its very nature a preparation for Christ; that the observance of the Mosaic Law was only pleasing to God inasmuch as it was done in the spirit; that it was abrogated by the New Covenant only as to the letter, not as to the spirit; that Sunday had taken the place of the Sabbath-day, being the day of a new spiritual creation; that the temple of Jerusalem had been destroyed in order to set up in the hearts of Christians another temple, spiritual in character and pleasing to God. In the second part (c. 18–21), he describes, with many quotations from the "Doctrine of the Apostles," the two

---

* According to Dr. Otto Bardenhewer, Patrologie, p. 35–36, an overwhelming majority of critics pronounce *against* the genuineness of the Epistle. He himself holds that the doctrines of the Epistle cannot, except by violence, be brought into harmony with those of St. Paul and the other Apostles. (R.)

ways of life, viz.: the way of light and the way of darkness, and shows what the Christian ought to do and avoid, in order to attain future resurrection and eternal happiness. The contents and scope of the entire Epistle form a parallel to St. Paul's Epistle to the Hebrews, while its simplicity and warmth of language remind us rather of the Epistles of St. John. "Stylum revera maiestate Apostolica dignum materiamque nascentis Ecclesiæ rebus accommodatam sapit." *

The first part of the Epistle contains fine passages, in particular, upon the divinity of Christ (c. 5, 7, 12); the object of the Incarnation (c. 5 and 14), the nature of justification as an inward sanctification (c. 6, 11, 16), faith working by love (c. 1, 4, 7), and other doctrines.

*Editions and Literature.* — The same as in the preceding paragraph. In the earlier known Greek MSS. of the letter, the first four chapters and a half were wanting, but the deficiencies have been supplied by the discovery of the Codex Sinaiticus, and the aforesaid Codex of Ph. Bryennius. — The first complete Greek editions were those of *Hilgenfeld* and *Gebhardt* (1877 and 1878). — *W. Cunningham,* The Epistle of St. Barnabas, a Dissertation, including a discussion of its date and authorship. London 1877. — *Ceillier,* Hist. gén. des auteurs sacrés et eccl. I. (éd. 1. Paris, 498–505). — *Nirschl,* Das Todesjahr des Apostels Barnabas, im "Katholik," 1881, p. 425; and "Lehrbuch der Patrologie," § 23. — *Braunsberger,* Der Apostel Barnabas. Mainz 1876. — *Funk,* in the Tübinger Theol. Quartalschr. 1884, p. 3–33.

---

* Fessler, Inst. Patr. I. 184.

### § 33. *St. Clement, Bishop of Rome.*

1. As to the life of this holy Father, the only certain facts handed down to us from Christian antiquity are, that he had close relations with the holy Apostles Peter and Paul; that he was Bishop of Rome, and identical with the Clement whom St. Paul mentions as one of his fellow-laborers in the Gospel.*  How and when he went to Rome, whether he was the immediate successor of St. Peter in the Roman See, or only followed Linus and Cletus, is as uncertain as the assertion of some old authors, that he was a cousin to the Emperor Domitian and a son of a Roman Senator, and, under marvelous circumstances, died a martyr's death in the sea, about A. D. 100.

2. Amongst the works ascribed to him, the first Epistle to the Corinthians, in 65 chapters, ranks as decidedly authentic, and is one of the finest literary monuments of Christian antiquity.  In it, with great force, yet with prudence and gentleness, Clement admonishes the Corinthians, who had been led into disobedience by factious men.  And in order to lead them back to sorrow and penance, to humility, obedience, and love, he points to the example of Christ, the evils of envy, and the terrors of the judgment to come.

On the other hand, the second Epistle to the Corinthians, in 20 chapters, is more than doubtful; and so are, in a still greater degree, the two "Letters to Virgins."  The former contains, in the form of a hom-

---

* Phil. IV. 3. . . . . " Help those women that have labored with me in the gospel with *Clement* and the rest of my fellow-laborers, whose names are in the book of life."  (R.)

ily, pressing exhortations to a truly Christian life, to contempt of a perishable world, to a striving after a blessed eternity, to a warfare against sin, and to works of penance. This letter was not ascribed to St. Clement according to Eusebius, who, indeed, repudiates the idea, and with regard to style and expression, it differs strikingly from the first Epistle.

Of the two Epistles to Virgins, i. e., the unmarried of both sexes, the first represents the beauty, but also the difficulties, of the state of virginity, and warns against idleness and mixed assemblies, while the second describes the manner of life in the single state, drawing examples from the Scriptures.

This latter Epistle contains, indeed, the same sublime simplicity and beauty as the first Epistle, but by reason of various allusions to events of later date, its authenticity is extremely doubtful.

The five Books of Decretals, the eight Books of Constitutions, and eighty-five Canones Apostolorum, as well as the twenty Homilies and Recognitions, together with an Epitome from them, are decidedly not genuine. The Decretal Letters contain the most excellent instructions upon the liturgy, the authority of the priesthood, and the duties of the faithful, as well as the most earnest admonitions to conversion from error. The first six books of the Constitutions, apparently composed towards the end of the 4th, or beginning of the 5th century, form one single and entire hand-book on religious subjects for priests and faithful, interspersed with many Biblical quotations. The seventh book, adorned with many extracts from the "Doctrine of the Apostles," embraces the outlines of a system of morals; and the eighth, besides an order of the Mass, gives instructions for conferring the various orders, with many formulas for blessings, and also some prayers. The eighty-five "Canones" joined to the eighth book, are of somewhat later origin, and contain directions about elections, ordination, official duties of priests, and such like. The Homilies and Recognitions are a kind of romance, Syrian in origin, and the product of a heretical spirit, endeavoring to justify Ebionitism, in opposition both to heathen polytheism and the Christian doctrine of the Trinity.

3. The first Epistle to the Corinthians, written in classical Greek, and giving proof of the high endowments and culture of the writer, is a splendid example of a pastoral letter, and furnishes beautiful testimonies to such doctrines as the inspiration of Holy Scripture,* the Trinity,† justification through faith and good works,‡ and the hierarchical orders in the Church.§ The cluster of legends that grew up around St. Clement's name, gives us an insight into the great esteem in which the Saint and his work were held by the early Christians.

*Editions and Literature.* — Apostolic Fathers as above, § 30. — *Migne*, S. gr. I, II. — A complete and reliable edition of the Greek text of both Epistles was only possible after the discovery of the Jerusalem codex at Constantinople by *Phil. Bryennius*, and was first published with critical commentary and notes by *Ad. Hilgenfeld:* Clementis Rom. Epistolæ, Lips. 1876. — Recently, *Germain Morin*, O. S. B., has brought to light a "Versio latina antiquissima S. Clementis Rom. ad Corinthios epistolæ" (4º Oxon.

---

* Chapters 45, 53.                    ‡ Chaps. 32, 33.
† Chap. 46.                           § Chaps. 42, 44.

1894), from a MS. belonging to the XIth century. — *Ceillier* l. c. I, 598–620. — *Brüll*, Der erste Corinther-brief des hl. Clemens. Freiburg 1883. — *Funk*, Die Apostol. Constitutionen. Rottenburg 1891. In this learned work is to be found a minute examination of the "Didascalia Apostolorum syriace," published by *de Lagarde*, Lips. 1854.

### § 34. *Hermas.*

1. A book belonging to the earliest days of Christianity, and most remarkable for its matter, form, and comprehensiveness, has come down to us under the name of "The Shepherd" (Ποιμήν, Pastor). The author calls himself Hermas, and tells us that, when still young, he was sold as a slave to a certain Rhode, and afterwards set free by her. He married, and amassed a considerable fortune, partly by dishonest trade, and led with his own family a life of little edification. In punishment of his sins he lost all his possessions, except one field, and had to suffer many hardships, which, however, brought about a moral reform of himself and family. He lived in Rome at the time of Pope Clement, and probably held the office of a lector in the Church. Whether he is the same Hermas to whom St. Paul sent greeting in his Epistle to the Romans,* or whether he is a brother of Pope Pius I. (140–155), is still a much disputed question. In favor of the former opinion may be adduced, not only the testimony of early Christian writers, such as Origen, Irenæus, Eusebius, and others, but also the circumstance that the writer represents himself † as a

---

* Rom. XVI. 14.  † Vis. II. 4.

contemporary of Clement of Rome, and that the book was recognized in the Eastern Church as the work of a disciple of the Apostles, and consequently considered to possess Apostolic authority, like the Epistles of Clement and Barnabas.    Against this ancient and for a long time generally prevailing opinion, various objections have been urged in modern times, the chief one being the so-called Muratorian fragment, which is a catalogue enumerating the books that are to be considered as canonical or uncanonical, dating from the end of the second century.    Here it is quite definitely stated that Hermas, a brother of Pope Pius I., was the author of "The Shepherd."    We are thus confronted with two directly contradictory opinions, both apparently well attested.    Dr. Nirschl and others have sought to reconcile them by making the older Hermas the real author of the work in Greek, and the younger the translator of it into Latin.    A third opinion maintains that it is the work of an entirely unknown person, and written soon after the time of the Emperor Trajan.

2. The work is written in the Apocalyptic style, and furnishes precepts and instructions as to the way of becoming a Christian, and how to live a truly Christian life.    It contains five Visions, twelve Commandments, and ten Similitudes.    In the first four Visions, the Church appears to Hermas under the figure of a matron, and teaches him ; but in the fifth Vision, which forms the transition to the Commandments and Similitudes, as well as throughout the latter, his informant is an angel of penance, appearing in the garb of a shepherd, whence the name of the whole book.

In Vision I. he receives instructions on purity of heart ;

In Vision II. on his relation to his wife and children.

In Vision III. he is shown the building of a tower, and how people are received and admitted into it.

In Vision IV. he is shown the afflictions of the Church, under the symbolical picture of a monster.

The Commandments treat of faith in one God, of simplicity, innocence, charity, truthfulness, lying, the duties of husband and wife, justice, patience, discernment of spirits and their inspirations, and struggle against concupiscence. They end with an admonition to Hermas to observe and make known these commandments.

The Similitudes are a series of telling images, illustrating various Christian truths and precepts, as, for instance, the harm of excessive solicitude for things temporal, the benefit the rich derive from the prayers of the poor, the merits of fasting, and so forth. In the tenth Similitude, the angel commands Hermas to exhort all men to penance, to the praise of God's works, the observance of his commandments, to patient endurance of suffering, and the practice of merciful kindness. The main purpose of all the communications made to Hermas in these Visions, Commandments, and Similitudes, is to awaken, not only in him and his family, but in all the faithful, a vigorous spirit of penance. As motives of penance, he points to the impending calamities of the Church, the end of the world, the second coming of Christ, or, in the image of the Vision, the completion of the tower.

3. The work abounds in beautiful passages and statements, some more, some less definite, on points of dogmatic and moral theology. For instance, the plurality of Divine Persons (Sim. IX, c. 12); the crea-

tion of man by God (Mand. XII, c. 4); original sin
and the necessity of baptism (Sim. IX, c. 16); the
free will of man (Mand. VI, c. 2); the necessity of
grace, to be obtained by prayer (Vis. III, c. 9); the
indissolubility of marriage (Mand. IV, c. 1); the
lawfulness of second marriage (Mand. IV, c. 4); the
observance of the commandments and striving after
perfection by the practice of good works (Sim. V, c.
2, 3); resurrection and eternal retribution (Sim. V,
c. 6, 7; VIII, c. 3; IX, c. 12. Vis. III, c. 7. Sim.
VI, c. 2; VIII, c. 6). But the author fails in accurately representing the doctrine of the Logos (Sim.
V, c. 5; IX, c. 1).*

The style of the book is simple, clear, but overladen
with imagery; it resembles, in many respects, the
Apocalypse of St. John, and on account of its solid
and important matter was held in high esteem from
the beginning in the Eastern Church, and, later on,
also in the West. St. Jerome calls it " a truly useful
book, and one from which many of the ancient writers
have drawn their testimonies." †

*Editions and Literature.* — *Migne*, S. gr. II, 818 —
1024. — *Hilgenfeld*, Hermæ Pastor, græce e codice Sin-
ait. ed. Lips. 1881. — *Haussleiter*, De Versionibus Pastoris Hermæ Latinis, Erlangæ 1884. — *Ceillier* l. c. I,
582-597. — *Nirschl*, Der Hirt des Hermas. Passau
1879 (an original and interesting discussion). — *Baum-
gärtner*, Die Einheit des Hermasbriefes. Freiburg

---

* The objection is that he confuses the Son of God and
the Holy Ghost. The confusion, however, is probably more
apparent than real. (R.)

† De vir. ill. c. 10. " Revera utilis liber, multique de eo
scriptorum veterum usurpavere testimonia; " (but he adds,
" Apud Latinos pæne ignotus est.") (R.)

1889. — Theolog. Quartalschrift, 1878, pages 44 and 354; 1888, page 51. — A collation of the Athos Codex of the Shepherd of Hermas, together with an introduction by *Sp. P. Lambros.* Translated and edited with a preface and appendices by *J. A. Robinson,* Cambridge 1888. — *C. Taylor,* The Witness of Hermas to the Four Gospels. London 1892.

### § 35. *St. Ignatius, Bishop of Antioch.*

1. Little is known of the life of *St. Ignatius,* who was also called Theophorus. All we know is, that he was a disciple of St. John the Evangelist, that he occupied the episcopal chair of Antioch (70–107) for thirty-seven years, as successor of St. Peter and Evodius, that during the persecution of Domitian, he encouraged and strengthened by prayer, fasting, and teaching the flock intrusted to him, and that he suffered martyrdom for Christ, according to his own ardent desire, in the Roman amphitheatre on Dec. 20, between 107 and 117, probably 107.*

With regard to the closing events of the life of the holy martyr, further details are contained in the "Martyrium S. Ignatii," written in a simple style, and, as is supposed, by eye-witnesses. It gives an account of how he discharged his episcopal office, how he was examined by the Emperor Trajan and gave testimony before him; it further describes his deportation, his stay at Smyrna, how he was visited by delegates from the neighboring churches, how he addressed letters to them, his further journey to

---

* See *Funk* in Kirchenlexicon VI, 582 (2 edit.). — *Nirschl,* Das Todesjahr des hl. Ignatius. Passau 1869.

Rome, and his death in the amphitheatre. In the conclusion the reason is given why this account was written. Its authenticity is greatly disputed, and the manuscript is declared to belong to the fourth or fifth century.*

2. We have seven Epistles of St. Ignatius, written on his last painful journey to Rome. Four of these, to the Ephesians, Magnesians, Trallians, and Romans, are written from Smyrna, while the other three, to the Philadelphians, the people of Smyrna, and to Bishop Polycarp, are written from Troas. These Epistles are veritable jewels of ancient Christian literature; they are full of unction, and every page bears witness to the episcopal fortitude, faithfulness, pastoral solicitude, and invincible faith of the great martyr. In them he endeavors to strengthen the faith of his brethren in the divinity and humanity of Christ, against the heresies of Ebionitism and Docetism, and as the best protection against all heresy he earnestly exhorts them to keep united amongst themselves and with their bishop. The authenticity of these Epistles, though much impugned, chiefly on dogmatical grounds, remains altogether beyond question. It is guaranteed first by the fact that Polycarp expressly states that he collected them all, that Irenæus, Origen, and Eusebius quote many passages from them, and that SS. Athanasius, Chrysostom, and Jerome appeal to them. In the next place, they bear the impress of a disciple of St. John, and of the Apostolic age. The remaining Epistles which profess to be written by St. Ignatius, are decidedly spurious, and owe their origin

---

* On the various acts of his martyrdom, see *Lightfoot*, The Apostolic Fathers, p. II, vol. II, and *Funk*, opp. Patr. Apost. I, 254 sqq. — *Nirschl*, Histor.-Polit. Blätter, 1879, vol. LXXXIV.

to an Apollinarist in Syria or Egypt, towards the beginning of the fifth century.

3. The genuine Epistles of St. Ignatius, whose great importance was acknowledged from the earliest times, bear magnificent testimony to the truth of the Trinity (Magn. c. 13; Eph. c. 9); to the doctrine of the divinity and humanity of Christ (Eph. c. 7, 18); the primacy of the Roman Church, which he calls " the president of the brotherhood " * [Rom. Introd.]; the threefold rank of the hierarchy (Philadelph. c. 7; Magn. c. 6); the Eucharist, which he calls the antidote of death and the means of immortality† (Eph. c. 5 and 20); Christian marriage in foro Ecclesiæ: — "It becometh men, and women too, when they marry, to unite themselves with the consent of the bishop, that the marriage may be after the Lord and not after concupiscence." (Polyc. c. 5.) Ignatius is a true copy of St. John, full of glowing love for Christ, whom he beholds represented in the bishops of the Church. His diction is generally powerful, but at times the language seems to struggle with the ideas, and becomes encumbered with heavy periods.

---

* In Bishop Lightfoot's translation the introductory words of the Epistle to the Romans run thus: "Ignatius . . . to the church that is beloved and enlightened through the will of Him, who willed all things that are, by faith and love towards Jesus Christ our God; even unto her *that hath the presidency in the country of the region of the Romans*, being worthy of God, worthy of honor, worthy of felicitation, worthy of praise, worthy of success, worthy in purity, and *having the presidency of love* ($\pi\rho o\chi a\vartheta\eta\mu\acute{e}\nu\eta$ $\tau\tilde{\eta}s$ $\dot{a}\gamma\acute{a}\pi\eta s$), walking in the law of Christ and bearing the Father's name." . . . (The italics are mine. R.)

† $\Phi\acute{a}\rho\mu a\kappa o\nu$ $\dot{a}\vartheta a\nu a\sigma\acute{\iota}a s$, $\dot{a}\nu\tau\acute{\iota}\delta o\tau o\nu$ $\tau o\tilde{\upsilon}$ $\mu\grave{\eta}$ $\dot{a}\pi o\vartheta a\nu\epsilon\tilde{\iota}\nu$.

*Editions and Literature.* — Apostolic Fathers as
above. — *Migne* S. gr. V, 10–996. — *Ceillier* l. c. I,
620–667. — *Nirschl*, Die Briefe des heiligen Ignatius.
Passau 1870 ; also, Lehrbuch, §§ 35–38, and Das Todesjahr des heiligen Ignatius. Passau 1869. — *Funk*, Die
Echtheit der Ignatianischen Briefe. Tübingen 1883,
and Wetzer and Welte's Kirchenlexicon, VI, 2 ed.
581. — A Syriac version of the three Epistles, in an
abbreviated form, was found, edited and commented
upon in several writings by *W. Cureton*, London
1845–1849. — *W. D. Killen*, The Ignatian Epistles
entirely spurious; a reply to the Rt. Rev. Dr. Lightfoot, Bishop of Durham, Edinburgh 1886. 8vo. — *R.
C. Jenkins*, Ignatian Difficulties and Historic Doubts :
a Letter to the Very Rev. the Dean of Peterborough.
London 1890. 8vo. — See *Bardenhewer*, Patrologie,
§ 10; *Fessler-Jungmann* l. c. §§ 36–37.

## § 36. *St. Polycarp, Bishop of Smyrna (d. about 166).*

1. *Polycarp* was the immediate contemporary and
friend of St. Ignatius, but nothing certain is known as
to his origin, or the place and time of his birth.   Irenæus, his disciple, tells us that he was instructed by
the Apostle St. John, and appointed by him Bishop of
Smyrna.   About the middle of the second century he
journeyed to Rome to consult with Pope Anicetus
regarding the time of Easter.   On this occasion he
brought back to the Church many who had been led
away by the Gnostics Valentine and Marcion.   It is
recorded that on meeting Marcion in the streets of
Rome, when the latter asked whether he knew him, he
replied that he knew " the first born of Satan."   He
was close on a hundred years old, when he died the

death of a martyr by the sword — having been miraculously preserved from death by fire — under Marcus Aurelius, about 166, or, according to others, about 155 or 156.

The particulars of the glorious end of St. Polycarp are given us in the " Martyrium S. Polycarpi," written by a certain Marcus, at the request of a Christian church of Asia Minor.   It contains a striking description of the personal appearance of the Apostolic disciple, the fearlessness of the Christians amidst the most terrible tortures, their enthusiastic love of the faith and veneration for their Bishop.   The authenticity of this valuable document, like that of the martyrdom of St. Ignatius, has indeed been contested in modern times, but the greater probability seems to be in its favor.

2. Of the letters which St. Polycarp, according to the testimony of St. Irenæus, wrote to the neighboring churches and to particular persons, we possess only that to the Philippians, whose authenticity is vouched for by Irenæus and Eusebius, and by the fact that it was publicly read in the churches, and that its subject is quite in harmony with the doctrine of the Apostles and the circumstances of the time and the author.

The Philippians had asked him to send them the letters of St. Ignatius.   To these he joined his own epistle, containing fourteen chapters of the most beautiful instructions on the Christian life and the duties belonging to its various states.

Five fragments of answers attributed to him, are doubtful; and the so-called " Doctrina Polycarpi," the " Epistola ad Athenienses," and the " Epistola ad Dionysium Areopagitam," are decidedly spurious.

3. The original text of the Epistle to the Philippians
is incomplete, but it is preserved complete in a Latin
translation. The Epistle is noteworthy for the following doctrinal points: The necessity of tradition
(c. 7); the divine and human nature of Christ (c.
1-2); intercession for friends and enemies (c. 12);
resurrection and judgment (c. 7). The style is
simple, clear, and powerful, interspersed with many
passages from the Old and New Testament, and, for
this reason, of special importance for the Canon of
Scripture. St. Irenæus speaks of him thus: —

" Polycarp was not only taught by the Apostles, and
had held intercourse with those who had seen Christ,
but was also appointed by the Apostles as bishop over
the Church of Smyrna, in Asia Minor, teaching always
the same things which he had learnt from them, and
which the Church also is handing down, and which
alone are true."*

*Editions and Literature.* — Apostolic Fathers as
above. — *Migne*, S. gr. V, 995–1046. — *Ceillier* l. c.
I, 672–683. — Much has been written both here and
abroad on the day and year of St. Polycarp's martyrdom. — *J. M. Cotterill*, in the Journal of Philology,
vol. XIX, 1891, p. 241–285, contended that the

---

* Adv. Haer. III, c. 3. "Πολύκαρπος οὐ μόνον ὑπὸ
" ἀποστόλων μαθητευθεὶς καὶ συναναστραφεὶς πολλοῖς τοῖς
" τὸν Χριστὸν ἑωρακόσιν, ἀλλὰ καὶ ὑπὸ ἀποστόλων κατασταθεὶς
" εἰς τὴν Ἀσίαν, ἐν τῇ ἐν Σμύρνῃ Ἐκκλησίᾳ ἐπίσκοπος . . . .
" ταὐτὰ διδάξας ἀεί, ἃ καί παρὰ τῶν ἀποστόλων ἔμαθεν,
" ἃ καὶ ἡ Ἐκκλησία παραδίδωσιν, ἃ καὶ μόνα ἐστὶν ἀληθῆ."
The German author gives no translation of the Greek passages he quotes. The English translation attempted in
this and other passages, is mine, but is probably too
literal to be good. (R.)

Epistle to the Philippians was written by a certain
Antiochus, a monk of Palestine, but he was refuted
by *C. Taylor*, in the same Journal, vol. XX, 1892,
p. 65–110. — See *Bardenhewer*, Patrologie § 11, 5–6.

### § 37. *St. Papias, Bishop of Hierapolis.*

1. *St. Papias*, often mentioned with distinction by
Christian antiquity, is said by St. Irenæus to have
been a disciple of the Apostle St. John and a friend
of St. Polycarp. He was a man of great erudition
and Biblical knowledge, and took special care to collect the oral traditions concerning the life and discourses of our Saviour. But he was rather deficient
in critical judgment and method, often taking figurative expressions in the literal sense. This, of course,
proved a fruitful source of other errors and mistaken
ideas. Whether he ended his pious and zealous life
by a martyr's death is uncertain.*

2. Of the work which he composed between 130–
150, under the name of Λογίων κυριακῶν ἐξηγήσεως
συγγράμματα, i. e. "Books of explanation of the Lord's
sayings," and which was still in existence in the thir-
teenth century, there are but ten fragments preserved
to us by Irenæus, Eusebius, and others. They contain notices of his studies, researches into the miracles of his time, and observations on the Gospels of
St. Mark and St. Luke, and on the four Maries mentioned in the Gospels.

3. It is worthy of note that Papias, according to a
quotation in Eusebius, prefers the verbal tradition of
the eye-witnesses of Christ to the written testimony.

---

* He is supposed to have lived between 80–160.

"I supposed the things written in books were not of such service to me as those learnt from the living and lasting voice." * He, too, seems to have been the first among the Fathers who adopted and taught the doctrine of the Millennium. St. Jerome says: "Hic dicitur mille annorum Judaicam edidisse δευτέρωσιν, quem secuti sunt Irenæus et Apollinaris et ceteri, qui post resurrectionem aiunt in carne cum sanctis Dominum regnaturum." †

*Editions and Literature.* — Apostolic Fathers, as above. — *Migne* S. gr. V, 1251–1262. — *Ceillier* l. c. I, 683–687. — *Routh*, Reliquiæ Sacræ, Oxonii 1846. I, 3–44.

## § 38. *The Unknown Author of the Letter to Diognetus.*

1. Up to the seventeenth century, St. Justin was thought to be the author of this remarkable though long unnoticed letter. However, it must be considered much older than the writings of St. Justin. For the author calls himself a disciple of the Apostles (c. 11) and represents Christianity as of quite recent appearance. Again, none of the older Fathers mention it amongst the works of St. Justin. The view, moreover, taken by the author of the Epistle as to Judaism and Christianity, is wholly different from that of St. Justin. Finally, there is a great difference of style and language between the two. No book of Justin is written so logically, clearly, and elegantly as this epistle. With regard to the person of Diognetus, all we know is, that he was a heathen of distinction,

---

* "Οὐ τὰ ἐκ τῶν βιβλίων τοσοῦτόν με ὠφελεῖν ὑπελάμβανον, ὅσον τὰ παρὰ ζώσης φωνῆς καὶ μενούσης." Hist. Eccl. III, 39.

† De vir. ill. c. 18.

who was desirous of a closer acquaintance with the Christian religion.

2. In this important letter the writer answers with great rhetorical skill and warmth the three following questions of Diognetus: —

(a.) Why do Christians reject heathenism and Judaism?

(b.) What God do they adore, who love each other even unto the contempt of the world and death?

(c.) If the Christian religion be the true one, why did it not come sooner into the world?

Answer to (a.) Because the gods of the heathens are senseless images of wood, stone, and metal, and the entire Jewish religion consists of empty ceremonies, and contains, moreover, much that is unreasonable. To (b.) The Christian religion is something supernatural, not like other religions invented by men, but revealed by God Himself, and for this reason it brings forth virtues unknown before. To (c.) It was, first of all, necessary that man should become convinced of his own spiritual poverty and helplessness, from which God alone could deliver him. This God did by sending his only-begotten Son into the world, and giving Him up to death, in expiation for the sins of mankind. In the last chapter Diognetus is invited to embrace the Christian religion, and to have a share in the true knowledge of God and in eternal salvation. Chapters XI and XII must be considered as a later addition, because they differ both in matter and form from the preceding ones.

3. This letter is also highly important from a dogmatical point of view. It contains, amongst others, the following doctrinal truths: a, that no man can, through his own endeavors, attain to the perfect knowl-

edge of God, but only through the Logos (c. 7, 8);
*b*, that Christ is God's own (ἴδιος) and only-begotten
(μονογενής), Son, the immortal (ἀϑάνατος) and incom-
prehensible (ἀπερινόητος) Logos, and far above the
angels (c. 7–9); *c*, that the Son of God became man
in order to reveal to us the divine mysteries (c. 7),
and to make satisfaction for our sins by His sacrificial
death (c. 9); *d*, that justification, besides cleansing
from sin, implies also interior sanctification (c. 7–9);
*e*, that the Church alone possesses the doctrine of the
Apostles (c. 11). The language of the letter is clear,
the style animated and florid, and the contents show
that the writer was of a spiritually elevated and
mystical turn of mind.

*Editions and Literature.* — Apostolic Fathers as
above. — *Migne*, S. gr. II, 1169–1186. — *Otto*, Corpus
apolog. christ. sæculi II, vol. I, 3 ed., Jenæ 1876–
1881. — *Ceillier* l. c. II, 38–42. — *Kihn*, Der Ursprung
des Briefes an Diognet. Freiburg 1882. — *Fessler-
Jungmann* l. c. § 46.

---

## SECOND EPOCH.

## GROWTH AND DEVELOPMENT OF PATRISTIC LITERATURE (150–325).

### § 39. *General Survey.*

During this period, Christian literature shows a remarkable development in many ways. Now was the
time to defend the Church against attacks from within
and without. Hence apologetical and polemical theology came naturally to the fore. Men preëminent in
learning and eloquence forsook idolatry and embraced

Christianity. These took up the defense of the Christian faith in a series of eloquent apologies, and, in conjunction with those who had been trained in the Christian schools, assailed the position of the Jews and Gentiles, as well as of the numerous heretics that sprang up, as the Gnostics, Montanists, Anti-Trinitarians, Novatians, and others. By this means they were able to bring out more and more clearly the nature and doctrine of the Church, and still further to consolidate her unity. The foundation of the catechetical schools at Alexandria, Antioch, and Cæsarea exercised a far-reaching influence upon the progress of Christian science and literature. In these schools, both Christian and heathen youths sought and obtained education in philosophical and Christian doctrine, and from them came forth a great number of learned men, bishops, saints, and martyrs. Towards the middle of this epoch, arose the first Latin authors, who, though but few in number at first, sent forth their light with all the more splendor.

*Editions and Literature.* — *Möhler* l. c. p. 179–187; 416–429. — *Simon,* Histoire de l'école d'Alexandrie. Paris 1845. — *Vacherot,* Histoire critique de l'école d'Alexandrie. Paris 1846–1851.

## CHAPTER I.

### GREEK FATHERS AND WRITERS.

#### A. APOLOGISTS.

§ 40. *St. Justin, Martyr* (*d. about 167*).

1. *Justin* was born about 100, at Flavia Neapolis (Sichem, Nablus) in Palestine, of rich heathen

parents, who could afford to give their son a good
education. From early youth he seemed to thirst for
a knowledge of things divine. He frequented in succession the schools of the Stoics, Peripatetics, Pytha-
goræans, and Platonists, but without finding in any of
them the realization of his ideal. Wandering one day
on the sea-shore, absorbed in thought, he was met by
a venerable old man, who directed his attention to the
study of the prophets, Christ, and the Apostles. The
assiduous perusal of the Sacred Books, and the constancy of the Christians under persecution, impressed
him deeply and led him at last to embrace Christianity
at the age of 33. Continuing to wear his garb of a
philosopher, he worked with great energy and skill,
by word of mouth and writing, for the defense and
propagation of the Christian religion. He undertook
long journeys in order to acquire a deeper knowledge
of its doctrines, and to win over to them the heathen
youth. He twice repaired to Rome, where he appears
to have established a school, and where, in public disputations, he attacked Marcion, the heretic, Crescen-
tius, the cynic, and other philosophers. Here, too,
he issued his apologies for the Christians. Having
been denounced as a Christian by his enemy Crescen-
tius, he was scourged and beheaded, apparently in
167.

2. The writings of St. Justin are so valuable that
they have earned for him imperishable glory and
renown in Christian theology. The following are
undoubtedly genuine:

(a.) " Apologia prima pro christianis," in 68 chapters, addressed to the Emperor Antoninus Pius, to his
son, Marcus Aurelius, to the Senate and people of
Rome. In the first part, he pleads in defense of the

Christians against their unjust persecution, that they are not evil-doers, but good citizens, and that the charges made against them of atheism and incontinency are unfounded. In the second part, he proves the truth of the Christian religion, and shows forth its blessings and fruits.

(b.) "Apologia secunda, vel minor," in 15 chapters. This is a continuation of his first Apology. In it he answers the scoffing questions of the heathens, as to why Christians did not kill themselves, in order to get the more quickly to God, and why God, if He be their protector, suffers them to be oppressed and put to death by the wicked.

(c.) "Dialogus cum Tryphone," in 142 chapters. Here he deals with three questions, in reply to Tryphon, the Jew. First, why do not Christians observe the Law given by God? Second, how can they worship the Redeemer both as God and as a crucified man? Third, why do they hold intercourse with heathens? In answer to these questions he proves from the prophets that Christ is the true God of the Jews and the Messiah expected by them, that the Old Covenant is dissolved, that Judaism has given place to Christianity, which is the true fulfilment of the Old Testament, and from henceforth the universal religion of the world. This dialogue is not strictly an account of a real disputation with the Jew Tryphon, but rather the outcome of conversations on religious matters which Justin had with the Jews, and of his experience thus gained. Nevertheless it is by far the most important of all the patristic apologies against Judaism. The work has not come down to us intact, for there is a gap in the 74th chapter.

The following are of doubtful authenticity: (a.)

"Oratio ad Græcos," in 5 chapters, in which the author assigns as his reason for embracing Christianity, the immorality of the heathen, and the purity and loftiness of the Christian, religion. (b.) "Cohortatio ad Græcos," in 38 chapters, in which he points out that the truth is not to be sought for in the heathen poets and philosophers, but in the prophets inspired by God. (c.) "De monarchia," in 6 chapters, wherein it is shown that the greatest heathen poets and philosophers were inclined to monotheism. (d.) "De resurrectione," a fragment in 10 chapters, in which the possibility and reality of our resurrection is inferred from the fact that Christ raised others and rose himself from the dead.

We have in favor of the genuineness of these writings the testimony of Eusebius, St. Jerome, and St. John Damascene; against it, the difference of the style, which is more polished than that of the Apologies.

The following are lost: (a) "Psaltes;" (b) "De anima;" (c) "Liber contra omnes hæreses." Other writings, as "Expositio rectæ fidei de Trinitate," "Responsiones ad orthodoxos," "Quæstiones gentilium ad Christianos," are wrongly ascribed to him.

In the writings of St. Justin, the Christian faith is explained with great erudition, depth, and precision. He expresses himself with remarkable clearness about original sin (Dialog. c. 88. 100); baptism (Apol. I. c. 61); divine service on Sunday (c. 65 and 67); the Eucharist (c. 66); the eternity of the punishments of hell (c. 12).

Justin was a philosopher of the school of Plato, and in common with Papias held Chiliastic views, without, however, maintaining them as part of the Christian faith and tradition (Dialog. c. 31, 32, 80, 81).

While maintaining that Christianity alone was in the
perfect possession of truth, he yet granted that
heathen philosophers possessed germs of truth
(σπέρματα τοῦ λόγου). Apart from digressions and
occasionally tiresome periods, his style is generally
dignified and forcible. Photius thus speaks of him:
"He is a man who has climbed the heights of philosophy, Greek as well as foreign; he is overflowing
with much learning and the riches of knowledge, but
he took no pains to adorn the natural beauty of his
philosophy with the arts of rhetoric."

*Editions and Literature.* — *Migne*, S. gr. VI.— *Ceillier* l. c. II, 1–73. — *Semisch*, Justin der Martyrer.
Breslau 1842.— *Aubé*, St. Justin, philosophe et martyr.
Paris 1861. — *Freppel*, St. Justin ("Les Apologistes
chrétiens au IIe siècle") Paris, 1886, 3d ed. — *Möhler*
l. c., p. 188–253. — *G. T. Purves*, The Testimony of
Justin Martyr to early Christianity. New York
1889. (London 1889.) 8vo. — *Funk*, in Kirchenlexikon, vol. vi. 2. edit.— *Fessler-Jungmann* l. c. § 49–53.

## § 41. *Tatian, the Assyrian.*

1. *Tatian*, born A. D. 130, was a disciple of St.
Justin. After having devoted himself in his youth to
rhetorical studies and the doctrines of heathen philosophy, he traveled through many lands, in order to
become acquainted with the manners, customs, and,
in particular, the religion of their inhabitants. The
heathen religion was repugnant to him, no less on
account of its irrationality and immorality, than of the
repulsive selfishness of the philosophers. On the
other hand, the Holy Books, with their sublime moral
principles, simple language and style, as well as the

pious life of the Christians, made so powerful an
impression upon him, that he embraced and joyfully
confessed the Christian faith. When at Rome, he
made the acquaintance of St. Justin, whom he calls an
admirable teacher. Some time after the death of the
latter, he returned to the East, where, out of wounded
pride, he adopted heretical principles, and was chosen
head of a sect of Gnostics, whose followers were
named Encratites, on account of their rejection of
marriage and abstinence from meat and wine, and also
Hydroparastatæ, because of their making use of water
instead of wine in the celebration of the Holy Eucharist. The time and place of his death are unknown.

2. Of the many works of Tatian, two only have come
down to us: (1) the "Oratio adversus Græcos," in 42
chapters, written about 170, before his apostasy, wherein he inveighs against the immoral excesses of the
Greeks and Romans, particularly the cruelty of the
gladiatorial games and the licentiousness of the thea-
tres. He expresses with lively indignation his contempt
of the Greek religion as being absolutely demoniacal,
and then proceeds to demonstrate the greater antiquity
of Christian wisdom as compared with that of the
Greeks, and the immorality and intemperance prevalent among heathens as opposed to the chastity and tem-
perance of Christians. (2) The "Diatessaron," which
is a harmony of the Gospels (the genealogy of Christ,
however, being omitted). This writing of Tatian,
whose original Syriac text had long been lost, was
found in the form of an Arabic translation in 1883, by
Father Augustine Ciasca, O. S. A., in a Vatican codex.
After being compared with another manuscript in
Arabic, preserved by a distinguished Copt, it was
translated into Latin, and published in 1888, in both

languages. It is of the highest value for the history of the Canon of the New Testament and the origin of Christianity.

3. Tatian's doctrines are not always correct and reliable. In the "Oratio ad Græcos" he teaches the eternity of God (c. 4–5); the creation of the world (c. 5); the origin of evil (c. 7); the resurrection of the body (c. 6); and describes, in an attractive style, the supernatural character and universality of the Christian religion (c. 32). He loses himself from time to time in long digressions.

In point of thought and style, he bears a striking resemblance to Tertullian. Irenæus testifies to his apostasy: "After the martyrdom of Justin he fell away from the Church, and lifted up by the thought of (being) a teacher and puffed up as if different from others (i. e. better than others), he set up a system of teaching of his own." *

*Editions and Literature.* — *Migne*, S. gr. VI, 801–888. — *Otto* l. c. vol. VI. — *Ciasca*, Tatiāni Evangeliorum harmoniæ arabice, nunc primum ex duplici codice editæ et latine translatæ. Romæ 1888. — *Ceillier* l. c. II, 123–131. — *Daniel*, Tatian der Apologet. Halle 1838. — *Mattes* in Wetzer and Welte's Kirchenlexicon, vol. X, Art. Tatian. — *Salvatori*, Il Diatessaron di Taziano. Firenze 1889. — *J. R. Harris*, The Diatessaron of Tatian: A Preliminary Study. London 1890. 8vo. — *M. Maher*, Recent Evidence for the Authenticity of the Gospels: Tatian's Diatessaron. London 1893. 8vo. — *J. H. Hill*, The earliest Life of Christ

---

* Adv. Haer. I, 23. "Μετὰ τὴν Ἰουστίνου μαρτυρίαν ἀποστὰς τῆς Ἐκκλησίας, οἰήματι διδασκάλου ἐπαρθεὶς καὶ τυφωθείς, ὡς διαφέρων τῶν λοιπῶν ἴδιον χαρακτῆρα διδασκαλείου συνεστήσατο."

ever compiled from the Four Gospels: being the
Diatessaron of Tatian (circa A. D. 160). Literally
translated from the Arabic Version. Edinburgh
1893. 8ᵛᵒ.

## § 42. *Athenagoras, the Philosopher.*

1. Of this writer we only know for certain that he
was born in heathenism, probably at Athens, that he
studied Greek philosophy, was converted to Christianity by the perusal of Holy Scripture, and that
he composed two excellent works. Everything else
reported concerning him is devoid of real foundation.

2. The two aforesaid writings are: "Legatio, sive
supplicatio pro christianis," in 37 chapters, and "De
resurrectione mortuorum," in 26 chapters. In the first
work, which was addressed to the Emperors Marcus
Aurelius and his son Commodus, about 177, he complains that Christians are put to death merely for their
name, and defends them against the charge of atheism,
Thyestian feasts, and incest. In the second, he refutes
the arguments brought against the resurrection, and
proves that fundamental Christian dogma by a process
of logical reasoning chiefly based upon the dual nature
of man, the necessity of a judgment upon both soul
and body, and the eternal destiny of man (c. 10–25).
The book "De vero et perfecto amore" is undoubtedly supposititious.

3. In both works there are to be found many beautiful passages, bearing on various points of doctrine,
as v. gr., the existence and unity of God (Legatio, c.
7–9); the trinity of persons in God (c. 10, 12); the
existence of angels and devils (c. 24, 25–27); the
power of the Christian religion for maintaining the
holiness of marriage and the observance of virginity

(c. 32, 33). Athenagoras was gifted with a philosophical intellect, refined by Grecian culture, and possessed a splendid style of writing. His Apology is
excellent both in matter and form. His treatise on
the resurrection shows depth of apprehension and skill
in reasoning, and is, in spite of some defects, very
important.

That Athenagoras became a Montanist is a ground-
less accusation. Natalis Alexander styles him:
" Virum acerrimi ingenii, singularis eloquentiæ, omni-
genæ eruditionis ac incredibilis in rem Christianam
studii " (Hist. eccl. III, 303), and Ceillier writes:
" Dans les écrits d'Athénagore on trouve beaucoup
d'esprit, d'érudition et d'éloquence, et une profonde
connaissance des mystères de notre religion " (Hist.
génér. des auteurs eccl. 1ʳᵉ. édit. II, 118.)

*Editions and Literature.* — *Migne*, S. gr. VI, 888–
1024. — *Ceillier* l. c. II, 112–123. — An edition of
both writings for schools and colleges has been arranged by *F. A. March* and *W. B. Owen* in Douglass'
Series of Christian Greek and Latin Writers, vol. IV.
New York 1876. 8ᵛᵒ.

§ 43. *St. Theophilus, Bishop of Antioch (d.
about 186).*

1. *Theophilus*, born and brought up in heathenism,
was led to the knowledge and profession of Christianity by means of the Holy Scriptures, which he had
resolved to read for the purpose of impugning them.
On account of his excellent qualities, he was chosen
Bishop of Antioch, A. D. 168. As such he vigorously
combated the Gnostics, and wrote several exegetical
and other works. He died between 181 and 186.

2. His beautiful treatise entitled " Ad Autolycum,"

in 3 books, was called forth by the scoffing remarks
of the heathen Autolycus upon the Christian doctrines
concerning God, the resurrection, and eternal happiness. It contains many instructive things. In the
first book, he explains the Christian doctrine of God,
whose Supreme Being is known by his works, and of
the resurrection. In the second, he shows the folly
of polytheism and the reasonableness of Christianity.
In the third, he proves that the heathen poets and
philosophers were wholly ignorant of a worthy way
of worshiping God. Christians, on the contrary,
have a fitting worship, as is shown by the virtuous
lives they lead. He also shows that the Holy Scripture, and therefore the Christian religion, are older
than the tradition of the Gentiles. Two other works,
against Marcion and Hermogenes, are lost, as also his
"Biblia catechetica," and commentaries on the Proverbs of Solomon, and the Gospel of St. Matthew.
The four books of " Allegoriæ in Evangelium," handed
down to us under his name, are a collection of scholia
on passages selected from the four Gospels, made
towards the end of the fifth century.

3. In the three above mentioned books to Autolycus,
which are a real " profanæ et sacræ eruditionis promp-
tuarium," we find discussed such points of doctrine as
the necessity of faith (I, 8), the incomprehensibility
of God (I, 3), the trinity of divine persons (II, 10,
15), the fall of man (II, 21), and the importance,
truth, and sanctity of the Christian faith (III, 9–15),
clearly and beautifully enounced and convincingly
proved. " Son style," writes Ceillier, " est élevé, poli
et bien diversifié; le tour des pensées vif et agréable;
les raisonnements justes et pressants " (Hist. génér.
II, 110.)

*Editions and Literature.* — *Migne* S. gr. VI, 1024–1168. — *Ceillier* l. c. II, 103–112. — *Otto* l. c. vol. VIII.— *W. Sanday*, A Commentary on the Gospels, attributed to Theophilus of Antioch. Studia Biblica (Oxford 1885) pp. 89–101.

## § 44. *Minor Apologists.*

Christian apologies have also been written at this period by other Fathers, as *Quadratus*, *Claudius Apollinaris*, and *Melito of Sardes*, and by ecclesiastical writers, such as *Aristides*, *Miltiades*, and *Hermias*.

1. (a.) St. Quadratus, a disciple of the Apostles, endowed with the gift of prophecy, presented to the Emperor Hadrian an Apology for the Christian religion, which is a monument of the purity of his faith and the depth of his knowledge. The Emperor, in consequence of this work, ordered a cessation of the persecution against the Christians. "Tantæ," says St. Jerome, "admirationi omnibus fuit, ut persecutionem gravissimam illius excellens sedaret ingenium" (Epist. 70 ad Magnum.) Unfortunately we are only in possession of a fragment preserved by Eusebius (Hist. eccl. IV, 3), in which Quadratus shows the difference between the miracles of Jesus and those wrought by the powers of demons.

(b.) St. Claudius Apollinaris, Bishop of Hierapolis, highly esteemed by his contemporaries on account of his great knowledge and virtues, wrote an Apology to the Emperor Marcus Aurelius, which was much praised by St. Jerome. He also wrote, as we learn from Eusebius, five books against the heathens, and two on truth against the Montanists. All these writings, however, with the exception of a few fragments, have been lost.

(c.) St. MELITO, Bishop of Sardes, of whose life nothing is known, ranks amongst the most brilliant lights of the Eastern Church of the second century, and the most learned men of that age. His literary labors extended to all the great ecclesiastical questions that agitated his time. Unfortunately, we only possess fragments of one or the other of his numerous literary works, amongst which the "Eclogæ" (extracts from Sacred Scripture in six books) was the most important, whilst his Apology, presented to the Emperor Marcus Aurelius, A. D. 170 or 171, was the last in point of time. His doctrine was not free from Anthropomorphism, nor from Chiliastic views. He died between 171 and 180. Eusebius calls him " a man who administered all things in the Holy Ghost." *

2. (a). ARISTIDES, whom St. Jerome calls " vir eloquentissimus," was an Athenian philosopher and a distinguished rhetorician. After his conversion to Christianity, he presented to Hadrian, or, as some say, to Antoninus Pius, an excellent Apology, in which he made use of the works of the heathen philosophers to vindicate the Christian religion. Of this long lost Apology, a considerable fragment in an Armenian translation, dating from the tenth century, was found in 1878 in an old còdex, by the Mechitarist monks in Venice, together with an oration ascribed to Aristides. But in the year 1889, J. Rendel Harris, an American palæographer, found in the Convent of St.

* Hist. eccl. V, 24. " Τὸν ἐν ἁγίω πνεύματι πάντα πολιτευ-σάμενον."

Catharine, on Mount Sinai, the entire Apology of Aristides, in a Syrian manuscript of the seventh century; and, soon after, Professor Robinson made the surprising discovery that the Greek text also was to be found, not only in manuscript, but actually printed, since 1832, in the " Vita Barlaam et Joasaph," found among the writings of St. John Damascene. Though the three texts agree on the whole, they differ from each other in many particulars, but the Syrian seems to be preferable.

(b.) MILTIADES, whom Tertullian calls " Sophista ecclesiarum," i. e. " Advocate of the Christians," composed, besides controversial works against heathens, Jews, and Montanists, a separate treatise in defense of the divinity of Christ, and a Christian Apology addressed to the civil power. From the few fragments preserved by Eusebius we may discern the ability of the entire composition, as well as the other writings of this author. St. Jerome says of him: "Scripsit et contra gentes volumen egregium . . . ut nescias, quid in illo primum mirari debeas, eruditionem sæculi, an scientiam Scripturarum" (Epist. 70 ad Magnum.)

(c.) HERMIAS. History gives us no information whatever respecting the time and life of this writer; neither do any of the ancient writers make mention of the work that has come down under his name, "Irrisio gentilium philosophorum." But he must have lived after Justin and Tatian, towards the beginning of the third century. In forcible and sarcastic language he deals with the doctrines of heathen philosophers on God, the world, the soul, pointing out their glaring contradictions, but failing at times to grasp or exhibit the pagan doctrines in their syste-

matic connection. Thus he testifies to the truth of
St. Paul's words: " The wisdom of this world is folly
before God." (I. Cor. iii, 19.)

*Editions and Literature.* — To 1. (a.) *Migne*, S. gr.
V, 1262–1266. — *Ceillier* l. c. I, 688–690. — To 1. (b.)
*Migne,* V, 1286–1302. — *Ceillier* l. c. II, 83–85. — To
1. (c.) *Migne*, S. gr. V, 1145–1250. — *Ceillier* l. c.
II, 75–79. — *Thomas*, Melito von Sardes, Osnabrück
1893. — To 2. (a) *Migne*, S. gr. V, 1267–1268. —
*Ceillier* l. c. I, 690–691. — Tübinger Quartalschrift,
1879, p. 289, and 1880, p. 109. — To 2. (b) *Migne*,
S. gr. XX, 473–476. — *Ceillier* l. c. II, 131. — To
2. (c) *Migne*, S. gr. VI, 1168–1180. — *Otto* l. c. vol.
IX. — *Ceillier* l. c. VIII, 554–556.

## B. GREEK CONTROVERSIALISTS.

### § 45. *St. Irenæus, Bishop of Lyons* (d. 202).

1. *Irenæus*, born between 130–140 in Asia Minor
(Smyrna?), had, from his earliest youth, the happiness
of being instructed by St. Polycarp and other Apostolic men. His deep attachment to the Christian
doctrine did not prevent him from studying the Greek
poets and philosophers, especially Homer and Plato.

With a view to missionary work, he journeyed to
Gaul, where he was ordained priest by Pothinus,
Bishop of Lyons, who suffered martyrdom in the persecution of Marcus Aurelius, A. D. 178. Irenæus
was nominated to succeed him as bishop by Pope
Eleutherius, to whom he had been sent on an ecclesiastical mission. In this office he showed untiring zeal
and energy for the good of the churches in Gaul.

Moreover, by means of his writings, in defense of the unity and purity of the faith, which was endangered by the Gnostics, he made his influence felt far beyond the limits of Gaul. Finally, he proved himself worthy of his name, Εἰρηναῖος, i. e., " the Peaceful," by affecting a happy compromise between the East and West in the dispute concerning Easter, which had gone so far as to cause an open rupture between the two sections of the Church.

In the great persecution under Septimius Severus, the shepherd suffered martyrdom with many of his flock (June 28th, 202).

2. Of the numerous writings of Irenæus, we have, besides a few fragments, only his chief work: " Detectio et eversio falso cognominatæ gnosis," (since St. Jerome generally, but less aptly, quoted as " Adversus hæreses,") in five books, and preserved for the most part in a Latin translation, but much interspersed with Greek expressions, and on this account rather difficult to understand. In this, at once the oldest and most solid and comprehensive work of the kind against the false doctrines of the Gnostics, Irenæus not merely testified to the truths of Christianity, but also defended them against the attacks of false philosophers, and sought to preserve the faithful from error, and to bring back those who had gone astray. The predominant thought throughout the whole work is this, that there is no truth, nor means of knowing the law of faith or morals, except in and through the Church.

3. Irenæus bears witness to the inspiration of Holy Scripture (II, 28, n. 3); its right interpretation in the Church (IV, 33, n. 8); tradition, as a source

of proof (III, 2, n. 2); the infallibility and immuta-
bility of the Church (I, 10, n. 2; III, 24, n. 1; V,
20, n. 1); the pre-eminence of the Roman Church,*
(III, 3, n. 2); belief in the Trinity (IV, 20, n. 1; 6,
n. 7); the object of the Incarnation (III, 16, n. 6;
18, n. 7); Mary, as the beginning of our salvation
(III, 22, n. 2–4); the free will of man (IV, 37, n. 1,
4); original sin (V, 16, n. 3); the perfectibility of
the human soul (IV, 39, n. 2); the sacrament of
baptism (III, 17, n. 2); the necessity of confession
of sins, ἐξομολόγησις (I, 13, n. 5, 7); and especially
the Holy Eucharist as a sacrament (V, 2, n. 3) and
sacrifice, (IV, 17, n. 5; 18. n. 1, 2, 4).

But in his views on the nature and immortality of
the human soul and on the Millennium, he deviates
from the doctrine of the Church. He was the first
who fully grasped the importance of the Catholic
principle of tradition, and used it with great dialectic
skill as a most powerful weapon against heretics. His
language is simple, natural, and generally animated.
Tertullian describes him as "omnium doctrinarum
curiosissimus explorator;" Eusebius aptly calls him
"a peacemaker," εἰρηνοπριός, while Epiphanius makes
honorable mention of him in these words: "Irenæus,
the aforesaid old man, being in all things furnished and
adorned by the Holy Spirit, and set up by Christ as a
true athlete, and anointed with those heavenly gifts
that are according to the true faith and knowledge,

---

* "Ad hanc enim ecclesiam propter potentiorem princi-
"palitatem necesse est omnem convenire ecclesiam, hoc est
"eos qui sunt undique fideles, in qua semper ab his qui sunt
"undique conservata est ea, quæ est ab Apostolis tradi-
"tio." l. c.

was able to beat down and overcome all their empty talk." *

*Editions and Literature.* — *Migne*, S. gr. VII. — (Reprint of Benedictine edition by *Massuet*, O. S. B. (d. 1716). — A separate and later edition by *W. W. Harvey*, Cambridge, 1857. — *Ceillier* l. c. II, 135– 196. — *Gouillaud*, St. Irénée et son temps. Lyon 1876. — *Freppel*, St. Irénée, etc. 3 éd. Paris 1886. — *Ziegler*, Irenæus, der Bischof von Lyon, Berlin 1871. — See also *Routh*, Reliq. Sacr. 2 ed. II, 1–36 and I, 47–68.

## § 46. *Caius, the Roman Presbyter* (*d. about 220*).

1. *Caius*, or Gaius, the place and time of whose birth are unknown, was most probably a disciple of St. Irenæus and lived at Rome under Pope Zephyrinus and the Emperor Caracalla. He became a priest of the Roman Church,† and seems also to have been a kind of bishop (ἐπίσχοπος τῶν ἐθνῶν). He gained great celebrity as an able defender of the doctrine of the Church against heretics, and was in particular a determined opponent of Chiliastic views (Millennium).

2. Caius wrote a "Disputatio adversus Proclum," who was considered the most learned and most able representative of the Montanists. The original work in Greek is lost. The fragments preserved by Euse-

---

* Adv. Haer. XXXI, 33. Εἰρηναῖος ὁ προειρημένος ἀνὴρ πρεσβύτης, ὁ κατὰ πάντα ἐκ Πνεύματος ἁγίου κεκοσμημένος, ὡς γενναῖος ἀθλητὴς ὑπὸ τοῦ Κυρίου προσβεβλημένος, καὶ ἐπαλειφθεὶς τοῖς ἐπουρανίοις χαρίσμασιν, τοῖς κατὰ τὴν ἀληθινὴν πίστιν καὶ γνῶσιν, καταπαλαίσας τε καὶ καταγωνισάμενος τὴν πᾶσαν αὐτῶν κενοφωνίαν."

† *Euseb.* H. E. II, 25. — *Photius*, Bibl. Cod. 48.

bius contain many interesting particulars of the spirit
and system of the heretics of that time. The "Parvus labyrinthus," as well as the work "De univer-
so," or "De causa universi," are the productions
of his contemporary Hippolytus.

*Editions and Literature.* — *Migne*, S. gr. X, 17–
36. — *Ceillier* l. c. II, 208–210. 239–241. — *Routh*,
Reliq. Sacr. II, 123–158 (2d ed.).

## § 47. *St. Hippolytus* (*d. about 235*).

1. *Hippolytus*, whose origin is unknown, was a
disciple of St. Irenæus, and lived at Rome where he
combated the Patripassianism of Sabellius and
Noëtus, though his own doctrine concerning the Logos
was not free from suspicion, and he held also rigoristic
views about the nature of penance. After the death
of Pope Zephyrinus, he came forward as Roman
Bishop (Episcopus Portus Romani), in opposition to
Pope Callistus, to whom he had a great aversion, and
thus caused the first schism in the papacy, which
happily did not reach very far nor last long. After
the death of Callistus, however, he was reconciled to
the Church, and on account of his great virtue and
work, was held in high veneration, and died a martyr
about 235. His admirers erected a costly marble statue
in his honor, which was discovered in the year 1551
with a partial catalogue of his works inscribed on it.

2. Besides some exegetical ("Explanatio in Genesin, in Danielem, in Psalmos, in Proverbia," etc.) and
homiletical works, Hippolytus also composed others
of a dogmatical and controversial nature, of which the
principal are the following: —

(a.) "Demonstratio de Christo et Antichristo," in
67 chapters, written about 200, wherein he shows, first,
that the Logos had already revealed his incarnation

to the prophets, and that he became man in order to
redeem the world.    Next, in order to fortify men
against the seductions of the Antichrist, he tries to
gather whatever information he can from Holy Scripture, concerning the person of the Antichrist, his origin
and characteristics, the time of his coming, his impos-
tures and impiety, who, he says, will proclaim himself
God and persecute the Church.

(b.) " Philosophumena, seu omnium hæresium
refutatio," in ten books, composed about 230, and,
with the exception of the second and third books, discovered in a manuscript of Mount Athos by Mynoides
Myna in 1842.   The work contains an explanation of
the Greek systems of philosophy, of magic, astrology,
and other superstitions; it describes furthermore the
doctrines of thirty-three Christian heretics, the teachings of the Essenians, Pharisees and Sadducees, and,
lastly, his own creed, not altogether free from error.

(c.) " Contra hæresin Noëti," in 18 chapters, containing a brief and solid defense against Noëtus, of
the dogma of the trinity of divine persons in the
unity of nature.

(d.) "Demonstratio adversus Judæos," in 10 chapters, wherein he proves the Messianic character of
Christ, the impiety of the Jews, and the divine justice
of their punishment.   The 38 so-called " Canones S.
Hippolyti," edited in Arabic by Haneberg, are, according to the learned researches of Funk, not the
production of Hippolytus, but extracts from the eighth
book of the Apostolic Constitutions.   Of the " Parvus
labyrinthus " (against the Antitrinitarian Artemon),
and of "De causa universi " (treating of the abode of
the souls of the departed till the judgment, and of
eternal retribution), as well as of his exegetical and
homiletical works, only fragments are left.

The work "Contra Beronem" and fragments on the
Trinity and Incarnation belong to a later period.
Several of his writings, as "Adversus omnes hær-
eses," "Contra Marcionem," "De charismatibus,"
"De resurrectione carnis," and others, have been
entirely lost.

3. Hippolytus, with his contemporaries Origen and
Tertullian, was indisputably one of the ablest and most
learned writers of his time. Apart from his erroneous
opinions on the Trinity and penance, his numerous
works, written in a clear and vigorous style, contain
the most telling passages on the inspiration of Holy
Scripture (Demonstr. de Christo et Antichr. c. 2);
on the invincibility of the Church (ibid. c. 59); on
baptism (Hom. in Theoph. c. 8, 10); the Eucharist
(Hom. in Prov.); the free will of man (Philos. X,
33); the resurrection and everlasting retribution
(De causa universi c. 2, 3). According to John
Zonaras, "Hyppolytus was a most holy and learned
man, Bishop of Portus Romanus, who also wrote
many works explanatory of different parts of Holy
Scripture." *

*Editions and Literature.* — *Migne*, S. gr. X, 261–
962. — *Duncker et Schneidewin*, Hippolyti refutationes
omnium hæresium; græce et lat. Goetting. 1859. —
*Haneberg*, Canones S. Hippolyti arabice e codicibus
romanis editi. Monachii 1870. — *Ceillier* l. c. II, 316–
374. — *Döllinger*, Hippolytus und Kallistus. Regensburg 1853. — *Hergenröther*, in Tübinger Quartalschr.
1852, pp. 416–441.— *Grisar*, Bedarf die Hippolytfrage

---

* "῾Ιππόλυτος ἀνὴρ ἱερώτατος καὶ σοφώτατος, ἐπίσκοπος
τοῦ κατὰ ῾Ρώμην Πόρτου γενόμενος, ὃς καὶ πολλὰ συγγράμματα συνεγράψατο, διάφορα τῆς θείας Γραφῆς ἐξηγη-
σάμενος."

einer Revision? Zeitschr. für Kath. Theologie, 3 Heft, Innsbruck 1878. — *Funk*, Zur Hippolytfrage. Hist.-polit. Bl. LXXXIX, 889 sq. — *Fechtrup*, in Wetzer and Welte's Kirchenlex. (2 Aufl.) vol. VI. — *Fessler-Jungmann* l. c. § 67. — *Ficker*, Studien zur Hippolytfrage. Leipzig 1893. — *Bunsen*, Hippolytus and his age. London 1852, 2 ed., 4 vols. 8$^{vo}$. — *C. Wordsworth*, St. Hippolytus and the Church of Rome in the early part of the 3d century. London 1853. 8$^{vo}$. — *Lightfoot*, The Apost. Fathers, II, 317–477.

## § 48. *St. Archelaus of Cascar [Carræ].*

*St. Archelaus* was bishop of Cascar in Mesopotamia between 276 and 282. Being a man of keen penetration and full of fire and vigor of soul, in order to prevent the further spread of Manichæism, he challenged Manes, the founder of the sect, to public disputation before heathens and Christians. The still preserved acts of this disputation form the most ancient and reliable source of the history of Manichæism. Archelaus displayed such great dialectic skill in refuting the Manichæan doctrine about the two principles of light and darkness, and in exposing the contradictions and weaknesses of their entire system, that he was adjudged the victory over Manes by the heathen umpires. In a later disputation, also, on the subject of the incarnation of the Logos, he gained a further victory over him by showing, that in denying the incarnation, he must necessarily also reject the resurrection and judgment. The acts of this disputation (Acta disputationis S. Archelai cum Manete, in 53 chapters), written by Archelaus in the animated Syrian style, but only preserved to us in a

Latin translation, are in so far of great value as they furnish the first authentic account of Manes and his doctrine. They have also materially contributed to the condemnation of the Manichæan system, and forcibly witnessed to such Christian doctrines as the incarnation of the Logos (Disp. c. 49, where Mary is expressly called Mother of God, Dei genitrix), the free will of man (c. 32), the ranks of the Christian hierarchy (c. 51).

*Editions and Literature.* — *Migne*, S. gr. X, 1406–1528. — *Ceillier* l. c. III, 333–344. — *Möhler* l. c. pp. 663–667. — *Kessler*, in his work "Mani, Forschungen über die manichæische Religion," Berlin 1889, denies with a great show of erudition the historical character of the above disputation between Archelaus and Manes, and considers the Acta as a compilation from older documents, written in the form of a dialogue in the beginning of the fourth century, with a view to counteract the spead of Manichæism. — *Dr. Bardenhewer*, too, does not consider Bishop Archelaus as a historical person and attributes the Acta disputationis to the imagination of a certain Hegemonius (Patrologie, § 47, No. 1).

## C. GREEK COMMENTATORS.

### § 49. *Pantœnus (d. about 200)*.

1. *Pantœnus*, probably a native of Sicily, and converted to Christianity by a disciple of the Apostles, applied himself chiefly to the study of Holy Scripture, without, however, abandoning his philosophical studies, which he had pursued from his youth. About the year 179, he was appointed teacher and president of the catechetical school of Alexandria. There, by-

his learned expositions of the Holy Scriptures, he gained so widespread a reputation that envoys were sent from India (Arabia or Ethiopia?) to ask him to come and preach the Gospel, which office, with the approval of his Bishop, Demetrius, he undertook and held for many years in those distant lands. After his return, he resumed his teachings in Alexandria till his death, about 200. He endeavored to combine the doctrines of the Stoic philosophy with those of Christianity, and helped to advance ecclesiastical learning by written as well as oral discourses and commentaries upon the Sacred Scriptures. Of his writings, however, only scanty fragments have reached us.[*]

*Editions and Literature.* — *Migne*, S. gr. V, 1327–1332. — *Routh*, Reliquiæ Sacræ I, 375–383. — *Ceillier* l. c. II, 237–239.

## § 50. *Clement of Alexandria (died about 215).*

1. *Titus Flavius Clemens* was born (at Athens or Alexandria) of heathen parents towards the middle of the second century, and received a heathen education. Dissatisfied with the results of Grecian and Egyptian science, which from an ardent desire for knowledge he had thoroughly sifted, he embraced Christianity at an early age. For the sake of advancing further in the blessed knowledge of the Christian truths, he sought out the most celebrated teachers of East and West, amongst whom was Pantænus, the "Sicilian bee, which gathered the honey from the flowers of the prophetical and Apostolical fields." The latter having set out for India to preach the Gospel, Clement was ordained priest by Demetrius, and appointed Presi-

---

[*] *Euseb.*, H. E. v, 10. — *Hieron.*, De vir. ill. c. 36.

dent of the catechetical school at Alexandria, in 189. In this capacity he acquired immortal praise by his learning, and many distinguished men received their training under him. During the persecution of Septimius Severus he fled from the town, in accordance with the admonition of our Lord,* and repaired to Flaviades in Cappadocia to his disciple Bishop Alexander, whom he later followed to Jerusalem. He died at an advanced age about the year 215, in what place is not known. He is not mentioned in the Roman Martyrology.

2. Of the works of this prolific writer we possess the following: —

(a.) "Cohortatio ad Gentes," in 12 chapters, in which, after a withering criticism upon the absurdity, folly, and emptiness of heathen religion and philosophy, he represents Christ as the divine Teacher, and His pure and lofty doctrines as the oldest and truly divine religion.

(b.) "Pædagogus," in 3 books, wherein he represents the Logos as the Tutor of those who are baptized, the principle of education being divine love, and its object to make men godlike. He next gives a practical instruction as to how to conform one's life to the precepts of the divine Tutor, and, finally, he sets forth in glowing colors, the true ideal of the Christian life.

(c.) "Miscellanea" ($\sigma\tau\rho\omega\mu\alpha\tau\epsilon\tilde{\iota}\varsigma$), in 8 books, a collection of various and somewhat disconnected discourses, partly religious and partly philosophical, wherein he tries to establish a rational basis for the doctrines of Christianity. The discussions they con-

---

* Matth. x, 23.

tain about the importance of the Old and New Testaments, the relation between faith and science, and the burning questions of the day upon morals, marriage, celibacy, asceticism and the like, give special importance to the book.

(d.) "Quis dives salvabitur?" in 42 chapters, in which the passages occurring in St. Matthew XIX, 21–24, are well and attractively explained, and where it is shown that the good use of earthly possessions can be made available for eternal salvation. Some of his works, as the "Adumbrationes," treatises upon fasting, patience, Easter, are lost, while only fragments remain of others, on the soul and Providence, etc.

3. The writings of Clement have opened the way to Christian philosophy. In them we meet with the finest passages on divers points of Christian doctrine and life, as, for instance, on the Trinity * (Pæd. III, 12); the true Church of Christ (Strom. VII, 16, 17); penance (II, 13; IV, 24); purgatory (VI, 14; VII, 12); the holiness and indissolubility of marriage (II, 23; IV, 20); prayer (VII, 7); fasting (VI, 12); the relation of science to faith (II, 4; V, 1), and other things. Clement was an Eclectic, but decidedly inclined towards Platonism. His "Cohortatio" and the "Stromata" testify to his prodigious erudition. His style is picturesque, but diffuse and heavy, his method indefinite. St. Jerome writes of him: "Clemens Alexandrinæ Ecclesiæ presbyter meo judicio omnium eruditissimus . . . Quid in (eius) libris indoctum, imo quid non e media philosophia est?" †

* "Εὐχαριστεῖν τῷ μόνῳ Πατρὶ καὶ Υἱῷ σὺν καὶ τῷ ἁγίῳ Πνεύματι, πάντα τῷ ἑνί ἐν ᾧ τὰ πάντα."

† *Hieron.*, Epist. 70 ad Magnum.

*Editions and Literature.* — *Migne*, S. gr. VIII-IX
(Reprint of Bishop J. Potter's edition, Oxford 1715,
and Venice 1757). — *Ceillier* l. c. II, 242–316. —
*Möhler*, l. c. 430–486. — *Reinkens*, De Clemente
Alex. homine, presbytero, philosopho, theologo. Vra-
tislav. 1851. — *Freppel*, Clemens d'Alexandrie. Paris
1866. — *Ch. Bigg*, The Christian Platonists of Alexan-
dria: Eight lectures preached before the University of
Oxford in the year 1886. Oxford 1886. 8vo. — An
English translation of Clement's works in the Ante-
Nicene Library, Clark, Edinburgh.

## § 51. *Origen* (*died 254*).

1. *Origen*, whon is styled Aeneus (*Χαλχέντερος*) on
account of his iron energy, and Adamantius
(*'Αδαμάντιος*), because of his genius and indomitable
perseverance, was born at Alexandria, A. D. 185, of
Christian parents, who watched with tender love
over his education, and instructed him well in the
Holy Scriptures. After the martyrdom of his father,
A. D. 202, a rich matron supplied him with the
means of studying theology under Pantænus and
Clement. At the same time he continued to apply
himself to the study of the profane sciences, and
became, at the desire of Bishop Demetrius, at the
early age of eighteen, President of the catechetical school of Alexandria, then the first in all Chris-
tendom. His brilliant talents, his power of teaching,
and the courage and steadfastness with which he suffered for the faith in the persecution of Septimius
Severus, made his name great among the Christians.
To the study of divine things he joined the practical
exercise of all Christian virtues. His zeal, however,

outstripped his discretion; for, he literally accepted and applied to himself the words of Our Lord in Matt. XIX, 12. For the sake of further improvement in philosophy, he frequented the schools of the Neoplatonic Ammonius Saccas, without neglecting, however, his theological studies. About 212 he journeyed to Rome, in order to see the "most ancient of all the churches." After his return, he resumed the office of catechetical teacher, took Heraclas, his former disciple, as his colleague, began also to teach the liberal arts and thus attracted many noble heathen youths to the cause of Christianity. At this time too he began the great work of the Hexapla, in which he was assisted by the liberal donations of the learned Gnostic Ambrose, whom he had converted to Christianity.

In the year A. D. 215 he undertook a journey to Arabia, in order to instruct an Emir in the Christian religion, and in 218 was summoned to Antioch to discharge a similar office for Julia Mammæa, the mother of the Emperor Alexander Severus. After ten years of persevering labor in Biblical exegesis, he was called to Greece to put down a schism, and on his way thither visited Palestine, where he was ordained priest in an uncanonical manner by the Bishops of Cæsarea and Jerusalem. This circumstance, as well as some erroneous sentences in the work " Περὶ ἀρχῶν," and perhaps also some displeasure on the part of Bishop Demetrius induced that prelate to degrade and excommunicate Origen in two synods.

The latter, hereupon, again withdrew to Palestine and founded a learned Christian school at Cæsarea, the reputation of which rivalled and almost surpassed that of Alexandria. He himself wrote many works.

In the persecution of Maximin, the Thracian, he took refuge in Cæsarea in Cappadocia, but returned, at the end of two years (238), to Cæsarea in Palestine; journeyed in 240 to Athens and Nicomedia, and in 244 to Bostra in Arabia, where he won the heretical Bishop Beryllus over to ecclesiastical orthodoxy, and brought back the Hypnopsychites to the truth.

In the last ten years of his life he composed his best works, especially the eight books against Celsus, delivered countless public homilies, besides his theological lectures, and wrote many letters. After unwearied labors in the cause of science, he died in 254, in the seventieth year of his age, in consequence of the cruel treatment received at Tyrus, in the Decian persecution.

2. The number of his writings is astounding, but the greater part of them are lost. Among them we may enumerate the following: —

(a.) *Biblical Exegetical Works*, amongst which his Hexapla, Octapla and Enneapla may be regarded as a kind of preliminary work. His expositions of Holy Scripture, which he knew by heart, are, in form, partly scholia, partly commentaries and homilies, and extend over nearly every portion of the Bible, but are now only extant in fragments. His Commentaries — in most part still preserved— on St. Matthew, St. John, and St. Paul's Epistle to the Romans, as well as the homilies upon St. Luke, are particularly valuable. As to his method of interpretation, he considers that the true interpreter should start with the grammatical and end with the allegorical-mystical sense.

(b.) *Apologetic and Controversial Works:* The eight books against Celsus, an Epicurean philosopher, who had published a work called "The True Word,"

wherein he brought together all the objections raised
by Jews and Gentiles against Christianity, both from a
religious and political point of view.   Origen answers
and refutes most of them with astounding erudition,
and in a brilliant style and with forcible arguments
shows that the Christian faith is most reasonable,
drawing his proofs from the wonderful extension of
Christianity, the cure of the sick and possessed, the
fulfilment of the prophecies, and the spotless morality
of the Christians in the midst of a world sunk in vice.
This work is the best of all the ancient Apologies, and
affords very excellent weapons even against modern
opponents of Christianity.

(c.) *Dogmatical Works*.   Several of these are lost,
as the books called " *Στρωματεῖς*," the books " On the
Resurrection " and " On Free Will ; " only a few fragments are preserved.   But his chief work, " De principiis," [*Περὶ ἀρχῶν*] has come down to us in a Latin
translation, and some passages of it also in the original.
The subjects treated in it are : in the first book, God
and the world of spirits ; in the second, man, his restoration and eternal destiny ; in the third, free will
and its relation to grace ; in the fourth, the interpretation of Holy Scripture.   The work forms a systematic treatment of the theology of his time, but, on
account of the errors contained in it, the author
made for himself many enemies and was the cause of
much disturbance.

(d.) *Practical Works and Letters*.   Among the
former we may mention, " De oratione," wherein he
explains the object, efficacy, and various kinds of
prayer, together with a commentary, full of meaning,
on the Pater Noster.   Also " Exhortatio ad martyrium," which contains a glowing explanation of the

motives for suffering martyrdom.    Of the letters, there only remain, with the exception of some fragments, an " Epistola ad Julianum Africanum," upon the authenticity of the story of Susanna, and one to Gregory Thaumaturgus.    Other works ascribed to him are spurious, the " Dialogus," etc.

3. Origen's works are not free from errors, especially the one entitled " De principiis."    He teaches a kind of subordinationism — inferiority of the Son and the Holy Ghost, not indeed as to their nature, but as to their origin.*    He likewise held the pre-existence of souls, a kind of transmigration, and the corporeal nature of the angels, and denied the eternity of hell. Apart from these errors, his writings contain a wealth of Christian doctrine, and the most magnificent testimonies on the Trinity (Hom. XII in Numeros); on prayer (De orat., c. 2, 5, 31); on the intercession of the angels and saints (ibid., c. 11; Contra Cels., VIII, 34, 57); on the necessity of  confession (Hom. III, in Levit. n.  4; hom. X, in Exod. n. 3).    As regards the Holy Eucharist, his language is guarded, on account of the " Disciplina arcani," still there are not wanting testimonies wherein he clearly affirms the doctrine of the real presence and of transubstantiation (Hom. XVIII in Jerem., n. 13; hom. XIII in Exod., n. 3.).

His style and language are flowing in his polemical writings, but prolix and tiresome in his commentaries and homilies.    Opinions differ very much as to his person, character, and merits.    St. Jerome, at first an

---

* Subordinationism as to origin only, and not in nature, is no heresy or error, but Catholic truth.    The author, therefore, expresses himself too vaguely.    [R.]

admirer, but afterwards an opponent of Origen, speaks of him thus : " Vult aliquis laudare Origenem? Laudet ut laudo. Magnus vir ab infantia et vere martyris filius, voluptates in tantum fugit, ut zelo Dei, sed tamen non secundum scientiam, ferro truncaret genitalia; calcavit avaritiam; Scripturas memoria tenuit, et in studio explanationis earum diebus sudavit et noctibus. Mille et eo amplius tractatus in Ecclesia locutus est; edidit innumerabiles præterea commentarios, quos ipse appellat τόμους. Quis nostrum tanta potest legere, quanta ille conscripsit? Quis ardentem in Scripturis animum non miretur? Quod si quis Judas zelotes opposuerit nobis errores ejus, audiat libere:

> Interdum magnus dormitat Homerus,
> Verum opere in longo fas est obrepere somnum.
>
> (Horat.)

Non imitemur ejus vitia, cujus virtutes non possumus sequi " [Epist. 84, ad Pammachium et Oceanum. Cf. *Vinc Lir.*, Commonit. c. 23.] The errors of Origen were not the fruit of a perverse will, but the echo of the Platonic philosophy he had so eagerly studied in his youth.

*Editions and Literature.* — *Migne*, S. gr. XI-XVII. — *Ceillier* l. c. II, 584–782. — *Möhler* l. c., pp. 485–576. — *Thomasius*, Origenes. Nürnberg 1838.—*Redepenning*, Origenes, sein Leben und seine Lehre. 2 vols. Bonn 1841–1846. — *Al. Vincenzi*, In Sancti Gregorii Nysseni et Origenis doctrinam et scripta nova recensio. 4 vols. 8vo. Romæ 1864–1865. — *Freppel*, Origène. 2 vols. 2 éd. Paris 1875. — *Harnack*, Dogmengeschichte I. 559–604; 2 ed. Freiburg 1888.

### § 52. *Friends of Origen.*

ST. GREGORIUS THAUMATURGUS, ST. PAMPHILUS, AND
ST. DIONYSIUS, THE GREAT.

Among the many friends and contemporaries of
Origen, the following deserve especial mention: —

1. *Gregorius Thaumaturgus*, whose real name was
Theodorus, was born about 210, of heathen parents,
at Neocæsarea in Pontus. Together with his brother
Athenodorus, he went to Berytus in Phœnicia, for the
purpose of studying jurisprudence. Thence he retired
to Cæsarea in Palestine, where both his brother and
himself were drawn towards Christianity by the per-
suasive eloquence of Origen, and received baptism in
239. After they had returned to their native town,
Neocæsarea, Gregory was appointed in spite of his
own opposition its first bishop. In the exercise of
his office he wrought countless miracles, to which
Gregory of Nyssa bears testimony in his biography,
which, however, is not wholly trustworthy. He took
part in the synod held A. D. 265 at Antioch, against
Paul of Samosata. At his death A. D. 270, there
remained in the city but 17 heathens, which was the
number of Christians he found when entering upon
his episcopal charge. The following of his writings
have come down to us: —

(a.) "Oratio panegyrica in Origenem," one of the
finest discourses in ancient Christian literature, and a
beautiful token of gratitude to his master, and of his
enthusiastic love of knowledge.

(b.) "Symbolum, sive expositio fidei," a sound
explanation of the doctrine of the adorable Trinity.

(c.) "Metaphrasis in Ecclesiasten" (in 12 chapters), which St. Jerome calls "brevis quidem, sed

valde utilis." Furthermore, an "Epistola canonica," containing important precepts regarding penance.

(d.) A theological treatise, addressed to Theopompus, upon the unity of nature in the three divine persons, and on the impassibility of God.

The "Expositio" is lost; other works, as "De anima ad Tatianum, Capitula 12 de fide," are spurious. Socrates gives the following testimony to the widespread fame of Gregory: —

"This Gregory is much spoken of in Athens, Berytus, and the whole province of Pontus, and, as it were, in the whole world."*

2. *Pamphilus*, born at Berytus in Phœnicia, completed his theological studies at Alexandria, and was ordained priest at Cæsarea in Palestine. He there distributed his rich patrimony, partly in alms and partly towards the foundation of a valuable library, which proved a treasure to his friend Eusebius, and, later on, to Jerome. He founded a Christian school, and was indefatigable in instructing heathens and in collecting and copying books. He died about 309 from the effects of imprisonment and tortures which he suffered on account of the faith under Maximin. Pamphilus was not an original writer. Even his "Apology for Origen," in six books, was the joint composition of himself and Eusebius. In it he endeavors by means of extracts from Origen's works to defend him against the charge of heterodoxy; the first book only has been preserved, in the inaccurate Latin translation of Rufinus. Eusebius calls him "a

---

\* *Socrates*, Hist. Eccl. lib. IV, 27: "Περὶ τούτου τοῦ Γρηγορίου πολὺς ὁ λόγος ἔν τε Ἀθήναις καὶ Βηρυτῷ καὶ ὅλῃ τῇ Ποντικῇ διοικήσει, ὡς δὲ εἰπεῖν, καὶ πάσῃ τῇ οἰκουμένῃ."

most distinguished and true philosopher in the manner of his life." *

3. *Dionysius*, the Great, of Alexandria, was born in that city, of noble heathen parents, about 190. The study of philosophy left him unsatisfied, while that of the Holy Scriptures deeply impressed him and drew him towards Christianity. He studied theology under Origen and Heraclas, and succeeded the latter in 232 as superior of the catechetical school, and was chosen Bishop of Alexandria about 247. The seventeen years of his episcopal administration were one unbroken chain of sufferings and of contests, partly with external foes, as Decius and Valerian, and partly with internal, as Novatian, Sabellius, Paul of Samosata, Nepos the Chiliast. He died A. D. 264. Only a few fragments remain of his writings and numerous letters, viz.: an " Epistola ad Novatianum," wherein he sternly rebukes Novatian for his schismatic proceedings, and exhorts him to return to Catholic unity; and an " Epistola canonica," addressed to the Lybian Bishop Basilides, on penitential discipline. Of his " Commentary on the Book of Ecclesiastes," and his " Explanation of the Gospel of St. Luke," as well as of his writings " De natura," " De promissionibus adversus Nepotem " and " Adversus Sabellium," there exist but fragments. His doctrine on the Logos, to whom he applied the term " creature " [ποίημα], was severely attacked and censured, but he tried to defend his use of the word in an orthodox sense, in a letter addressed to Pope Dionysius, part of which is still preserved. With critical penetration,

---

* *Eusebius*, H. E. VII, 32: " ᾿Ελλογιμώτατον αὐτῷ τε βίῳ ιλόσοφον ἀληθῆ."

comprehensive learning, glowing zeal, and indomitable
courage, he combined admirable humility and charity.
Christ, in his History of Greek Literature, says:
"His letters bear witness to the great and marked literary progress which Christian writers had made in the
schools of the rhetoricians." * Ceillier characterizes
him thus: "St. Denys avait un génie très élevé, une
érudition profonde, une connaissance exacte du dogme
et de la discipline de l'Eglise; il était modeste dans ses
sentiments, persuasif dans ses discours, plein de zèle
pour l'honneur de la religion, pour la pureté de la foi,
la paix et l'unité de l'Eglise" [l. c. III, 279.]

4. Among the personal friends of Origen, besides
the above mentioned, were also the Bishops of Arabia,
Bishop Alexander of Jerusalem, Theoctistus and
Firmilian of Cæsarea in Cappadocia, and the chrono-
grapher Sextus Julius Africanus.

*Editions and Literature.* — To 1. — *Migne*, S. gr.
X, 963-1206. — *Ceillier* l. c. III, 307-325. — *Ryssel*,
Gregor Thaum., sein Leben und seine Schriften.
Leipzig 1880. — To 2. — *Migne*, S. gr. X, 1529-
1558. — *Routh* l. c. III, 485-512; IV, 339-392. —
*Ceillier* l. c. III, 435-448. — To 3. — *Migne*, S.
gr. X, 1233-1344, 1575-1602. — *Ceillier* l. c. III,
241-279. — *Möhler* l. c., pp. 624-637. — *Hagemann*, Die Römische Kirche in den ersten 3 Jahr-
hunderten (Freiburg 1864), pp. 411-453. — *Dittrich*,
Dionysius der Grosse von Alexandrien (Freiburg
1867). — To 4. — *Migne*, S. gr. X, 202-206, and X,
36-94. — See also the articles under the respective names

* "Seine Briefe zeugen von den grossen formalen Fort-
schritten, welche die chrislichen Schriftsteller in den Schulen
der Rhetoren gemacht haben." [2. Aufl., München 1890.]

in the Kirchenlexion. — Also *Bardenhewer* l. c., p. 173.

## § 53. *St. Methodius, Bishop of Olympus* (*d. about 312*).

1. *Methodius*, Bishop of Olympus, the particulars of whose life are unknown, was one of the many opponents of Origen, both during his lifetime and after his death. He is described by contemporary writers as a man of great penetration of mind, of high education and profound learning. He died the death of a martyr under Maximinus Daza, in the Diocletian persecution, about 312.

2. In his writings, Methodius defends celibacy, opposes the errors of Origen, impugns heathenism, and comments upon the texts of Holy Scripture. Chief of his works, still preserved in the original text, is the " Convivium decem Virginum, sive de virginitate " [Συμπόσιον ἡ περὶ ἀγνείας].

In the form of a dialogue, the writer describes with perfect enthusiasm, and with all the wealth of the Greek language at his command, the exalted idea of absolute continency or virginity, and in this way sets before his readers the great difference between Christian and pagan ethics in one of the most important points. The dialogue consists of 24 verses, sung by Thecla, the Chantress, to each of which a choir answers a refrain [ὑπακούει]. Only extracts and fragments remain of his works: " De libero arbitrio et unde malum," " De resurrectione," and " De rebus creatis." The three dialogues upon Simeon and Anna, Palm-Sunday, and the cross and passion of Christ, are not genuine. A defense of the Christian religion against Porphyrius, a commentary upon Genesis, the

Canticle of Canticles, and Job, and a sermon on the martyrs, are almost entirely lost.

3. The writings and fragments that are extant suffice to give us an idea of his high mental endowments, his classical education, and the originality of his mind. The latter gift is particularly conspicuous in his doctrine of the incarnation (Conviv. orat. I, c. 4; orat. III, c. 4. 6.) and its relation to the Church and the faithful (orat. VIII, c. 5. 6.). Methodius teaches that the origin of evil lies not in matter, but in the abuse of free will. In his doctrine concerning the resurrection, he follows more or less Athenagoras, and keeps the midway between the spiritualistic tendencies of Origen, and the gross conceptions of the Chiliasts. The body, he maintained, being a constituent part of man, must also have a share in the immortality of the soul, and their reunion and glorification are the fruit of the redemption. Epiphanius describes Methodius as " a clever man, and one who battled hard for the truth." *

*Editions and Literature.* — *Migne*, S. gr. XVIII, 9–408. — *Jahn*, St. Methodii opp. 4° Halis 1865. — *Ceillier* l. c. IV, 26–45. — *Pankow*, Methodius von Olympos. Mainz 1888. — *Fritschel*, Methodius und seine Philosophie. Leipzig 1879. — *Bonwetsch*, Methodius' von Olympus Schriften. Leipzig 1891.

---

* " Ἀνὴρ λόγιος καὶ σφόδρα περὶ τῆς ἀληθείας ἀγωνισάμενος." (Haer. LXIV, 63.)

## CHAPTER II.

### LATIN FATHERS AND WRITERS.

§ 54. *Tertullian, Priest of Carthage (d. about 240)*

1. *Quintus Septimius Florens Tertullianus*, born at Carthage about 160, being endowed with the most splendid intellectual gifts, acquired early in life a surprising amount of knowledge in philosophy and Greek and Roman literature. He devoted himself to the study of law, and later on became professor of rhetoric in his native town; but in matters of religion and morality he occupied a very low position, all his aims being confined to the pleasures of life. Still, the shameful immorality of the heathen religion and life did not fail to disgust him, while the pure lives of the Christians and the steadfastness of their martyrs, deeply impressed and attracted him. Soon after, he embraced Christianity, in the thirtieth year of his age, and, though married (to a Christian), entered the priesthood. Henceforth he devoted the wealth of his intellect and learning to the service of the Church. In one continuous succession of writings he vehemently attacked and combated all her opponents, heathens, Jews and heretics. But, later on, between 202 and 205, he fell away and passed over to the sect of the Montanists, more congenial to the natural rigorism of his character. He founded a stricter Montanist party, that of the Tertullianists, which lasted down to the fifth century, and attacked the Catholic Church with all the bitterness peculiar to heretics. It is very questionable whether he returned to the Church before his death, which occurred about 240.

2. Tertullian's works, which contain a rich store of

philosophical, historical, juridical, and physical knowledge, extend over every department of the religious life. They are divided into apologetical, dogmatical (polemical), and practical.

To the *apologetical* works belong: —

(a.) " Apologeticus," in 50 chapters, a large, important work, composed about 198, addressed to the procurators of the Roman Empire. In it he complains above all that Christians are not allowed a chance or opportunity of defending themselves, and that they are condemned merely on account of their name. He indignantly repudiates the charges, made against them by the heathens, of child-murder, of unnatural crimes in their religious assemblies, of impiety and disloyalty. True, Christians will not, indeed, render divine honor to the emperors, but they remain faithful and loyal to them even amidst the hardest persecutions, and pray for them. In conclusion he compares their doctrine and life with that of the philosophers. This Apology is as sweeping a condemnation, as it is a brilliant defense of Christianity, and is distinguished both by its matter and form.

(b.) "Ad nationes," in 2 books, a further and still more severe attack upon paganism, but containing some very obscure and unintelligible passages.

(c.) "De testimonio animæ," a small but ingenious work, wherein Tertullian shows that the human soul is naturally Christian ; that it gives testimony to the existence of a just God and of evil spirits or demons, and that it is its own witness of immortality.

(d.) "Ad Scapulam," in 5 chapters, a warning to the Proconsul Scapula not to draw down upon himself the anger of God by his cruel persecution of the Christians.

(e.) " Adversus Judæos," in 14 chapters, a demonstration of the fulfilment of the prophecies in and through Christ, and an exposition of the relation of the Mosaic to the natural and Christian law.

His *dogmatical* (*polemical*) writings are : —

(a.) " De præscriptionibus hæreticorum," in 44 chapters, wherein he shows that the doctrine of Christ is only to be found with the organs of tradition, lawfully transmitted and succeeding each other, [præscripto veritatis] ; that the genuine tradition is also the oldest and Apostolic, whilst every heresy is of later origin [præscriptio principalitatis] ; and that heretics, being outside the Church, have no right to the Holy Scriptures [præscriptio proprietatis]. The author uses his best style and the most forcible arguments to vindicate and justify in a scientific manner the Catholic principle of tradition. This is one of the most valuable and important of Tertullian's works.

(b.) " De baptismo," in 20 chapters, with many dogmatical and practical remarks upon the nature, necessity, effects, and administration of baptism, of infant-baptism, which he is desirous of delaying, and of the baptism of heretics, which he holds to be invalid.

(c.) " Adversus Marcionem libri V," " Adversus Valentinianos," " Adversus Hermogenem " — all against the heresy of the Gnostics.

(d.) " De anima," in 58 chapters, a refutation of philosophical and heretical opinions concerning the soul, in which, however, error is freely mixed with truth.

(e.) " Adversus Praxeam," in 31 chapters, a demonstration of the Trinity.

(f.) " De carne Christi," in which the doctrine of

the Incarnation is well grasped and ardently defended against the Gnostics.

(g.) "De resurrectione carnis," in 63 chapters, a demonstration against the Gnostics, from reason and Holy Scripture, that the body, as the instrument of the soul, will be raised up and reunited to it.

To Tertullian's *practical* works belong the following: —

(a.) "Ad martyres," in 6 chapters, for the encouragement and consolation of the Christians languishing in prison under sentence of death.

(b.) "De spectaculis," in 30 chapters, an earnest warning to Christians and catechumens against frequenting public shows, those "privata consistoria impudicitiæ."

(c.) "De idolatria," in 24 chapters, an admonition against direct and indirect participation in idolatrous worship.

(d.) "De corona militis," in 15 chapters, showing that it is not lawful for a Christian soldier to wear a wreath upon his head after the heathen fashion.

(e.) "De fuga in persecutione," in 14 chapters, urging that instead of flying from martyrdom, we ought much rather to covet it.

(f.) "Scorpiace contra Gnosticos," in 15 chapters, on the unlawfulness of denying the faith and on the meritoriousness of martyrdom.

(g.) "De patientia," in 16 chapters, an extremely beautiful and eloquent description of patience.

(h.) "De oratione," in 29 chapters, on the Lord's Prayer and the manner of praying in general.

(i.) "De pœnitentia," in 12 chapters, on the nature and necessity of penance, and the manner of practicing it rigorously.

(j.) "De pudicitia," on purity, in which, contrary to his former opinion, he limits the forgiveness of sin to lesser faults.

(k.) "Ad uxorem," in 17 chapters, advice to his wife against marrying again, and of the unlawfulness of marrying a heathen, on account of the great dangers besetting the faith.

(l.) "De cultu feminarum," in 2 books, in which he censures female extravagance in dress, and extols the virtues of a Christian life, particularly modesty.

(m.) "De pallio," in 6 chapters, a trenchant self-justification for having exchanged the philosopher's cloak for the toga.

(n.) "De exhortatione castitatis," in 13 chapters, warning to a friend not to marry again.

(o.) "De monogamia," in 16 chapters, in which second marriage is utterly rejected as "species stupri."

(p.) "De virginibus velandis," that virgins, as well as married women, should wear a veil.

(q.) "De jejunio adversus psychicos," in 17 chapters, a severe attack upon Catholics on the subject of fasting.

The last four works, as well as the "De corona militis" and "Fuga in persecutione," "Scorpiace" and "De pudicitia," are written in the Montanist spirit. Some works are lost, others, as "Libellus adversus omnes hæreses," "Epistola de cibis judaicis," and others, are incorrectly ascribed to him.

3. The various works of Tertullian contain, though interspersed with many errors, some of the finest arguments for the Catholic faith. His character, too, is revealed in his writings. Ardor and earnestness, acuteness and knowledge, were in him harmoniously blended together. These qualities made St. Jerome

exclaim: "Quid Tertulliano eruditius? quid acrius? 'Apologeticus' ejus, et contra gentes libri cunctam sæculi obtinent disciplinam" [Epist. 70. ad Magnum.] He knew how to handle the most difficult questions of dogma and morals in such a way that we almost seem to read a writer of our own days. Tertullian recognized the will of God as the supreme and first rule of man's life and action, but he failed to see that the divine will is made known to us by the Church alone. He consequently fell into the errors of Montanism, which was more in harmony with the rigor of his character. His language, like his character, is harsh and austere, his diction laconic and cutting, almost always concise and obscure. "Pene quot verba, tot sententiæ, quot sensus, tot sunt victoriæ" [Vinc. Lirin., Commonit. c. 24.] Amongst his best writings, we may count the "Apologeticus," "Liber de præscriptionibus," "De pœnitentia," "De patientia," "De oratione," and "Exhortatio ad martyres." Tertullian is the father of the Latin language of the Church.

*Editions and Literature.* — *Migne*, S. lat. I–II. 1. — Tertulliani opp., pars I, in Corp. script. eccl. lat. vol. XX, ed. *Reifferscheid* et *Wissowa*. Vindob. 1890. — *Ceillier* l. c. II, 374–529. — *Möhler* l. c. pp. 701–789. — *Freppel*, Tertullien. 2e éd. Paris 1872. — *Hauck*, Tertullian's Leben und Schriften. Erlangen 1877. — *Nirschl*, Lehrbuch § 76. — *Bonwetsch*, Die Schriften Tertullians nach der Zeit ihrer Abfassung. Bonn 1878.— *Kolberg*, Verfassung, Cultus und Disciplin der christl. Kirche nach den Schriften Tertullians. Braunsberg 1886. — *Nöldechen*, Tertullian. Gotha 1890, criticized in the Zeitschr. für Kathol. Theol. (Innsbruck 1892), pp. 529–534. — *Esser*, Die

Seelenlehre Tertullians.    Paderborn 1893. — English
translations of the Apologeticus by *W. Reeve*, London 1889, 1894; and by *T. H. Bindley*, London
1890. — Also, Tertulliani de præscript. haer., ad martyres, ad Scapulam, edited with introduction and notes
by *T. H. Bindley*, Oxford 1894. 8vo.

## § 55. *Minucius Felix.*

1. Of the life of this ecclesiastical writer, we only
know that, according to St. Jerome, he was celebrated
in Rome as a lawyer and orator ["insignis causidicus
Romæ," Hieron.], and that he continued to follow the
same profession after his conversion to Christianity,
which occurred in his later years, in the time of the
Emperors Antoninus Pius or Marcus Aurelius.  He
had two friends, Octavius Januarius, a lawyer and a
Christian like himself, and Cæcilius Natalis, a heathen.
These, while journeying from Rome to Ostia, entered
into a disputation upon heathenism and Christianity,
which gave occasion to Minucius Felix, who had been
chosen umpire, to compose his Apology for Christianity, under the title "Octavius," in 40 chapters.

2. In the form of a dialogue the author shows, first,
how Octavius exposes the absurdity of paganism, and
how he refutes the ordinary charges, brought up by
Cæcilius, against the Christians, of worshiping the head
of an ass, of being atheists and enemies of the State,
and of indulging in immoral practices.  He then proceeds to show how Octavius set forth with warmth and
enthusiasm the truth and beauty of the Christian religion, so far as to gain his opponent to its cause.
Both conquered, the one over his adversary, the other
over his error.  "Ego Octavio meo plurimum quantum

eadem tranquillitate, qua vivimus, sed et mihi gratulor, nec expecto sententiam. Vicimus, et ita haud improbe usurpo victoriam; nam, ut ille mei victor est, ita ego triumphator erroris " (c. 40.)

3. This is probably the most ancient of the Latin apologies that we possess, and it has this great advantage, that the differences between polytheism and monotheism (c. 20–28), between the heathen and the Christian views (c. 31–38), are drawn directly from life. It contains, moreover, many interesting details about heathen demon-worship, and the position and life of the Christian Church of those days. But, strange to say, there is no shadow of an attempt at Scriptural proof, or demonstration of specific Christian doctrines, such as the Trinity, redemption, and others. The reason of this omission no doubt is to be sought in the particular purpose of the work, and in the immediate circle of its readers. The style is brilliant, and the expressions most happy. The power of mind, the subtlety and depth of argument, the charm of description and variety of imagery are admirable. Both arrangement and subject bear witness to the high philosophical culture and juridical precision of the writer. " Minucius Felix non ignobilis inter causidicos loci fuit. Huius liber, cui 'Octavius' titulus est, declarat, quam idoneus veritatis assertor esse potuisset, si se totum ad id studium contulisset " [Lactantius, Instit. V, 1, et I, 2.]

*Editions and Literature.* — *Migne*, S. lat. III, 201–672. — *Halm*, Corp. script. eccl. lat. vol. II. Vindob. 1867. — *Ceillier* l. c. II, 222–234. — *Rich. Kühn*, Der Octavius des Minucius Felix. Eine heidnisch-philosoph. Auffassung des Christenthums. Leipzig 1882. — *Grillnberger*, Der Octavius keine heid-

nisch-philos. Auffassung des Christenth., Jahrb. für
Philosophie und specul. Theol. III (1889), 104 sq. —
*Kihn*, art. Minucius Felix, in Wetzer and Welte's
Kirchenlex. (2 Aufl.).

## § 56. *St. Cyprian, Bishop of Carthage* (d. 258).

1. *Thascius Cæcilius Cyprianus*, born of a wealthy
and distinguished heathen family at Carthage, in the
beginning of the third century, was a man of great
genius and talent. He followed the profession of a
teacher, and his fame as a rhetorician became so
great that it brought him not only distinction, but also
considerable wealth. These advantages, however,
proved no spiritual blessing to him; they only afforded greater facility for indulging in dissipation and
worldly pleasures. A change, however, came about
in 246, when Cyprian was converted to Christianity
by the priest Cæcilius, whose name he henceforth
adopted out of regard and esteem for his new teacher.
Having distributed his earthly goods to the poor, the
new convert began to devote himself with great ardor
to the study of the Sacred Scriptures and the writings
of Tertullian. In 247 he was ordained priest, and two
years later consecrated Bishop of Carthage. When
the Decian persecution broke out, in 250, he considered it prudent to retire for a while from the city and
to provide for the necessities of his flock by means of
letters written from his place of concealment. In 251
he returned to Carthage, where new trials and sufferings awaited him. During a terrible pestilence and
during the persecution of Gallus, he inspired his
Christian flock with courage and hope, both by word
of mouth and example. He also held many synods

respecting the schism of Novatus and Felicissimus, but fell unfortunately into a dispute with Pope Stephen regarding the baptism of heretics. Cyprian, while hotly pursuing the controversy, never pushed it to the verge of schism. In the persecution of Valerian he was banished to Kurubis, but after a year's exile brought back to Carthage and put to death by the sword as an enemy to the gods of Rome, on September 14th, 258. Cyprian is one of the most illustrious bishops of the Catholic Church.

2. Of his writings, besides 81 letters (65 from and 16 to him), which are of great importance for a knowledge of the ecclesiastical affairs and history of the African and Roman churches of that time, we possess the following: —

### A. *Apologetical Works.*

(a.) " Epistola ad Donatum," or, " Liber de gratia Dei," in 16 chapters, describing in a pleasant style the corruption of the pagan world, his own former unhappy condition, his conversion to Christianity, and the effect produced by baptism in his soul.

(b.) " De idolorum vanitate," in 15 chapters; a work similar to the " Octavius " of Minucius Felix, wherein he impugns heathen idolatry, and defends Christian monotheism and the Christological truths.

(c.) " Testimoniorum adversus Judæos libri tres," treating of the temporary character of Judaism, of the person and mission of Christ, and ending with an instruction upon a good Christian life.

(d.) " Ad Demetrianum," in 25 chapters, a letter in defense of Christianity against various charges.

### B. *Practical Works.*

(a.) "De habitu virginum," in 24 chapters, a graceful admonition to simplicity in dress and modesty of life.

(b.) "De unitate ecclesiæ," in 27 chapters, an invaluable dogmatical work, in which the principle, "Salus extra ecclesiam non est," is explained by the remark: "Habere jam non potest Deum patrem, qui ecclesiam non habet matrem. Si potuit evadere quisque extra arcam Noe fuit, et qui extra ecclesiam foris fuerit, evadit" (c. VI). In the conclusion, Cyprian earnestly exhorts those who are separated from the Church, to return to her bosom; and all the faithful to exercise charity and brotherly love.

(c.) "De mortalitate," in 26 chapters, a treatise full of noble faith and magnanimous courage, against the fear of death entertained even by Christians during the time of pestilence.

(d.) "De exhortatione martyrii," in 13 chapters, an admonition to steadfast confession of the faith and a warning against apostasy.

(e.) "De lapsis," in 36 chapters, expressing his joy at the constancy of many during the persecution, and his sorrow for those who had fallen, with directions concerning their rëadmission into the Church.

(f.) "De oratione dominica," an explanation of the Pater noster, accompanied by the most beautiful reflections, greatly praised by St. Augustine.

(g.) "De opere et eleemosynis," "De bono patientiæ," and "De zelo et livore," all very instructive and elegantly written.

Other treatises ascribed to him are doubtful, such

as "De spectaculis," "De disciplina et bono pudi-
citiæ," "De laude martyrii."

The following are not genuine: —

"De singularitate clericorum," "De rebaptis-
mate," and some poems. Also the treatise "De
aleatoribus," in 11 chapters, containing very important testimonies on such points of Catholic doctrine as
the primacy of the Roman Bishop, the sacrament and
sacrifice of the Holy Eucharist, the necessity of the
confession of sins, and others. This work is not by
St. Cyprian, but was very probably written by a
bishop who lived a little later.

3. From the works of St. Cyprian, we may cull the
most beautiful passages upon the Church, the nature
of penance, the Christian life, and especially on the
crown of martyrdom and virginity. His highest moral
principle, asserted on almost every page, is con-
formity to the Church of Christ in all the relations of
human life. His writings are full of sweet beauty,
charming simplicity, fascinating language, and masterly eloquence. "They run," says St. Jerome,
"like the sweet and placid waters of a pure fountain;
they are clearer than the sunlight." * For the rest, St.
Cyprian has drawn a good deal from Tertullian, whose
writings, together with Holy Scripture, formed his
favorite reading, according to the maxim of St. Jerome: "Admiramur ingenium, damnamus hæresin."
He is, however, not so rich in thought, nor so telling and pregnant in expression as that writer, but
rather inclined to be prolix by multiplying synonyms,

---

* "Beatus Cyprianus instar fontis purissimi dulcis incedit
et placidus" (Ep. 58, ad Paulinum.) "Sole clariora sunt
opera ejus" (*Idem*, De vir. ill., c. 67.)

and by recourse to the arts of rhetoric. In his moral principles he steers clear of the repelling rigorism of Tertullian, strives for wise moderation and tries to reconcile opposite views. Ennodius says of him: —

> Vatis Cypriani et martyris
> Cor, lingua, sensus, dignitas
> Mortem ferendo proferunt.
> Dictis fuit perfulgidus,
> Et ore dives unico,
> Torrentis unda gurgitis,
> Impacta cornu spicula
> Sermone vincens promulo.    (Carm. lib. I, 12.)

*Editions and Literature.* — *Migne*, S. lat. IV and V, 9–80. — *Hartel*, Cypriani opp. omnia. Vindob. 1868–1871. — *Ceillier* l. c. III, 1–224. — *Möhler* l. c. pp. 809–893. — *Reithmayr*, Gesch. des heiligen Cyprian. Augsburg 1848. — *Peters*, Der heilige Cyprian. Regensburg 1877. — *Fechtrup*, Des heiligen Cyprian Leben. Münster 1878. — *Freppel*, S. Cyprien et l'église d'Afrique au 3me. siécle. 3me. éd. Paris 1890. — *E. W. Benson* (Archbishop of Canterbury), Cyprian: His Life, His Times, His Work. New York, 1897. (See Catholic criticism on this work by H. I. D. Ryder, D. D., in the American Eccles. Review, January, 1898.)

§ 57.    *Cornelius (d. 252), Stephanus (d. 257), and Dionysius (d. 269), Bishops of Rome.*

1. *Cornelius*, a Roman by birth, was invested with the highest ecclesiastical dignity, A. D. 251. The very outset of his short pontificate was saddened by the appearance of an anti-pope in the person of Novatian.

He wrote several letters to Bishops Fabius of Antioch and Cyprian of Carthage, mostly referring to the schismatical proceedings of Novatian and his party, or also to the lapsed, who had returned to the unity of the Church. His letters to St. Cyprian form an invincible proof of the primacy of the Roman Church, and are a splendid testimony to the spirit of peace and concord which animated both bishops. Cornelius died a martyr on September 14th, 252.

2. *Stephanus*, chosen Bishop of Rome in 253, earned great fame by his vigor and energy. He provided for the spiritual and corporeal wants of the faithful, both at home and abroad, watched zealously over ecclesiastical unity and discipline, and strenuously upheld the lawfulness of the baptism of heretics against Cyprian and Firmilian. He probably died a martyr in 257. Only fragments remain of his letters to the bishops of Gall with reference to the schism at Arles, and to Cyprian and Firmilian, concerning baptism.

3. *Dionysius*, by his virtues and eminent theological learning an ornament of the Roman clergy, had sided with Pope Stephen in the dispute about the baptism of heretics, and was raised to the chair of St. Peter in 259, which he held till 269. We possess only three of his letters, which are eloquent testimonies to his pastoral solicitude and learning: —

(a.) "Epistola encyclica adversus Sabellianos," in refutation of contemporary errors regarding the blessed Trinity.

(b.) A letter to Dionysius of Alexandria, inviting him to clear himself from the suspicion of heresy.

(c.) " Epistola ad ecclesiam Cæsariensem," consoling that church under the calamities caused by the barbarian invasion. Eusebius relates that Dionysius of Alexandria called Dionysius of Rome a "learned and wonderful man." [Ἀνὴρ λόγιος καὶ θαυμάσιος.]

*Editions and Literature.* — To 1. — *Migne*, S. lat. III, 697–888. — *Ceillier* l. c. II, 573–583. — *Bollandists*, Sept. IV., 143 sq. — To 2. — *Migne*, S. lat. III, 1016-1046. — *Ceillier* l. c. III, 282–285. — *Schrödl*, Geschichte der Päpste (Mainz 1873), p. 272. — To 3. — *Migne*, S. lat. V, 100–136. — *Ceillier* l. c. III, 326–328. — *Hagemann*, Die römische Kirche in den ersten 3 Jahrh. (Freiburg 1864), p. 334. — *Hergenröther*, Kirchengeschichte (Freiburg 1876) I, 200.

## § 58. *Novatian, the Schismatic.*

1. *Novatian*, of unknown origin, but probably a Phrygian by birth, while still a catechumen at Rome, is said to have suffered from demoniacal attacks and to have received private baptism when in danger of death. Although he took no care, after his recovery, to have the usual solemn ceremonies of baptism supplied, and to receive the sacrament of confirmation, he was yet, in spite of his irregularity and of the opposition of the Roman clergy, ordained priest on account of his former good conduct. At first he seemed to answer every expectation. Soon after, however, he abandoned his own principles, which he had declared in a former letter to St. Cyprian, and placed himself at the head of that rigorous party which wished to exclude the lapsed from being received back again into the Church. When the virtuous priest Cornelius, who belonged to the moderate side, was elevated to the episcopal see of Rome, Novatian sought episcopal consecration at the hands of three ignorant bishops, and set himself up as anti-

pope, A. D. 253. A synod of Rome, and another at Carthage, however, excommunicated him, and even his own party abandoned him. Nevertheless, the evil principles he had disseminated, and which Novatus had helped to foster, on the subjects of penance and the Church, continued to grow, and gave rise to a very dangerous sect, whose followers styled themselves the " Pure " [καθαροί], and who spread over Asia and Africa, Gaul and Spain, and existed till the seventh century. The date of Novatian's birth and death is unknown.

2. Of his numerous works and letters, all written in an easy, pleasant style, we only possess : —

(a.) " Liber de Trinitate sive regula fidei," in 31 chapters, a controversial work, and mostly written in syllogistic form, wherein the author endeavors to refute those who held Christ to be a mere man, and those who maintained that the Son and the Holy Ghost are but different modes or manifestations of the Father, and thus denied the reality of three distinct divine persons. The authenticity of this work is, however, not quite certain.

(b.) " De cibis judaicis," in 7 chapters, upon the precepts of the Old Testament regarding food, which had but a typical meaning, and, therefore, no longer applied to Christians, who, the author contends, should bestow all the more care upon the practice of self-denial.

(c.) " Epistola cleri Romani ad Cyprianum episcopum." This weighty and dignified encyclical, composed and signed by Novatian in 251, is chiefly concerned with the readmittance of the lapsed, and is based upon principles much less severe than those he insisted on at a later period.

3. Novatian was a man of talent and culture with considerable knowledge of philosophy. In his work on the Trinity, he treats with great acuteness, depth, and solidity of the doctrine of the Godhead, in opposition to the errors of the Gnostics; then proves that Christ is true God and true man, and impugns the heresy of Sabellius; he also touches upon the doctrine of the Holy Ghost, and endeavors to harmonize the doctrine of the three Divine Persons with the unity of nature. In his moral principles, he resembled Tertullian. "Novatien écrivait avec beaucoup d'agrément et de douceur. Son discours est méthodique et bien suivi" (*Ceillier* l. c. III, 296.)

*Editions and Literature.* — *Migne,* S. lat. III, 889–1000. — *Ceillier* l. c. III, 290–296. — *Hagemann* l. c. pp. 371–411. — Wetzer and Welte's Kirchenlex., IX, 544 (2 ed.).

## § 59. *Arnobius* (*d. after 325.*)

*Arnobius,* an African and heathen by birth, and a teacher of rhetoric by profession, was for a long time a strenuous opponent of Christianity. The folly and immorality of polytheism on the one hand, and the grandeur and power of the Christian doctrine on the other, inclined him to the religion of Christ and, in consequence of a dream, he asked to be baptized. In proof of the sincerity of his conversion, he wrote, at the request of the Bishop of Sicca, his "Disputationes adversus nationes," in 7 books. The work, however, is not so much a defense of the Christian doctrine — a task for which his insufficient knowledge did not qualify him — as an exposure of the hollowness of heathenism, with which he was intimately acquainted.

The first two books are of an apologetic character; one dealing with the objection that all public calamities are due to the Christians, and with the adoration of a crucified God; the other with the reasons of belief (motiva credibilitatis), viz.: the wonderful spread of Christianity, the heroism of the martyrs, the miracles of Christ, and such like. The other five books are controversial, showing the absurdity of heathen mythology (III, IV, V) and the foolishness of the heathen religion with its worship of many gods, animal sacrifices, and soothsaying (VI, VII). His doctrine concerning God, the world, and the human soul, is not always correctly expressed, and besides there are other errors, especially in Christology. The writer's style is bombastic and full of pathos, and betrays, in many parts, an uncertainty in his Christian convictions. St. Jerome speaks rather disparagingly of it: "Arnobius inæqualis et nimius et absque operis sui partitione confusus" (Epist. 58 ad Paulinum.) Ceillier likewise: "Il n'y a ni ordre ni méthode dans ses ouvrages; son stile est dur et enflé" (l. c. III, 385.)

*Editions and Literature.* — *Migne*, S. lat. V, 350–1372. — *Reifferscheid*, Arnobii adversus nationes libri VII, in Corp. script. eccl. lat. vol. IV. (Vindob. 1875). — *Ceillier* l. c. III, 373–387. — *Leckelt*, Ueber des Arnobius Schrift "Adversus nationes" (Neisse 1884). — *Röhricht*, Die Seelenlehre des Arnobius (Hamburg 1893). — *Freppel*, Commodien, Arnobe et autres (Paris 1893).

## § 60. *Lactantius Firmianus* (d. about 330).

1. This writer was born in Africa of heathen parents and trained under Arnobius. His Symposium

(Συμπόσιον), consisting of 100 enigmas, each in three hexameters, induced the Emperor Diocletian to summon him to Nicomedia, as teacher of Latin rhetoric. The small number of his disciples, the dry and sterile nature of his occupation, the hollowness of heathen philosophy, poverty, and want of the barest necessaries of life, awakened in him a desire for knowledge and happiness of a higher kind, and led him, about 303, to embrace Christianity, which he thenceforward most strenuously vindicated against the unjust hatred of the heathens. He died in poverty at an advanced age, in 330, probably at Treves, whither he had been summoned by Constantine, the Great, as tutor to his unfortunate son Crispus.

2. We are in possession of the following of his works : —

(a.) "Institutionum divinarum libri VII," a comprehensive apology for Christianity, in which he endeavors to show to the learned, by arguments from reason, what is true philosophy; and to the ignorant, what is true religion. Each book has its own title.

Book I, "De falsa religione," treats, first of the unity of God and the divine government of the world; next of the falsity of the polytheistic worship;

Book II, "De origine erroris," of the origin of heathenism, which Lactantius traces back to the influence of demons;

Book III, "De falsa sapientia," of the contradictions in heathen philosophy on the most essential questions;

Book IV, "De vera sapientia," of divine revelation, the Incarnation and Passion of our Lord, and Christian doctrine as opposed to heresy;

Book V, "De justitia," of justice, viz., of the worship of God in deed and truth, and of true fraternal love;

Book VI, " De vero cultu," of the true way of honoring God and showing kindness to men;

Book VII, "De vita beata," of eternal happiness, as the last end of man and the reward of a good life. Then follows a description of the end of the world, the coming of the Antichrist, the resurrection and the general judgment. The writer draws largely from Tertullian, Minucius Felix, and Cyprian, and often quotes from Cicero and Virgil.

A later abridgment of the compendious work, " Epitome institutionum divinarum ad Pentadium fratrem," in 72 chapters, contains many new and beautiful thoughts and illustrations.

(b.) " De opificio Dei," a work somewhat savoring of the Stoic philosophy, wherein the author dwells on the beauty and fitness of the human frame, in order to draw a proof from it of the goodness and power of God.

(c.) " De ira Dei," in which the author demonstrates with learning and eloquence, that God by his very nature must punish the wicked and reward the good.

(d.) " De mortibus persecutorum," in 52 chapters, wherein he shows by the examples of Nero, Domitian, Valerian, Diocletian, Galerius, and others, that God had punished and humbled all the persecutors of the Christian religion, while he had exalted the Christians. In recent times, there are some to whom the style of this book, and especially its vehement language, seem incompatible with the gentle, peaceful sentiments of Lactantius, and who, therefore, deny the authorship of the work.

Other works of his, such as the "Symposium,"
"Hodeporicum" (a poetical description of travels),
"Grammaticus," and a collection of letters comprising a number of learned treatises, are lost.    The poems
"De passione Domini," in 80 hexameters, and "De
resurrectione Domini," in 55 distichs, are not genuine,
but that entitled "De Phœnice," in 85 distichs, is
now generally ascribed to him.

3. The writings of Lactantius contain much that is
beautiful and instructive upon the relations of the
human soul to God and divine revelation, upon the
way in which philosophy and religion minister to the
glory of God and happiness of men (Instit. IV, 3, 4 ;
III, 9–12 ; 27, 28) ; on the necessity of grace ("De ira
Dei" c. 1 ; Instit. II, 3), and the confession of sins
(Instit. IV, 17 ; VI, 24), and such like subjects.    His
"Institutiones" are particularly remarkable for their
learning, skillful arrangement, and brilliant style.    In
consequence of his imperfect learning in Christian
theology, however, the author does not always express
himself correctly or in such a way as to exclude mis-
understandings ; his views are decidedly Chiliastic
(VII, 14 sqq.).    Nevertheless, he ranks amongst the
most eminent ecclesiastical writers, and, on account of
the purity of his Latin and the perspicuity of his style,
is called "the Christian Cicero."    Eusebius writes in
his Chronicles : "Lactantius vir omnium suo tempore
eloquentissimus, sed adeo in hac vita pauper, ut ple-
rumque etiam necessariis indiguerit, nedum deliciis"
(II, 191).

*Editions and Literature.* — *Migne*, S. lat. VI,
VII. — *Brandt* et *Laubmann*, Lactantii opp., in Corp.
script. eccl. lat. XIX (Vindob. 1890). — *Ceillier* l. c.
III, 387–434. — *Stöckl*, Philosophie der patristischen

Zeit, pp. 249–263. — *Heinig*, Die Ethik des Lactantius (Grimma 1887). — *Marbach*, Die Psychologie des Lactantius (Halle 1889).

---

## THIRD EPOCH.

## FULL GROWTH OF PATRISTIC LITERATURE, A. D. 325–461.

### § 61. *General Survey*.

Many circumstances combined during this epoch in giving a new and most powerful impetus to the development of Christian doctrine, and in bringing patristic literature to its prime. On the one side, there were the last efforts of pagan struggle against Christianity, succeeded by the rise of mighty heresies; on the other, the growth and activity of the schools of Christian learning at Alexandria, Antioch, Cæsarea, and Edessa. The interval of external peace allowed ecclesiastical learning to expand more freely, and from the contests forced upon it by the Arian, Macedonian, Eutychian, and Sabellian heresies, it drew fresh strength and vigor. In consequence, Christian literature not only increased in dimensions, but also in order and arrangement, inasmuch as its various branches were separated and specially treated. Eusebius of Cæsarea made a beginning of Church history. Apologetics found brilliant exponents in Athanasius and Augustine, who laid the first foundation of Christian philosophy. The discipline of sound exegesis was greatly developed by St. Chrysostom, St. Jerome, and others; systematic theology was attempted by St. Gregory of Nyssa, St. Augustine, and others; while St. Ambrose endeavored to systematize moral theology. Macarius, the Great, and Dionysius, the Areopagite, enlarged the field of mystical theology; practical theology was also extensively cultivated in catechetical instructions, homilies, and sermons; and even sacred poetry found able and promising representatives in Gregory Nazianzen, Ephraem, the Syrian, Prudentius, Sedulius, and others.

---

## CHAPTER I.

### GREEK AND ORIENTAL FATHERS AND WRITERS.

§ 62. *Eusebius, Bishop of Cæsarea (d. about 340).*

1. *Eusebius Pamphili*, born in Palestine about 265, was educated and ordained priest at Cæsarea. After the martyrdom of his teacher Pamphilus (A. D. 308), whose name he adopted out of respect for him, he repaired first to Tyre, then to Egypt, where he suffered imprisonment for some time. On the cessation of the Diocletian persecution, he was chosen Bishop of Cæsarea, about 314, and enjoyed the particular favor of the Emperor Constantine. Soon, however, partly from weakness of character, partly from fear, lest, by accepting the doctrine of the " homousia," he might fall into Sabellianism, he sided with Arius. But, at the special wish of the Emperor, he signed, after long deliberation, the Symbol of the General Council of Nicea (325), without, however, entirely breaking with the Arian party. Being a court bishop, he con-

formed his conduct to the whims and wishes of the Emperor. He took part in the Arian Synod of Antioch, in which Bishop Eustathius was deposed (330), and in that of Tyre (335), where a similar fate befell Athanasius. Still, he refused to accept the vacant see of Eustathius. He died at Cæsarea between 338 and 340.

2. Of his works, the following are still extant: —

## A. *Historical.*

(a.) " Historia ecclesiastica," in 10 books, containing the early history of the Church, from the Incarnation of Our Lord to the year 323, and supplying the most valuable information upon Church discipline, the heresies and Christian persecutions of that time — a distinguished work, which won for its author the honorable title of " Father of Church History."

(b.) " Chronicorum libri II," compendium of the history of the world from the creation, drawn largely from the Chronography of Julius Africanus. It is extant in a Latin and Armenian translation.

(c.) " De vita Constantini M." and " Oratio de laudibus Constantini M.," two panegyrics not free from flattery.

(d.) " De martyribus Palæstinæ," accounts of martyrs during the persecution of Diocletian.

(e.) "Acta passionis S. Pamphili et sociorum," a fragment of the lost work " De vita Pamphili."

## B. *Apologetical.*

(a.) "Præparatio evangelica," in 15 books, in which he shows the absurdity of idolatry and the reasonableness of the Jewish and Christian religions, and furnishes the reasons why Christians prefer Judaism to heathenism.

(b.) "Demonstratio evangelica," in 20 books, of which, however, only the first ten are extant. The author shows that there is proof for the truth of the Christian religion, that there is a connection between Christianity and Judaism, and that the prophecies of the Old Testament are fulfilled in the person of Christ.

(c.) "Eclogæ propheticæ," in 4 books, allegorical interpretations of Messianic passages from the Psalms and Prophets.

(d.) "Theophania," in 5 books, a resumé of the "Præparatio" and "Demonstratio," extant in a Syriac translation and in some Greek fragments, containing a magnificent apology for Christianity, based upon arguments drawn from the life, teachings, and miracles of Our Lord and the conversion of the world.

(e.) "Adversus Hieroclem," in 48 chapters, showing that Apollonius of Tyana can in no wise be compared to Christ, and that his supposed miracles are either mere fictions, or diabolical delusions.

## C. *Dogmatical and Controversial.*

(a.) "Contra Marcellum libri II," wherein the author sharply rebukes and accuses Marcellus of Amyra of Sabellianism.

(b.) "De ecclesiastica theologia libri III," in proof of the hypostatic union of Christ. In this work, written against the same Marcellus, there are some erroneous statements about the Holy Ghost.

(c.) "De solemnitate paschali," of which but a fragment exists, treating of the fulfilment of the Jewish Passover in the New Testament.

(d.) Fourteen sermons, or smaller treatises, on various subjects, as "De resurrectione," "De incorporali anima," etc., full of vigorous thought and written in a lively style.

## D. *Exegetical.*

(a.) "Topica sive de locis Hebraicis," a topography of Palestine, still extant in a Latin translation, together with an alphabetical list of Biblical places.

(b.) "Evangelici canones," a kind of Gospel harmony, in which is gathered together what all or several Evangelists narrate, and what is peculiar to each of them.

(c.) "Quæstiones ac solutiones evangelicæ," in 3 books, an attempt to reconcile passages apparently contradictory in the Evangelists. Only fragments remain.

(d.) Commentaries upon the first 118 Psalms; upon Isaias (almost complete) and Daniel; on the Proverbs and the Gospel of St. Luke (fragmentary).

Of his letters there remain but two: "Ad Cæsarienses," principally upon his conduct at the Council of Nice, and "Ad Constantiam Augustam," upon images of Christ. Many of his numerous writings, as the "Apology for Origen," in 5 books, a biography of Pamphilus, in 3 books, the "Life of the Prophets," and other writings, are wholly or partially lost.

3. Though Eusebius was the most learned theologian of his time, yet his grasp of dogmatical truths was wanting in depth and clearness. His vacillating character also has greatly tarnished the fame of his learning, his love of peace, and his zeal for the Church. His Church History, though not free from inaccuracies, is, nevertheless, most valuable, on

account of the great number of facts gathered from
ancient documents and from official records. His
apologetic works are of greater merit than the dogmatical, in which he often speaks of the divinity of
Christ in an Arian sense, and represents the Holy
Ghost, not as a Divine Person, but as a creation of
the Son (διὰ τοῦ Υἱοῦ γενόμενος). In his Biblical exegesis, he distinctly favored the allegorical interpretation. It is worthy of notice that Eusebius, in his
Commentary on Luke xxii, 57, calls Peter the
head of the Apostles (ὁ δὲ πάντων αὐτῶν προκεκριμένος
ἀπόστολος). His style is generally dry and devoid of
grace, and has, therefore, little attraction for those
who are influenced by eloquence; but it is well calculated to afford instruction to those who are seeking
the truth, and prefer to see it apart from all rhetorical
adornment.

Photius says: "As to his diction, he is neither
pleasing nor brilliant, but he is a very learned man,
though wanting in quickness of mind, steadiness of
character, and accuracy, especially on dogmatical
points." *

*Editions and Literature.* — *Migne*, S. gr. XIX-
XXIV. — *Ceillier* l. c. IV, 202–445. — *Stein*, Euse-
bius nach seinem Leben etc. (Würzburg 1859). —
*Harnack*, Gesch. der altchristl. Literatur (I. Leipzig
1893), p. 551 sq. — An English translation of his
Church History in "Select Library of Nicene and Post-
Nicene Fathers," etc., Ser. II, vol. I (New York

---

* Biblioth. c. 13: " Τὴν φράσιν οὐκ ἔστιν οὐδαμοῦ οὔτε
ἡδὺς οὔτε λαμπρότητι χαίρων. Πολυμαθὴς δὲ ἐστιν ὁ
ἀνήρ, εἰ καὶ τὴν ἀγχίνοιαν καὶ τὸ σταθηρὸν τοῦ ἤθους, ὡς
παρὰ τὴν ἀκρίβειαν τὴν ἐν τοῖς δόγμασιν ἐνδεέστερος."

1890). — Special editions of his Church History by
*E. Burton* (Oxford 1838, in 2 vols. 8ᵛᵒ); of Præpar.
evangel. by *Th. Gaisford* (Oxford 1843, in 4 vols.
8ᵛᵒ), and of Demonstrat. evang., by the same
(Oxford 1852, in 2 vols. 8ᵛᵒ) — *Gaisford* has also
edited Eclogæ propheticæ, Adv. Hieroclem, Contra
Marcellum, De ecclesiastica theologia (Oxford 1842–
1852).

## § 63. *St. Peter, Archbishop of Alexandria* (*d. 311*).

1. *St. Peter* was educated at Alexandria by Archbishop Theonas, whom he succeeded in that see A. D.
300. In the third year of his episcopate, during
the Diocletian persecution, he was obliged to flee from
Alexandria to save his life. He sent out a warning
against Meletius and excommunicated Arius. He
presided over the Church of Alexandria with glory
and imparted great luster to its see by his deep
piety and learning; until, by order of the Emperor
Maximin, he was suddenly seized and beheaded, A.
D. 311.

2. Of his various writings there are but fragments
in existence. He wrote a book on penance, in reference to the great number that fell during the Diocletian persecution; of this there are still 15 canons
extant; a book on the Divinity, and a treatise on the
advent of Christ, wherein he clearly affirms the
divinity of Christ and the consubstantiality of Father
and Son; also a discourse upon the soul against the
doctrine of pre-existence. A fragment on Easter
is considered to be doubtful, though it contains
nothing that would not harmonize with his time.
Eusebius says, he was "Divinum episcoporum

exemplar propter vitam et virtutem et in sacris literis
peritiam." *

*Editions and Literature.* — *Migne*, S. gr. XVIII,
449–522. — *Ceillier* l. c. IV, 17–25. — *Peters*, in
the Kirchenlexikon (2nd ed.) IX. — *Harnack* l. c.,
p. 443 sqq.

## § 64. St. Athanasius, Archbishop of Alexandria (d. 373).

1. *Athanasius* was born of Christian parents at
Alexandria, between 296 and 298. Early in life, he
attracted the attention of Bishop Alexander, who took
him into his house and gave him a careful religious and
theological training, particularly in Holy Scripture and
in the works of Origen. He was likewise taught the
spirit and practice of Christian asceticism under the
guidance of St. Anthony. Bishop Alexander, who
had conferred upon him the diaconate in 319, took
him to the Council of Nice in 325, and destined him
for his successor in the see of Alexandria, to which he
was actually elected after Alexander's death in 328,
in spite of his own opposition. The election, however,
aroused the envy and rage of the Arians, who were
leagued with the Meletians, and they brought the most
grievous charges against him in their synods. Though
he successfully refuted all their accusations, through
the intrigues of the Arians he was banished five times,
but his return was always, especially on the last occasion, in 365, hailed with joy by the people. As bishop,
he ceaselessly combated, by word of mouth and writ-

---

* *Hist. eccles.* IX, 6: " Θεῖον ἐπισκόπων χρῆμα, βίου
τε καὶ ἀρετῆς ἕνεκα καὶ τῆς τῶν ἱερῶν λόγων συνασκήσεως."

ing, the heresies of Arius and the Apollinarists, and in consequence, suffered innumerable afflictions. The last years of his life, spent in comparative peace, he devoted to the duties of his pastoral charge, to literary labors, to purging the Church from error and increasing her glory. To his great consolation he lived to see the decline of Arianism. He died at an advanced age, May 2d, 373.

2. Among his numerous works are the following: —

## A. *Dogmatical and Apologetical.*

(a.) "Oratio adversus gentes," in 47 chapters, an exposition of the origin and detestable character of heathenism ; a demonstration of the existence of God and of the omnipotence, goodness, and wisdom of the Logos.

(b.) "Oratio de incarnatione Verbi," in 57 chapters, on the necessity and possibility of the Incarnation, on the death of Christ upon the cross, and on the wonderful effects of Christianity as a proof of its divine origin.

Both works, written with equal learning and literary skill, form in their connection a whole.

## B. *Dogmatical and Controversial.*

(a.) "Orationes IV adversus Arianos," on the eternity and consubstantiality of the Son; the unity of nature and the distinction of persons in the Father and Son; the duality of nature and unity of person in the God-man, and on the difference between Father and Son.

(b.) "Epistolæ IV ad Serapionem," to confute

those who, though they acknowledged the Son as God, yet held the Holy Ghost to be a creature.

(c.) " Expositio fidei," against various heretics, especially the Arians.

(d.) " In verba: ' Omnia mihi tradita sunt a Patre meo,' " against the Eusebians, who urged this text in favor of their position. Athanasius opposes the text, "Omnia quæcumque Pater habet, mea sunt."

(e.) "Oratio maior de fide," in proof of the doctrine of the Trinity, and of the Logos (incomplete).

(f.) " Ad Iovianum de fide," an excellent exposition of the faith, written at the request of Jovinian.

(g.) " De incarnatione Verbi Dei et contra Arianos," treating also of the divinity of the Holy Ghost, and of his procession from the Father and the Son. Its authenticity, however, is questionable.

(h.) " Epistola ad Epictetum episcopum contra hæreticos," much esteemed in ancient times.

(i.) " Epistola ad Adelphium episcopum contra Arianos," an energetic refutation of Arianism and the later heresies of Nestorianism and Eutychianism.

(j.) "Epistola ad Maximum philosophum," confuting the errors concerning the Person of the Redeemer.

(k.) " De incarnatione Domini nostri Jesu Christi contra Apollinarium libri II," in which the author not only refutes all the errors of the Apollinarists, but also defends the most important of the Christological doctrines with invincible force. This is one of the best works upon this subject, but its authenticity is doubted by some.

## C. *Historical and Dogmatical.*

(a.) Three apologies, viz., "Apologia contra Arianos," in self-defense; "Apologia ad imperatorem Constantium," a splendid refutation of calumnies, and "Apologia de fuga sua," against the reproach that he had abandoned his flock through cowardice.

(b.) "Epistola encyclica ad episcopos," informing them of the violent proceedings of the Arians.

(c.) "Epistola ad episcopos Aegypti et Libyæ contra Arianos," warning the bishops of Egypt against the Arians and their writings.

(d.) "Epistola de decretis Nicænæ synodi," a vindication of the Nicene decrees.

(e.) "Epistola de Dionysio episcopo Alexandriæ," on the orthodox doctrine of Dionysius concerning the Trinity and the Logos.

(f.) "Epistola ad Serapionem fratrem de morte Arii."

(g.) "Epistola de synodis Arimini et Seleuciæ celebratis."

(h.) "Historia Arianorum ad monachos" (ab 335–357), containing a number of documents, but curtailed at the beginning.

(i.) "Tomus ad Antiochenos" and "Epistola ad Rufinianum," regarding the rëadmission of Arians into the Church.

(j.) "Epistola ad Afros," a warning against the Arians.

(k.) "Epistolæ II ad Luciferum," in which he praises the firmness of this courageous adversary of the Arians.

(l.) "Vita et conversatio S. Patris nostri Antonii,"

in 94 chapters, a charming biography of his former master, St. Anthony.

### D. *Exegetical.*

(a.) "In interpretationem Psalmorum epistola ad Marcellinum," in 33 chapters, an impressive admonition to study the Psalms.

(b.) "Expositiones in Psalmos," a short and chiefly mystical interpretation of the first 146 Psalms.

(c.) "De titulis Psalmorum," a kind of paraphrase of separate Psalm verses, with an explanation of the titles of Psalms.

### E. *Moral and Ascetical.*

(a.) "Epistola ad Dracontium, monachorum præfectum, episcopatum fugientem," an effective admonition to accept the charge of the episcopate.

(b.) "Epistola ad Amunem monachum," upon indeliberate stains of soul and body; on marriage and celibacy, the former, as he says, yielding a threefold reward, the latter a hundredfold.

(c.) "Epistolæ festales XV," a kind of Lenten pastoral letters upon fasting, extant in a Syriac translation.

The "Symbolum Athanasianum," so-called, belongs to a later period; other works ascribed to him are either doubtful or spurious. Of his commentaries on the Psalms, Canticle of Canticles, St. Matthew, St. Luke, and the First Epistle to the Corinthians, only fragments are preserved.

3. So great was the sanctity of Athanasius, so wonderful his firmness of will and penetration of mind, so unblemished his orthodoxy, that St. Gregory Nazianzen

called his life " the pattern of the episcopate " (ὅρος ἐπισκοπῆς); his doctrine " the law of orthodoxy " (νόμος ὀρθοδοξίας); himself " a column of the Church " (στῦλος τῆς Ἐκκλησίας), " a man of God " (ἀληθῶς ἄνθρωπος τοῦ θεοῦ), and " a great guide of souls " (μέγας τῶν ψυχῶν οἰκονόμος).* His works bear admirable witness to every point of faith, and particularly to the mystery of the Trinity, which he expounds with wonderful clearness and depth. He also teaches that the Holy Ghost proceeds from the Father and the Son; calls Mary the Mother of God; acknowledges in the Eucharist the real Body and Blood of Christ; regards the Holy Scripture and tradition as the chief sources of faith; explains to catechumens and heathens the " disciplina arcani; " gives instructions on lay-communion, on the assemblies of the faithful, the mutual relations between the bishop and his flock, on the primacy of the Roman Church, and other similar subjects. His principal works are distinguished for dialectic skill, clearness of expression, and a well-sustained development of thought. He knew how to combine simplicity with loftiness of thought and how to add force and ardor of feeling to both, so that none of his contemporaries can be compared to him. He is one of the greatest men of all times, and fully deserves the surname of " the Great" and " the Father of Orthodoxy."

*Editions and Literature.* — *Migne*, S. gr. XXV– XXVIII. — *Ceillier* l. c. V, 150–372. — *Möhler*, Athanasius der Grosse (2 Aufl. Mainz 1844). — *Atzberger*, Die Logoslehre des Athanasius. München 1880. — *Pell*, Lehre des heiligen Athanasius von der Sünde und Erlösung (Passau 1888). — *Sträter*, Die

---

* *Gregor. Naz.*, Orat. in laud. S. Athanasii.

Erlösungslehre des hl. Athanasius (Freiburg 1894).—
An English translation of the chief works of St.
Athanasius, in "Select Library," etc.  Ser. II. Vol.
4 (New York 1892). —The Festal Letters of Athanasius, discovered in an ancient Syriac version and
edited by *W. Cureton* (London 1848, 8ᵛᵒ). — An
annotated translation of St. Athanasius by *J. H.
Newman* (Parker).

§ 65. *St. Ephraem, the Syrian (d. not before 379).*

1. *Ephraem,* surnamed the Syrian, or also the Edes-
senian, probably on account of his long sojourn in
Edessa, was born, according to his own account, of
Christian parents, at Nisibis, about 306.   As a youth,
he seems to have been troubled by doubts and difficulties on divine Providence.   He received his education, secular and ecclesiastical, from the learned Bishop
Jacob of Nisibis,  whom  he accompanied, at a later
period, to the Council of Nice, and who also appointed him  to  teach  Syriac in  the school he had
founded.  When Nisibis was repeatedly besieged by the
Persian King Sapor II., Ephraem stood by his fellow-
citizens, helping them by wise counsels.   But when
the city surrendered to the Persians (363), he withdrew and repaired to Edessa, where, uniting the
contemplative to the active life, he labored most successfully in combating heresies, preaching the Gospel,
assisting the poor, in the study of Scripture, and the
composition of many able and excellent works.   In
370 he visited Basil the Great at Cæsarea, and then
journeyed to the monks of Egypt.   As he preached a
panegyric on St. Basil, who died January 1st, 379, his
own death must be placed at a later date.   He was

held in the highest esteem in the East on account of
the holiness and austerity of his life, as well as because of his learning and good works, and was called
"Pillar of the Church" and "Syrorum Propheta."
It is questionable whether he was a priest, because,
in his last will, he calls himself a deacon.

2. His numerous works, which fill six folios, may be
divided into exegetical, dogmatical, moral and ascetical, all written in Syriac, but, at an early date, translated into Armenian, Arabic, Ethiopian, Greek, and
later, though much too freely, into Latin.

## A. *Exegetical.*

(a.) "Commentarii," embracing almost all the
books of Holy Scripture, and explaining them, some
briefly, others more fully, both according to the grammatical-historical and the allegorical-mystical sense.
The latter is especially resorted to in his sermons and
hymns for ascetical purposes. Most of these Commentaries exist only in the form of summaries.

(b.) "XII sermones exegetici," among others on
the Prophet Jonas and on Lazarus, and "Sermones
varii recentius a Lamy publicati," amongst which
those on Joseph are the most remarkable.

(c.) "Evangelii concordantis expositio," a commentary upon Tatian's Harmony of the Gospels, now
only preserved in the Armenian translation. [A Latin
translation edited by G. Mösinger.]*

---

* Evangelii Concordantis expositio facta a S. Ephraemo,
Doctore Syro. In Latinum translata a R. P. *J. B. Aucher*,
Mechitarista, cujus versionem emendavit, annotationibus
illustravit et edidit *G. Mösinger*. Venetiis 1876. 8vo.
(R.)

### B. *Dogmatical.*

(a.) " Sermones polemici LVI adversus hæreses," in which the divinity of Christ is defended against the Gnostics, Arians, and Eunomians, and the Church praised and exalted.

(b.) " Sermones polemici LXXX adversus Scrutatores, *i. e.* hæreticos ; VII de margarita ; III de fide," in defense of the Trinity, the divinity and Incarnation of Christ, divine Providence and the perfections of God.

(c.) " Sermo adversus Judæos," on the fulfilment of the types and prophecies of the Old Testament.

(d.) " Sermo de Domino nostro, *i. e.* de ejus incarnatione."

(e.) " Sermones II contra hæresiarchas, et carmina IV contra Julianum Apostatam."

(f.) " Carmina XV de Paradiso Eden," a poetical description of the earthly, as a symbol of the heavenly, paradise.

(g.) " Sermones et hymni de festis Domini," both thoughtful and graceful.

(h.) " Sermones de sanctis," on the saints of the Old Law, whose virtues are praised and held up for imitation. The work also contains hymns to the Blessed Virgin and panegyrics on several of the Apostles and martyrs, particularly on the Forty Martyrs of Sebaste.

### C. *Moral and Ascetical.*

(a.) " Sermones IV de libero humanæ voluntatis arbitrio," proving the existence of free will, which, though weakened and in need of the assistance of grace, is not extinct.

(b.) " Sermones morales et ascetici," treatises on

virtues and vices; on the means of combating the latter and acquiring the former, especially on the monastic life, its privileges and duties.

(c.) "Sermo de sacerdotio," on the utility, dignity, and sanctity of the priesthood.

(d.) "Paræneses LXXVI seu hortationes ad pœnitentiam," full of impressive earnestness, with continual reference to death, judgment, and hell.

(e.) "Carmina Nisibena," on the joys and sorrows of the city of Nisibis, the merits of her bishops, the iniquities of her inhabitants, and many doctrinal subjects.

(f.) "Sermones de rogationibus," exhortation to prayer and penance, to avert the divine chastisements.

(g.) "Necrosima seu canones funebres LXXXV," a poetic description, in varied metre, of the virtues of bishops, priests, deacons, monks, etc., with a detailed description of funeral obsequies.

(h.) "Testamentum," a summary of loving counsels and exhortations to his brothers, a request for prayer, and a protest against burial with costly solemnities.

The following are doubtful: A sermon on virtues and passions; another on Abraham and on the woman who was a sinner; also maxims and sayings of Ephraem.

These are spurious: A discourse to the monk John, a treatise on idle words, two hymns, a prayer for the departed.

3. In Ephraem's writings, the moral and ascetical aspect predominates. Still, there are many dogmas expounded, such as the Trinity, the Godhead and manhood of Christ, the sinlessness and unspotted virginity of the Mother of God, the necessity of baptism

and the confession of sins, the presence of Christ in
the Holy Eucharist, the invocation and worship of the
angels and saints, and intercession for the departed.
He takes a deep and earnest view of the Christian,
and especially the priestly, life and gives also a minute
description of the monastic life. His chief aim in all
his sermons and exhortations, which are mostly in metrical form, is to impress the hearts of his readers. His
style, therefore, is, generally speaking, warm, picturesque, and flowing, at times perhaps overladen with
pictures and similitudes. His hymns are of real poetical value, and have gained him the beautiful name of
" Lyre of the Holy Ghost."

*Editions and Literature.* — Ephraemi Opera omnia
(græc., lat. et syr.) 6 fol., Romæ 1732–1746; —
arabice absque versione latina, 4 voll. 8ᵛᵒ, Venetiis
1835. — S. Ephraemi Syri Hymni et Sermones, quos
e codd. Londin., Par., Dublin., Rom. et Oxon. de-
scriptos edidit *Th. J. Lamy*, 3 tom. 4° Mechlinæ
1882–1889. — *P. Zingerle*, Ausgewählte Schriften. 6
vols. Innsbruck 1830–1837. — *Ceillier* l. c. VIII,
1–119. — *Eirainer*, Der hl. Ephräm der Syrer. Kempten 1889. — *Fessler-Jungmann* l. c. §§ 132–236. —
See also an article by *Th. J. Lamy* in the Dublin
Review, 1885, Vol. XIV, pp. 20–44.


§ 66. *St. Cyril, Bishop of Jerusalem (d. 386).*


1. *Cyril*, born in 315, probably in or near Jerusalem, passed his youth in solitude, received the
deaconship in 334 from Bishop Macarius, and the
priesthood from Bishop Maximus, who also appointed
him to the office of instructing the catechumens

[φωτιζόμενοι] and newly-baptized (νεοφώτιστοι). The episcopal dignity, to which he was raised in 351, after the death of Bishop Maximus, involved him in many afflictions. Twice, in 358 and 360, he was driven away from his see by the intrigues and rancor of Acacius, the Metropolitan of Cæsarea, who favored the Arians. After having been recalled in 362, by Julian, whose attempt to rebuild the Temple of Jerusalem he personally witnessed, he was banished once more in 367, by the Arian Emperor Valens, upon whose death, however, he returned to Jerusalem (378) and strove to restore order in the Church and to lead back to her communion the many who had fallen away. He was present at the Second General Council of Constantinople in 381, and died on March 18th, 386, after an episcopate of 35 years, 16 of which had been passed in exile.

2. Of his works we possess the following: —

(a.) "Catecheses XXIV," the first 18 of which were addressed to those about to be enlightened, i. e. baptized (κατηχήσεις φωτιζομένων), the rest to those who had been newly enlightened (κατηχήσεις μυσταγωγικαί). These instructions treat in a simple and touching manner, not only of the necessity and dignity of baptism and preparation for it, but furnish, likewise, explanations of all the other articles of the Christian faith. The objection against their authenticity is based upon Protestant prejudice rather than upon any serious argument. The excellence and merit of these "Catecheses" have been recognized at all times.

(b.) "Homilia in Joann. v, 2–16."

(c.) "Epistola ad Constantium Imperatorem," in which he transmits to the Emperor the report of the

appearance of a fiery cross in the heavens at the time
of his accession to the episcopate.

Some of his writings are lost; others are incorrectly
ascribed to him, as, "Homilia in occursum Domini"
(presentation of Jesus in the Temple), "Historia
ecclesiastica et mystagogica," "Chronologia," and
others.

3. Cyril's "Catecheses" are exceedingly important, because they ably explain, prove, and vindicate
the dogmas of the faith, and supply valuable information as to the ancient liturgy of the Church.   Cyril, in
refuting error, gives an exposition of almost every
doctrine of the Church; thus combining dogma with
apologetics.   In particular, he bears witness to the
universality of original sin (XII, c. 15); the Catho-
licity of the Church (XVIII, c. 23, 26); the twofold nature in Christ (XII, c. 1); the effects of
confirmation (XXI, c. 3); The Real Presence in the
Sacrament of the Altar (XXII, c. 1. 3); the sacrificial
character of the Eucharist (XXIII, c. 7, 8) etc.   But
upon the doctrine of the Trinity, he lacks precision,
so that some, though unjustly, have accused him
of Arianism.   Despite his deep learning, his style is
natural and simple.   The Greek Menologium (March
18th) calls him "The ready champion of the Apostolic dogmas" — "Τῶν ἀποστολικῶν δογμάτων προθύμως
ὑπερμαχῶν."

*Editions and Literature.* — *Migne*, S. gr. XXXIII. —
*Ceillier* l. c. XIII, 241–407. — *Delacroix*, S. Cyrille
de Jérus., sa vie et ses oeuvres. Paris 1865. — *Nirschl*
l. c., §§ 106–108. — *Mader*, Der hl. Cyrillus, Bischof
von Jerusalem, in seinem Leben und seinen Schriften,
nach den Quellen dargestellt.   Einsiedeln 1891.

## § 67. *St. Basil, the Great, Archbishop of Cæsarea* (*d. 379*).

1. *St. Basil* was born in Cæsarea in Cappadocia, A. D. 329, of wealthy and pious parents. His literary and scientific education he received at Cæsarea, Constantinople, and, together with St. Gregory of Nazianzen, at Athens. Influenced by his pious relations, he became more and more detached from the world, and determined to visit the monks of Syria, Palestine, and Egypt, in order to learn the true art of living by personal observation (360–361). After his return, he bestowed his goods upon the poor, withdrew with his mother Emmelia and grandmother Macrina into monastic retirement, where, with his younger brother, St. Gregory of Nyssa, and St. Gregory of Nazianzen, he led the strictest ascetical life. Having been ordained priest in 364, and raised to the archiepiscopal dignity in 370, he showed himself the intrepid defender of the Nicene faith and the rights of the Church. He was as patient in bearing his own personal sufferings, as he was generous in alleviating those of others ; a great theologian, an eloquent preacher of the word of God, a rigid ascetic, a bright example of the episcopal order, and the real father of the monastic rule still existing in the East. He died on January 1st, 379, worn out by the rigor of his austerities and the labors of his episcopate.

2. The following works of St. Basil are worthy of note : —

(a.) " Libri V, quibus impii Eunomii Apologeticus evertitur," a keen refutation of Bishop Eunomius of Cycicus, who taught that the Son is of a different nature from the Father ($\dot{\alpha}\nu\acute{o}\mu\omega\iota\varsigma$), and a de-

fense of the " homousia " of the Son and the Holy
Ghost.

(b.) " Liber de Spiritu Sancto ad Amphilochium
Iconii episcopum," in 30 chapters, against those
Arians who denied the unity of nature of both the
Son and the Holy Ghost with the Father (Pneuma-
tomachi).

(c.) " Homiliæ IX in hexaëmeron," an explanation
of the six days of creation, which attracted admiration
even in the writer's own time. It contains, in spite
of many erroneous ideas common to all the early ages
on the subject of natural history, a great number
of excellent discussions, edifying exhortations, and
splendid descriptions of the power, wisdom, and goodness of God and the beauty of the universe.

(d.) " Homiliæ XIII in Psalmos," each of which
explains a psalm, according to the literal, moral, and
allegorical sense.

(e.) " Commentarius in Isaiam," with excellent
moral applications, but incomplete and less finished
in style.

(f.) " Homiliæ XXIV de diversis," some dogmatical, some moral, and some panegyrical. Amongst the
moral homilies, the one addressed to young men on
the subject of reading pagan authors with profit,
deserves special mention. The readers, he says,
should be like bees, appropriating only the true and
beautiful.

(g.) " Ascetica," containing treatises on various
subjects, as, for instance, the excellence of the religious
life and the duties of monks; the judgment of God;
faith; 80 different rules of conduct; 55 longer and
313 shorter rules for monastic life, together with counsels for monks and penances for breaches of discipline

appropriate both for monks and nuns. By his monastic rule, St. Basil organized and consolidated the religious life in the Eastern Church. He also gave the name to a liturgy which spread widely in the East.

(h.) " Epistolæ 365, historicæ, dogmaticæ, morales, asceticæ, disciplinares, consolatoriæ, commendatitiæ et familiares," written in the very best style, and often displaying keen wit.

A commentary on Job and a treatise against the Manichæans are lost. Other works ascribed to him are either doubtful or spurious.

3. The writings of St. Basil are a rich mine for the doctrines of the Church. To mention but a few: The necessity of ecclesiastical tradition (De Spir. S. c. 27, n. 66, 67); the efficacy of baptism (Hom. in s. Bapt. c. 5.); the preparation required for the reception of the Holy Eucharist as the body and blood of Christ; contrition, confession, and satisfaction, as parts of the Sacrament of Penance (Reg. brevis 229, 288). As an interpreter of Holy Scripture, he gives preference to the literal sense. As a moral and ascetical writer, he lays stress on the practical part of religion, especially active charity, without, however, neglecting or depreciating the speculative element of theology. Like Athanasius, Basil is deservedly surnamed "The Great;" for he was great as a theologian, as an ascetic, and as a bishop, and was held in the highest esteem both by Christians and heathens. Rufinus of Aquileja calls St. Basil " Virum fide et operibus et omni sanctitate sat clarum." His sermons and discourses are full of fire and dignity; his style is pure and elegant, his language flowing. Photius writes of him : " The great Basil is excellent

in all his orations; able, like none other, in the use of
a pure, clear, masterly, wholly popular and festive
diction.  He is said to be first, and second to none, in
the systematic order and clearness of his thoughts; he
was a lover of persuasion, sweetness, and brilliancy;
fluent in speech, and like water welling fresh from the
fountain." *

*Editions and Literature.* — *Migne*, S. gr. XXIX-
XXXII. — *Ceillier* l. c. VI, 60–433. — *Klose*, Basilius
der Grosse.  Stralsund 1835. — *Fialon*, Étude histor.
et littér. sur S. Basile.  Paris 1869. — *Probst*, Die
Liturgie des hl. Basilius, "Katholik" II (1882), and
I (1883.) — *Fessler-Jungmann* l. c. §§ 100–105. — An
Anglo-Saxon version of St. Basil's Hexaëmeron was
published from a MS. in the Bodleian Library, together
with a translation and a life of the author, by *H. W.
Norman*, London 1848, 8$^{vo}$; and the treatise on the
Holy Ghost was translated, with analysis and notes, by
*G. Lewis*, London 1888, 12$^{mo}$.

§ 68. *St. Gregory of Nazianzen, Bishop of Sasima*
(*d. about 390*).

1. *Gregory* was born at Arianzus, about 329, and
received a good religious education from his pious
mother, St. Nonna.  His higher education he sought
in the schools of Cæsarea, Alexandria, and Athens,
where he became acquainted with Julian and formed

* "'Άριστος μὲν ἐν πᾶσιν τοῖς αὐτοῦ λόγοις ὁ μέγας
Βασίλειος· λέξει τε γὰρ καθαρᾷ καὶ εὐσήμῳ καὶ κυρίᾳ καὶ
ὅλως πολιτικῇ καὶ πανηγυρικῇ δεινός, εἴ τις ἄλλος, χρήσασθαι
νοημάτων τε τάξει καὶ καθαρότητι πρῶτος, ἀλλ᾽ οὐδενὸς
δεύτερος ᾄδεται· πιθανότητος δὲ καὶ γλυκύτητος καί γε
λαμπρότητος ἐραστής, καὶ ῥέων τῷ λόγῳ, καὶ ὥσπερ ἐξ
αὐτοσχεδίου πηγάζων τὸ ῥεῖθρον." Bibl. Cod. CXLI.

an intimate friendship with St. Athanasius and St. Basil. After his return home in 359 he was baptized and then retired with St. Basil, in order to devote himself to the practice of asceticism and literary labors; but soon after he found himself involved in the religious disputes of the day. The priesthood was unexpectedly forced upon him, in 361, by his aged episcopal father, at the urgent request of his flock. Once more he withdrew to his longed-for solitude, only to forsake it again in 362, in order to render assistance to his aged father. At the instance of St. Basil, and after long opposition, Gregory allowed himself to be consecrated Bishop of Sasima, but refused the administration of that newly-founded diocese, and withdrew to his father to Nazianzen, whose coadjutor he became till his death, laboring successfully in the cause of the faith. From fear of being appointed as his successor to the bishopric, in 375, he again fled for a time into solitude, at Seleucia. In 379 he went, at the request of his friends, to Constantinople, where, in spite of the machinations of the Arians, he succeeded by his eloquence in gaining a triumph for the orthodox faith. By the Second General Council (381) he was elected to the see of Constantinople, which, however, he abdicated again, in consequence of the objections raised by some Egyptian bishops, who arrived after the opening of the Council. He returned to Nazianzen and took charge for some time of the see vacated by his father's death. He passed the remainder of his days in the exercise of literary labors and in the practice of an ascetic life. He died in his native place, A. D. 389 or 390.

2. His works are: —

(a.) "Orationes theologicæ," on the divinity of

the Son and the Holy Ghost, and the relation of both to the Father.

(b.) "Orationes invectivæ contra Julianum imperatorem," an animated indictment against the apostate Emperor, for attempting to stifle the growing life of Christianity by denying to its followers the means of a higher education.

(c.) "Oratio apologetica de fuga," in 117 chapters, wherein he explains the motives of his flight, namely, his love of solitude and sense of unworthiness; and the reasons for his return, namely, a longing after his parents and friends, but especially the will of God. There are other sermons of his on the feasts of Our Lord and the anniversaries of the martyrs, as well as some funeral and other discourses.

(d.) Five hundred and seven poems, some longer, some shorter, and in various meters, on such subjects as the Trinity, Creation, Providence, the Fall, Incarnation, the religious life, virginity, marriage, his own life and experiences ("Poema de vita sua"), and other contemporary events. Among them there are 129 epitaphs and 94 epigrams.

The poetical merit of these compositions varies considerably.

(e.) Two hundred and forty-four letters, chiefly of friendship or of condolence and recommendation, all thoughtful, clear, and brief, and very important for contemporary history.

The following are doubtful: "Annotatio de quatuor animalibus apud Ezechielem;" "Paraphrasis in Ecclesiasten Salomonis;" "Tractatus de fide." The tragedy "Christus patiens" is not genuine.

3. Gregory was a model bishop, the fearless champion of the mystery of the Trinity, and a great master

of the ascetical life. In his doctrine of the Trinity, which forms the primary subject of his writings, we may especially notice his illustrations of the mystery taken from the sun, its light and rays ; or from the eye, fountain, and stream : * " For the source (eye), fountain, and stream are one in number, but different in appearance." †

In spite of his honorable name of " The Theologian," he ranks below Athanasius in originality and grasp of dogmatical truths. His greatness lies chiefly in his eloquence as a preacher. A man of deep piety and an ardent lover of solitude, he had little taste or talent for matters of practical life. Though his discourses are distinguished by purity of diction, variety of figures and illustrations, aptness of inference, and elevation of thought, they are yet often too diffuse and overburdened with antitheses and other oratorical licenses. His poems combine depth of thought with richness of imagination, and according to a German writer, reveal a genuine sense of nature and a profound religious spirit, enlightened by true philosophy (Christ, l. c., p. 742). Rufinus, in

---

* Orat. theol. v. 31–33: " Ὀφθαλμόν τινα, καὶ πηγήν, καὶ ποταμὸν ἐνενόησα . . . . ὀφθαλμὸς γάρ, καὶ πηγή, καὶ ποταμὸς ἕν ἐστιν ἀριθμῷ, διαφόρως σχηματιζόμενα. — Πάλιν ἥλιον ἐνεθυμήθην, καὶ ἀκτῖνα, καὶ φῶς . . ."

† The author seems to me to make a mistake here. These words do not express the doctrine of Gregory, but a Sabellian difficulty against the illustration. For, after having admitted that there are some good points in the illustration, he thus continues: " Sed subiit me timor primum ne fluxio quaedam Divinitatis stabilitatis expers admittatur. Deinde ne per hanc similitudinem unum numero introducatur. Oculus enim et fons et fluvius unum sunt numero, varie efformata." (R.)

the prologue to his translation of St. Gregory's works, pays the following magnificent tribute to him: " Gregorius vir per omnia incomparabilis, qui verbo et operibus clarus, splendidissimum lumen scientiæ Christi Ecclesiis præbuit.... Hujus neque vita aliquid probabilius et sanctius, neque eloquentia clarius et illustrius, neque fide purius et rectius, neque scientia plenius et perfectius inveniri potest." And Basil calls him " A vessel of election, a deep well, or rather the mouth of Christ." *

*Editions and Literature. — Migne*, S. gr. XXXV-XXXVIII. — *Ceillier* l. c. VII, 1–306. — *Hergenröther*, Die Lehre von der Trinität nach Gregor von Nazianz. Regensburg 1850. — *Ullmann*, Gregor von Nazianz. Gotha 1867. — *Weiss*, Die grossen Kappadocier als Exegeten. Braunsberg 1872. — *Benoît*, S. Grégoire de Nazianze; sa vie, ses oeuvres et son époque. 2 vols. 2me ed. Paris 1885. — *Hümmer*, Des hl. Gregor von Nazianz Lehre von der Gnade. Kempten 1890. — *C. W. King*, Julian, the Emperor. London 1888. 12mo. (Contains a translation of Gregory's two orations against Julian.)

§ 69. *St. Gregory, Bishop of Nyssa* (*d. about 395*).

1. *Gregory of Nyssa*, born about 331, owed his literary education entirely to private study and to the care of his elder brother, Basil, the Great, whom he often called his instructor and father. Having for some time followed the profession of a rhetorician,

---

* *Basil.*, Ep. 8: " Σχεῦος ἐκλογῆς καὶ φρέαρ βαθύ· λέγω δὲ τὸ τοῦ Χριστοῦ στόμα Γρηγόριον."

Basil and Gregory Nazianzen won him back to the clerical state, to which he had at first devoted himself. In 371 his brother Basil consecrated him Bishop of Nyssa, where he soon incurred the displeasure and ill-feeling of the Governor, Demosthenes, on account of some supposed maladministration, and in 375, the Arian bishops, on the pretense that his election had been illegal, succeeded in banishing him from his diocese. After wandering about for the space of three years, he was allowed, through the favor of the Emperor Theodosius, to return to his diocese, amid demonstrations of triumph. He took so prominent a part in the General Council of Constantinople (381), that he was often called "Pater Patrum," and was intrusted with a mission to Arabia, to allay the disturbances caused by the Apollinarists.

Towards the end of his life, besides his frequent contests with the heretics, he suffered grievous injuries from his bitter enemy Archbishop Helladius of Cæsarea. He died about 395.

2. His works embrace nearly every part of Christian faith and life.

### A. *Exegetical.*

(a.) "Explicatio apologetica in hexaëmeron," written in order to complete, explain, and defend the work of his brother Basil.

(b.) "De hominis opificio," in 30 chapters, wherein, in connection with the preceding work, he treats of the creation of man and his likeness to God, of his state before and after the fall, and his future state after the resurrection. He also condemns Origen's doctrine of the pre-existence of souls.

(c.) "De vita Mosis seu de virtutis perfectione," a

guide to Christian life with references to the deeds of Moses.

(d.) "In Psalmorum inscriptionem libri II," treating of the purpose, order, and division of the Psalms.

(e.) "Accurata expositio in Salomonis Ecclesiasten," 8 homilies, natural and pleasing, but incomplete.

(f.) "Homiliæ XV. in cantica canticorum," describing the union of the soul with God.

(g.) "Epistola de Pythonissa ad Theodosium episcopum," wherein he contends that in I Reg. xxviii, 8, it was not the soul of Samuel that appeared to Saul, but an evil spirit in the form of a prophetess.

(h.) "Homiliæ V de oratione," a pleasing explanation of the Lord's Prayer.

(i.) "Homiliæ VIII de beatitudinibus," in which the grammatical interpretation is beautifully blended with the allegorical, and a number of striking illustrations are used.

### B. *Dogmatical.*

(a.) "Libri XII contra Eunomium," in which he proves the doctrine of the "homousia" of the Son and Holy Ghost with the Father, and defends his brother Basil against the calumnies of Eunomius. This is one of the best controversial works against Arianism.

(b.) "Antirrheticus adversus Apollinarem," in 59 chapters, and a supplement to the same, "Adv. Apollinarem ad Theophilum episc. Alexandrinum," proving that Christ could only be our pattern and our Redeemer by the assumption of a perfect and complete human nature. Both works are remarkable for style, depth of thought, and power of argument.

(c.) " Oratio catechetica magna," in 40 chapters, a kind of religious philosophy, written for the benefit of heathens, Jews, and heretics, and proving the chief tenets of the Christian religion by arguments drawn both from reason and revelation.

(d.) "Ad Ablabium: quod non sunt tres Dii;" " Ad Simplicium tribunum de fide;" " Contra fatum, disputatio cum ethnico philosopho" (in defense of the free will); " De anima et resurrectione," a dialogue, in which Gregory makes his dying sister give utterance to her thoughts on the soul, death, resurrection; " De infantibus qui præmature abripiuntur," why God often allows children to die young; and other similar treatises.

## C. *Practical and Ascetical*.

Sermons on various subjects, as Contra usurarios, fornicarios; de pauperibus amandis; de mortuis; adverus eos qui differunt baptismum. Also sermons for feast-days, funerals, and other occasions. Furthermore: " Quid nomen et professio Christianorum sibi velit;" " Liber de perfectione, summaria descriptio veri vitæ asceticæ scopi;" " De sacris et religiosis peregrinationibus," and, in particular, the beautiful treatise " De virginitate," in which he views perfect self-abnegation as the most certain means of union with God. Finally 25 letters, important for the dogmatic controversies and ecclesiastical discipline of the time.

The following are of doubtful authenticity: —

(a.) Two sermons on I. Mos. i, 26; (b.) a sermon on the nativity of Our Lord and the massacre of the innocents at Bethlehem, and another on our Lord's

presentation in the Temple; (c.) an exposition of
I Cor. xv, 23–28, and (d.) " Electa testimonia adversus Judæos ex veteri Testamento," having reference
to the Trinity, the birth and resurrection of Our Lord,
and similar subjects.

3. In his treatises on dogmatical subjects, Gregory's chief aim is to advance from faith to understanding, to let the superior light of truth shine and
speak for itself, and to defend it from heretical per-
versions.   In his interpretation of Scripture, he shows
spirit and independence of mind, but oversteps, perhaps, the due bounds in the application of the allegorical method.   As an ascetical writer, he seeks to
develop and deepen the inner religious life of the soul.
The subject which chiefly engaged his attention and
demanded his skill and zeal, was the unity and trinity
of God.   The unity he seeks to explain and derive from
the very idea of God as the most perfect Being, while
he tries to illustrate the trinity by the analogy of the
human soul viewed as $\psi\upsilon\chi\acute{\eta}$, $\lambda\acute{o}\gamma o\varsigma$, and $\nu o\tilde{\upsilon}\varsigma$.   With
regard to the origin of the soul he inclines more to
Generationism than to Creationism, rejects decidedly
the belief in its pre-existence and transmigration, and
teaches that the body and soul come into existence
together.   His Eschatology is less correct, inasmuch
as he favors erroneous views about the resurrection,
eternity of punishment in hell, and kindred subjects.
Gregory was endowed with admirable simplicity and
kindness of heart; and to these virtues were added
great learning and skill in writing, an intellect rich
and fertile in ideas.   Inferior to his brother Basil in
depth of feeling and in practical ability, and inferior
also to his namesake in point of eloquence, he surpassed both in richness of thought.   The Greek

Menology says in his praise (January 10th): "Omni genere sermonis et bona virtutis fama palmam adeptus est." *

*Editions and Literature* — Migne, S. gr. XLIV–XLVI. — *Ceillier* l. c. VIII, 200–343. — *Buse*, Der hl. Gregor von Nyssa. Leipzig 1848. — *Stöckl*, Gesch. der patrist. Philosophie, pp. 288–317. — *Al. Vincenzi*, In S. Gregorii Nysseni doctrinam nova recensio. Romæ 1864. — *Weiss* l. c. — *Hilt*, Des hl. Gregor von Nyssa Lehre von dem Menschen. Köln 1890. — For an English translation of a number of St. Gregory's writings see "Select Library of Nicene and Post-Nicene Fathers of the Christian Church," Ser. II, vol. V. New York 1893.

§ 70. *Diodorus, Bishop of Tarsus* (*d. about 394*).

1. Towards the end of the third century, there arose a theological school at Antioch as well as at Alexandria. These two schools developed in the course of time quite different systems of teaching. The school of Antioch limited the inspiration of Holy Scripture to matters of faith and morals (res fidei et morum), cultivated chiefly the literal or verbal-historical interpretation, and favored the Aristotelian philosophy in its theological disputations. The Alexandrian school, on the contrary, extended the inspiration of Scripture to every sentence and word, adopted chiefly the allegorical method of interpretation, and showed marked preference for the Platonic philosophy. Both schools

---

* "Διὰ πάσης ἐλθὼν ἰδέας λόγων καὶ ἀρετῆς εὐδοκιμήσει τὸ κράτος ἐδέξατο."

brought forth men of distinction and learning. Diodorus of Tarsus belongs to the school of Antioch.
Born of a noble Antiochian family at the beginning of
the fourth century, he studied humanities at Athens,
and received an excellent theological and ascetical
training at Antioch. This enabled him, at a later
period, when he had become a priest, to take up arms
with zeal and courage against the enemies of the
faith, and, being gifted with talent for teaching, to
train young men and make them excellent theologians.
He is the chief exponent and representative of the
literal, or historico-grammatical method of interpretation, as opposed to the allegorical-mystical.

The Emperor Julian looked upon him with a deep
hatred on account of his generous and self-sacrificing
defense of the Symbolum Nicænum. In grateful
acknowledgment of his sterling and unshaken fidelity
even amidst persecution, Bishop Meletius of Antioch
chose him in 378 as Bishop of Tarsus, in which
capacity he attended the Second General Council of
Constantinople (381), and consecrated Nectarius
bishop of that city. After a worthy episcopate, he
died, probably before 394.

2. Among the numerous writings of Diodorus, of
which only small fragments escaped the fury of the
Arians, were the following : —

A. *Apologetical and Dogmatical.*

Treatises against the Manichæans, Sabellians, Macedonians, and Apollinarists. Some of these works, as
may be seen from the arguments, contained the hidden germs of the later Nestorian heresy.

## B. *Exegetical.*

Commentaries on most of the books of the Holy Scripture, in which, however, he too often overlooks the supernatural and prophetic element.

3. Diodorus, whom St. Chrysostom styles " a living martyr," and whom an imperial decree mentions as one of the vouchers for the Nicene orthodoxy, died in the faith of the Church. Although in speaking of Christ's two natures, he had made use of the (afterwards) heretical expression of the " logos *dwelling in* the man Christ " (ἐνοίκησις), and had thus prepared the way for Nestorianism, he did so from a laudable desire to uphold the two perfect natures of Christ against the Arians and Apollinarists. Therefore, it is but fair to interpret his words in a milder sense. In any case, he cannot be said to have broached a formal heresy. Amidst incessant labors he found time for the severest ascetical practices. As an interpreter of Scripture, his judgment is clear, sober, and happy in the development of the literal sense. Photius calls him " a pious, pure, and judicious man in these things." *

*Editions and Literature.* — *Migne,* S. gr. XXXIII, 1546–1628. — *Ceillier* l. c. VII, 693–708. — *Ph. Hergenröther,* Die antiochenische Schule. Würzburg 1866.

§ 71. *Theodore, Bishop of Mopsuestia (d. 428) and Polychronius, Bishop of Apamea (d. about 430).*

### I.

1. *Theodore* was born at Antioch about 350, where, together with St. Chrysostom, he received his literary

---

* " Ἔστιν ἐν τούτοις εὐσεβῶν καὶ καθαρός τε καὶ εὐκρινὴς ὁ ανήρ."

education from the Sophist Libanius, and his theological training from Diodorus. At the age of 20, renouncing the lucrative career of a lawyer, he withdrew into a monastery to give himself up to the practice of ascetical life and the study of Holy Scripture. But before long he changed his mind, left the monastery, and resolved to marry. Persuaded however, by his fellow-student Chrysostom, to relinquish this decision, he was ordained priest by Bishop Flavian of Antioch in 383. For ten years he was very active, and exercised great influence in the sacred ministry. By his discourses he attracted many excellent disciples and his interpretation of Scripture earned him the name of "The Interpreter," which he bears among the Nestorians to this day. In 392 he was raised to the bishopric of Mopsuestia. As bishop, he took an active part in all the ecclesiastical affairs of the time, and attended, in 394, a synod at Constantinople, where he excited the admiration of Theodosius, the Great, by one of his sermons. He passed his life chiefly in the pursuit of literary labors, strenuously opposed to Arianism and the heresy of the Apollinarists, but strongly favoring the views of the Nestorians and Pelagians, for which reason his works were condemned by the Fifth Œcumenical Council in 553. He died in 428, having held his episcopal see for 36 years.

2. His writings were numerous: Commentaries on almost all the books of Holy Scripture; "De incarnatione Filii Dei;" "Contra Apollinarem;" "Contra Eunomium;" "Contra defensores peccati originis," "Liber ad baptizandos," etc. But only the Commentary on the Twelve Minor Prophets is preserved complete. A Latin translation of his Commentary on the Epistles of St. Paul is nearly complete.

3. Theodore was a man of great endowments, of remarkable learning and energy, and of impulsive temperament. Although wanting in originality and creative power, he showed no lack of boldness in asserting his ideas and views. Being a thorough rationalist, he totally rejected the allegorical method of interpretation, restricted the number of Messianic passages in the Old Testament, greatly depreciated the authority of several of the canonical books, as well as of the older interpreters, and fell into many dogmatical errors besides. Thus he maintained that there were two persons in Christ; denied the divine maternity of Mary, original sin, and the necessity of grace. His writings show great antipathy to all philosophy, particularly the Platonic. His style is generally obscure, diffuse, and insipid. Photius says: "In his diction, he is neither clear nor very accurate; he often repeats himself, and seems, somehow, without any grace or sweetness." *

## II.

*Polychronius*, brother of the above-mentioned, and Bishop of Apamea, composed commentaries on Daniel, Ezechiel, and Job, of which only detached though very important and valuable fragments are preserved in the Catenæ. The Commentaries ascribed to him on the Proverbs, Canticle of Canticles, Jeremias, and Baruch, as well as the fragment on the "Causes of the Obscurity of Holy Scripture," cannot be from his pen, on account of the disparity of style.

---

* " Τὴν δὲ φράσιν οὐδὲ λαμπρός, οὐδὲ λίαν σαφής· ταὐτολογεῖ δὲ τὰ πλεῖστα, καὶ ἄχαρίς πως, καὶ ἀηδὴς εἶναι δοχεῖ."

The genuine fragments, however, clearly show that Polychronius possessed a true exegetical spirit and instinct, that he held fast to Scriptural inspiration, acknowledged the full canon of sacred books, favored the historical method of interpretation, and was profoundly versed in archæology and profane history. He possessed all the talents of his brother without any of his faults, except, perhaps, that of slightly inclining to his rationalistic method. He and Theodoret of Cyrus, are considered the most illustrious interpreters of the Antiochian School.

*Editions and Literature.* — *To I.* — *Migne*, S. gr. LXVI, 9–1020. — *Ceillier* l. c. X, 488–496. — *Specht*, Theodor von Mopsuestia und Theodoret von Cyrus. München 1871. — *Kihn*, Theodor von Mopsuestia. Freiburg 1880. — The Latin translation of the Commentary on St. Paul's epistles was newly edited by *H. B. Swete*, Cambridge 1880–1882, in 2 vols. 8vo, with the " Fragmenta dogmatica " in the appendix. — See also " Theodorus of Mopsuestia," by the same author, in the Dictionary of Christian Biography, vol. IV. — *To II.* — *Migne*, S. gr. CLXII. — *Bardenhewer*, Polychronius, etc. Freiburg 1879.


§ 72. *Didymus, the Blind* (d. about 395).

1. *Didymus*, born about 309, or 310, became blind at the early age of five. But in spite of this and other obstacles, he succeeded in acquiring so vast a store of profane and sacred knowledge,* that he became one of

---

* *Rufin.*, H. E. II, 7. " Miscebat tamen precibus studia ac laborem et juges continuatasque vigilias non ad legendum, sed ad audiendum adhibebat, ut quod aliis visus, hoc illi conferret auditus. . . . Ita brevi Deo docente in tantam

the most celebrated masters of the Alexandrian School. It was from his writings that Jerome, Rufinus, Palladius, Isidore of Pelusium, and others, drew their knowledge and training. He was an ardent admirer of Origen and a staunch defender of his work " Περὶ ἀρχῶν." Three centuries later, the erroneous doctrines of both writers were anathematized in the Sixth (680) and Seventh General Councils (787).

2. Of his dogmatical and exegetical works, the following have been preserved : —

(a.) " De Trinitate libri tres," against the Arians ; an orthodox and acute defense of the Catholic doctrine ; of the first book there are six chapters wanting.

(b.) " De Spiritu Sancto," in 63 chapters, on the divinity, personality, and operations of the Holy Ghost, with a spirited refutation of the objections of the Pneumatomachi. This work, one of the best on the subject amongst ancient writings, is now only extant in a translation of St. Jerome.

(c.) " Contra Manichæos," in 18 chapters, a refutation, chiefly from reason, of the Manichæan doctrine of two principles, and of the sinfulness of matter.

(d.) Fragments of his commentaries on the Psalms, Job, Proverbs, Second Epistle to the Corinthians, Acts of the Apostles, Gospel of St. John, and Seven Catholic Epistles, abounding in beautiful thoughts and useful reflections. Among his lost works, the most celebrated is the defense of Origen's " Περὶ ἀρχῶν."

3. Didymus was a layman and married. Jerome praises the correctness of his doctrine on the Trinity,

divinarum humanarumque rerum eruditionem ac scientiam venit, ut scholæ ecclesiasticæ doctor existeret."

but censures him for having favored Origen's opinions, and, in particular, for having taught the pre-existence of souls.  His style is simple, clear, and agreeable; his interpretation, though mostly allegorical and mystical, is yet natural; his method of reasoning definite.   Rufinus makes this beautiful remark about him: "Velut lampadem quandam divina luce fulgentem, Didymum Dominus accendit" [Hist. eccl. II, 7.]

*Editions and Literature.* — *Migne*, S. gr. XXXIX, 131–1818. — *Ceillier* l. c. VII, 724–747.

## § 73. *St. Macarius, the Great* (*d. 390*).

1. *Macarius*, called the Egyptian or the Elder, to distinguish him from the Younger, of Alexandria, was born about 300 in Upper Egypt.  From youth he felt drawn to a life of penance and solitude, and about 330 retired into the desert, where he spent the last sixty years of his life in the exercises of a rigorous asceticism.  He was ordained priest in 340, and had to endure many afflictions for the faith under the Emperor Valens.  His brother monks held him in the greatest veneration on account of his sanctity and wonderful power of healing the sick and the possessed.  Palladius says of him that so great were the mortifications he underwent that he was called the "'young old man,' because he advanced more quickly in virtue than in age." *

2. Of his works we still possess 50 homilies, 2 beautiful prayers, and, besides, some maxims ( " Apoph-

---

* " Τοσαύτῃ ἐχρήσατο καρτερίᾳ πόνων ἀσκητικῶν, ὥστε καλεῖσθαι αὐτὸν παιδαριογέροντα διὰ τὸ θᾶττον τῆς ἡλικίας ταῖς ἀρεταῖς προκόψαι."

thegmata " ) on the practice of the ascetical life;
2 epistles, in which he recommends to the monks the
exercise of the Christian virtues, particularly of
humility. The " Opuscula ascetica," which contain
7 treatises: "De custodia cordis," "De perfectione
in spiritu," "De oratione," " De patientia et discretione," "De elevatione mentis," " De caritate,"
and " De libertate mentis," is not by Macarius himself,
but consists of extracts compiled from his works by
Simeon Logotheta in the twelfth century.

3. The homilies treat of asceticism, of the nature,
degrees, and difficulties of perfection, as also of
temptations. They contain an admirable explanation
of the various forms of mysticism. The style is
unadorned, simple, but wanting in order, nor are the
numerous illustrations always well chosen.

*Editions and Literature.* — *Migne*, S. gr. XXXIV,
1–968. — *Ceillier* l. c. VII, 709–724.


§ 74. *St. Epiphanius, Bishop of Salamis* (*d. 403*).

1. *Epiphanius* was born between 310 and 315, of
Jewish parents, in a village of Palestine. After their
death, owing to the influence of the monks, especially
the Abbot Hilarion, he became a Christian, monk,
priest, and abbot of a monastery founded by himself
in his own native place. This he governed for the
space of thirty years, universally venerated for his
piety and learning. In 367 he was elevated to the
metropolitan see of Salamis in the island of Cyprus.
In 382 he journeyed to Rome, for the purpose of
putting an end to the schism at Antioch. His almost
exaggerated zeal for the purity of the Christian doctrine, the extraordinary restlessness of his character,

as well as want of keen judgment and worldly experience, led him sometimes into injudicious actions. He was the most determined opponent of the errors of Origen, and it was he who, by his proceedings against Bishop John of Jerusalem, an admirer of Origen, was the real cause of the Origenistic controversy. Moreover, he listened to the intriguing Theophilus of Alexandria, and shared in his opposition against St. Chrysostom, a supposed favorer of Origenism, and was even ready to take part in a pretended council convened against him. Discovering, however, that he had been duped by Theophilus, he left Constantinople before the council assembled, and sailed for Cyprus, but was overtaken by death during the voyage, A. D. 403.

2. We possess the following of his works: —

(a.) "Panarion" (medicine-chest), that is, a remedy, or antidote against heresy. It is generally quoted as "Hæreses." This work contains an exposition and refutation of 80 heathen, Jewish, and Christian errors, taken chiefly from the writings of Justin, Irenæus, and Hippolytus; furthermore an "Expositio fidei," which is an appendix to it, and the "Recapitulatio," an abridgment of it.

(b.) "Ancoratus," in 121 chapters, in which, with a view of strengthening the faith of believers, he treats extensively, though often diverging from his subject, of the doctrines of the Trinity and the Incarnation, the resurrection, judgment, and eternal life.

(c.) "De mensuris et ponderibus, scil. s. Scripturæ," in 24 chapters, in which he explains the name and value of the different weights and measures mentioned in Holy Scripture. He also speaks of the

Greek Septuagint, and of Origen's Hexapla, and makes observations, especially geographical, which are important for the science of Biblical Introduction.   Besides the 24 chapters in Greek, there exists a Syriac version, in sixty chapters.

(d.) "De duodecim gemmis," an allegorical explanation and description of the miraculous power of the twelve gems in Aaron's breast-plate.

(e.) Two letters, translated into Latin, in one of which he censures Bishop John of Jerusalem for his esteem of Origen, and in the other praises Jerome for his opposition to him; also a Commentary on the Canticle of Canticles.*

The following are spurious: —

(1.) " De prophetis eorumque obitu ac sepultura;" (2.) VIII Homiliæ; (3.) "Tractatus de numerorum mysteriis," and (4.) " Physiologus," in 49 chapters, a book much read in the Middle Ages, and containing wonderful accounts of animals whose characteristic qualities are made to illustrate Christian doctrines.

3. The writings of Epiphanius give proof of his great learning, his lively but often extravagant zeal for orthodoxy, monasticism, and asceticism.   He knew five languages ($\pi\varepsilon\nu\tau\acute{\alpha}\gamma\lambda\omega\tau\tau\sigma\varsigma$), a rare accomplishment in those days, and enjoyed a high reputation for piety and learning.   St. Jerome calls him " Patrem pæne omnium episcoporum et antiquæ reliquias sanctitatis " (Apol. II adv. Rufin.) and, according to St. Augustine, Epiphanius was " apud Græcos vir inter magnos habitus et a multis in catholicæ fidei sanitate

---

* This Commentary, says Bardenhewer, is now generally ascribed to Bishop Philo of Carpasia in Cyprus, at the beginning of the 5th Century.   (Patrologie § 54.)   (R.)

laudatus '' (De hæres. ad Quodvultdeum). His style, however, is weak, diffuse, and unmethodical.

*Editions and Literature.* — *Migne*, S. gr. XLI–XLIII. — *Ceillier* l. c. VIII, 631–744. — *Gervais*, L'histoire de la vie de S. Epiphane. 4°. Paris 1738.— *Eberhard*, Die Betheiligung des Epiphanius an dem Streit über Origenes. Trier 1859.

## § 75. *St. Chrysostom, Patriarch of Constantinople* (*d. 407*).

1. *John*, afterwards styled *Chrysostom*, on account of his remarkable eloquence, was born at Antioch in 347. After the early death of his father, an officer of high rank, his pious mother Anthusa took charge of his education, and had him instructed by the best masters of the day. He studied rhetoric under Libanius, who considered him his most able disciple, and philosophy under Andragathius. After following, with great success, the profession of an advocate, at a time when his prospects were the most brilliant, he withdrew from public life, received holy baptism in 369, and devoted himself in tranquil retirement to an ascetical life and theological studies. The offer of a bishopric, in 373, he declined and avoided by flight, taking up his abode with some solitaries in the neighborhood of Antioch, until the failure of his health compelled him to return to his native city, where he was ordained·deacon, in 381, by Bishop Meletius, and priest, in 386, by Bishop Flavian, who entrusted him with the charge of preaching in the Cathedral. By his sermons and writings he acquired such fame that the Emperor Arcadius, under some crafty pretext, enticed him to Constantinople in 397, where, much against his will, after the death of

Nectarius, he was unanimously elected and declared Patriarch, in 398. St. Chrysostom was a model bishop; he was indefatigable in preaching; he founded hospitals and alms-houses, reformed the clergy and sent missionaries abroad. He took especially to heart the conversion of the Goths, and, by his preaching, wrought wonders among the most barbarous populations. But, by his Apostolic zeal, he drew upon himself the hatred of all the worldly-minded and licentious. The crafty, jealous Theophilus of Alexandria, in league with the Empress Eudoxia, whose vanity the holy doctor had wounded, persuaded the Emperor Arcadius, first to banish Chrysostom, in 403, then to recall him as speedily, and to banish him again, in 404. In painful journeys, and afflicted with bodily ailments, ill-used even by the clergy, the holy Patriarch wandered through Bithynia, Phrygia, Cappadocia, and Armenia, as far as Cucusus in Cilicia. Three years later, he was to be removed from the latter place (June, 407), and ordered to Pityus in Colchis, on the Eastern shore of the Black Sea. He succumbed, however, to the hardships of the journey and the ill-usage of his tormentors, and with his favorite motto on his lips, " Glory be to God for all " (" δόξα τῷ θεῷ πάντων ἕνεκα ") breathed forth his great soul on September 14, 407, at the age of sixty. His remains, which 31 years later were solemnly translated to the Church of the Apostles at Constantinople, in presence of the deeply-afflicted Emperor Theodosius, now rest in the Basilica of St. Peter at Rome.

2. His numerous works are as follows: —

I. *Scriptural Commentaries,*

which extend over nearly all the books of the Old and

New Testament, and are mostly arranged in the form of homilies. In the first part, he explains the meaning of the text and context, and in the second, draws moral and ascetical lessons from them.

His most celebrated expositions of the Old Testament are: —

(a.) Sixty-seven homilies and nine sermons on Genesis.

(b.) "Expositiones in Psalmos 3–12; 41–49; 108–150."

(c.) "Sermones V de Anna."

(d.) "Homiliæ III de Davide et Saulo."

(e.) "Interpretatio in Isaiam prophetam" (i–viii, x), one of the finest works of the Saint.

(f.) "Homiliæ VI in illud: Vidi Dominum Is. vi, 1."

(g.) "Homiliæ II de prophetiarum obscuritate."

Among his best New Testament homilies are reckoned: —

(a.) Ninety "Homiliæ in Matth.," all very valuable; the most celebrated amongst them are those on the Sermon of the Mount.

(b.) Eighty-eight "Homiliæ in Joannem," short, and sometimes controversial.

(c.) Fifty-five "Homiliæ in Acta Apostolorum," less perfect in style.

(d.) Two hundred and forty-six "Homiliæ in epistolas S. Pauli Apostoli," all of which, especially those on the Epistle to the Romans, are most valuable and brilliant.

II. *Ecclesiastical Homilies and Sermons.*

(a.) Dogmatical and controversial: — "XII Homiliæ contra Anomœos;" "VIII Homiliæ adversus Judæos;" "Homiliæ in resurrectionem mortuorum."

(b.) Sermons for feasts and panegyrics: " Homilia in diem natalem D. N. J. Chr.;" "Homilia de resurrectione et de ascensione Domini;" "Homiliæ II de festo Pentecostes;" "Homiliæ III in omnes ss. martyres;" "Homiliæ VII de laudibus S. Pauli Apostoli," in which the preacher gives a brilliant description of the immense work and activity of the Apostle of the Gentiles.

(c.) Sermons for special occasions. Amongst these the most distinguished in point of eloquence are the "Homiliæ XXI de statuis ad populum Antiochenum," in which St. Chrysostom endeavors to pacify the people of Antioch, who, enraged at the imposition of new taxes, had smashed the statues of the Emperor; he inveighs, however, at the same time, against the wickedness prevailing in the city.

(d.) Moral and ascetical discourses: " Homiliæ IX de pœnitentia," on the necessity and various kinds of penance; " Sermones de consolatione mortis;" "Catecheses ad illuminandos," on preparation for baptism and the obligations of those about to be baptized.

### III. *Dogmatical and Controversial.*

(a.) " Adversus Judæos et Gentiles demonstratio quod Christus sit Deus," a demonstration that Christ is the Messiah and God, drawn from the fulfilment of the prophecies.

(b.) "Liber in S. Babylam et contra Julianum et Gentiles," to show the miracles of the Apostles and martyrs, particularly those worked by St. Babylas, during the translation of his relics, ought to have convinced Julian that Christianity is a divine religion; but as he persisted in his infidelity, God punished him by a premature death.

### IV. *Moral and Ascetical.*

(a.) "De sacerdotio libri VI," wherein he explains, too rhetorically perhaps, the reasons of his flight from the episcopal burden, and the dignity and responsibility of the priesthood, as well as all the qualities required, but rarely met with, in those who aspire to the priesthood.

(b.) "Adversus oppugnatores vitæ monasticæ libri III," a defense of the monastic life, and "Comparatio regis cum monacho;" a monk is richer and happier than a king, both in life and death.

(c.) "De compunctione cordis libri II," on the ways and means of interior compunction.

(d.) De providentia libri III ad Stagirium," exhortation to trust in divine Providence in time of affliction.

(e.) "De virginitate," exposition of the passage I Cor. vii, 38, full of instruction and edification.

(f.) "Adhortatio ad Theodorum lapsum libri II," in which he admonishes and urges Theodore, in impressive language, to return to the Church.

(g.) "Ad viduam juniorem libri II," condolence on the loss of her husband; on the privileges of widowhood, and the difficulties of the married state.

(h.) "De subintroductis," a sharp rebuke administered to those priests who cohabit with consecrated virgins.

(i.) "Liber, quod, qui seipsum non lædit, nemo lædere possit," a thoughtful little work.

(j.) "Liber adversus eos, qui scandalizati sunt ob adversitates," upon the sufferings which are laid upon the just, that they ought not to cause distrust in the Providence of God.

## V. *238 Letters.*

These are very important for a knowledge of contemporary history, and of the life and character of this great Doctor of the Church.

*Doubtful Works:* — " Interpretatio in Danielem prophetam ; " " Orationes de fato et providentia ; " " Homiliæ duæ de precatione," " Homilia de Psalmo L." There are, besides, a great number of supposititious homilies.

3. Chrysostom regarded everything more from a practical than a speculative point of view, and consequently excels more in moral than in dogmatic theology. There is nothing very peculiar or striking in his doctrine of God and the divine Nature, but in his anthropology and soteriology he shows great originality. The relations of grace and free will are well discussed and explained. In the art of exposition and illustration he is unsurpassed, and by his skillful choice of examples from Bible history he was enabled to bring home to the individual soul the practice of virtue in the most forcible manner. In treating of the means of salvation, he extolls above all prayer, which he speaks of in language full of beautiful imagery. In exegesis he endeavors to unite the method of the two great schools of Antioch and Alexandria; for he would not reject altogether the employment of allegory, though he did not consider it necessary or essential to the interpretation of

Scripture. His knowledge extended to almost every branch of science. His style is natural, earnest, and serious, neither rigid nor lax. He knew how to combine sweet gentleness and warm affection with earnestness. The arrangement of his sermons, in which depth of thought vies with brilliancy of expression, is simple and skillful, his method of teaching sound; his instructions are easy to understand, his descriptions and narrations pleasing. In him the qualities of a great doctor were united with those of a great preacher of the Gospel. He is the first and most celebrated of all the Greek Doctors, and is praised by St. Nilus as "The greatest light of the universe" ("ὁ μέγιστος φωστὴρ τῆς οἰκουμένης"), and by St. Isidore of Pelusium as "The eye of the Church of Byzantium and the entire Church" ("ὁ τῆς ἐν Βυζαντίῳ Ἐκκλησίας καὶ πάσης ὀφθαλμός.")

*Editions and Literature.* — *Migne*, S. gr. XLVII–LXIV. — *Ceillier l. c.* IX, 1–790. — A revised edition of the Greek text of the 90 Homilies on St. Matthew, by *F. Field* (3 vols. 8ᵛᵒ. Cambridge 1839), and of the Homilies to the Epistles of St. Paul (5 vols. 8ᵛᵒ. Oxford 1849–1855).— An English translation of many of St. Chrysostom's writings in the "Select Library," etc., vol. IX–XIV. (New York 1888–1890). Leaves from St. John Chrysostom, selected and translated by *M. H. Allies* (London 1889. 8ᵛᵒ). — *Hermant*, Vie de S. Chrysostome (2 vols. Paris 1683).— *Neander*, Der hl. Chrysostomus und sein Verhältniss zur antiochenischen Schule (Gotha 1859). — *Martin*, S. Chrysostome, ses oeuvres et son siècle (2 vols. Montpellier 1860). — *Ph. Hergenröther* l. c. p. 29. — *Rochet*, Histoire de S. Jean Chrysostome (2 vols. Paris 1866). — *Ludwig*, Der hl. Chrysostomus in

seinem Verhältniss zum byzantin. Hofe (Braunsberg
1883). —*R. W. Bush*, Life and Times of Chrysostom
(London 1885).— *Ph. Schaff*, St. Chrysostom and St.
Augustine, in "Studies in Christian Biography"
(London 1891. 8ᵛᵒ). — On his liturgy, see *C. E.
Hammond*, The Ancient Liturgy of Antioch, etc.
(Oxford 1879. 8ᵛᵒ). — See also *Bardenhewer*, Patrol-
ogie, § 57.

§ 76. *Synesius, Bishop of Ptolemais (d. about 413).*

1. *Synesius*, the descendant of an ancient and distinguished race, was born at Cyrene, in Africa, between
370 and 375, and was taught mathematics and the
Neo-Platonic philosophy by the celebrated female philosopher Hypatia, at Alexandria. Later on he went
to Constantinople, where he spent three years full
of painful experience, and thence to Athens, in
search of that peace which neither philosophy nor
the world can give. He returned once more to Alexandria, residing there from 402 to 404, where he
married. The mystical tendency of his mind, as
well as the influence of his wife, gradually inclined
him in favor of Christianity. At length, A. D. 409,
without ceasing to be a Neo-Platonist, he received
Christian baptism from Theophilus, Bishop of Alexandria. Before a year had elapsed, the clergy and
the people petitioned for his elevation to the episcopate, on account of his personal qualifications and
the services he had rendered to his country and
native city, which he had saved from the power
of the Moors.

After strenuous resistance, from a feeling of his
own unworthiness and a sense of the awful dignity

and responsibility of the office, he received episcopal consecration.

He governed his diocese by word and deed at a time of peculiar difficulty, with prudence, zeal, and great success. Weighed down by grief over the indescribable troubles of that period and the premature death of his three sons, he died A. D. 413.

2. Of his works the following are preserved : —

(a.) One hundred and fifty-six letters, which bear ample testimony to his philosophical mind, his sensitive soul, and his untiring activity.

(b.) A Sermon on the Duty and Office of Kings, preached, in 397, at Constantinople, in the presence of Arcadius, in which he censures the vices of kings and the luxury of the court with manly courage, and inculcates sound maxims of government.

(c.) Various treatises : as, " Dion vel de ipsius vitæ instituto," a recommendation of the study of philosophy; " Calvitii encomium," a mock panegyric on baldness, in derision of the Sophists, who talk merely for the sake of talking; " De insomniis," a rather confused treatise on the origin and meaning of dreams; " Ægyptius seu de providentia," allusions to contemporary events, and the party intrigues of the Byzantine court; " De dono astrolabii," in praise of astronomy, on the occasion of the presentation of a precious astrolabe.

(d.) Two fragments of homilies, two sermons, and ten hymns, all of which reflect the deeply spiritual character of the author.

3. With the exception of his hymns, which breathe a spirit of true lyric poetry and genuine Christianity, the works of Synesius contain but few specifically Christian doctrines. They are rather a mass of syncretistical

doctrines clothed in heathen and Neo-Platonic phrases and formulas. The books written before his conversion to Christianity often savor of antipathy to the monastic state and the Christian priesthood; but in those composed by him as a Christian and a bishop, his positive faith subdues his love for Neo-Platonism and his heathen imagination is transformed by Christian ideas. Still he never wholly succeeded in throwing aside Neo-Platonism and entering into the full and genuine spirit of Christianity. His style is ornamental, and not unfrequently poetical. Synesius knew how to unite with Platonic depth and grace of expression the eloquence of a Demosthenes. For this reason he was called " Suavissimus philosophus et piarum delicium Musarum."

*Editions and Literature.* — *Migne*, S. gr. LXVI, 1021–1752. — *Ceillier* l. c. X, 496–517. — *Krabinger*, in Wetzer and Welte's Kirchenlex. X (1 Aufl.), Art. Synesius. — *F. X. Kraus*, Studien über Synesius, in the Tübinger theol. Quartalschr. 1865. — *Druon*, La vie et les oeuvres de Synésius. Paris 1878.

## § 77. St. Cyril, Patriarch of Alexandria (d. 444).

1. *Cyril*, of whose birth, youth, and literary training nothing is known, was a nephew of the Patriarch Theophilus. He studied the sciences in or near Alexandria, under good and competent masters, and theology under Bishop John of Jerusalem. He took an active part in his uncle's opposition to St. Chrysostom, and was, after the death of the former, but not without difficulty, promoted to the patriarchal see of Alexandria (412). The commencement of his episcopate was marked by riots and disturbances. He

closed the churches of the Novatians, chastised the Jews, who had shed Christian blood, embroiled himself with the Governor Orestes, venerated as a martyr a certain monk who had been beaten to death for having publicly insulted the Governor, and was the cause of a popular excitement which resulted in the murder of the highly-esteemed pagan philosopher Hypatia (415). Later on, however, having been disabused by St. Isidore of Pelusium, he gave satisfaction to Chrysostom (419), for the injustice done him by his uncle. He distinguished himself greatly in the controversy with Nestorius, whom, in his capacity of Papal Legate, he deposed at the Third General Council (in 431) for his obstinate assertion of two persons in Christ. But Cyril himself was deposed by the opposite party of 43 bishops, and imprisoned for two months by order of the Emperor Theodosius II., who had been misinformed about him. He lived, however, to see as the result of his untiring labors the happy return to unity of the greater part of the schismatical faction. He died June 27th, 444.

2. His writings, though not remarkable for beauty of style, are, nevertheless, distinguished by dogmatical precision, depth, and clearness. We are in possession of the following of his works: —

### I. *Dogmatical and Apologetical.*

(a.) " De sancta Christianorum religione adversus atheum Julianum," 10 books against Julian, who had published a cleverly written work against Christianity, which had the effect of shaking the faith of some Christians and of reviving the drooping spirits of the pagans. In this apology, which is dedicated to the Emperor Theodosius II., Cyril follows the example of

Origen in his work against Celsus. Attacking his adversary point by point, he treats of the relations of Christianity to Judaism and heathenism; demonstrates by arguments drawn from reason the folly and shamefulness of paganism, and the reasonableness and sanctity of Christianity. The whole work comprised probably 30 books; but of the other 20 only fragments are perserved.

(b.) "Thesaurus de sancta et consubstantiali Trinitate," a kind of "Summa" on the Trinity against the Arians and Eunomians.

(c.) Seven dialogues on the consubstantiality of the Father and the Son.

(d.) "De recta fide ad religiosissimum imperatorem Theodosium lib. I, et ad piissimas imperatrices (i. e. Eudoxia, the wife, and Pulcheria, the sister, of the Emperor), libri II," written in order to strengthen their faith against the errors of Nestorius.

(e.) "Scholion de incarnatione Unigeniti," the best introduction to Cyril's Christological doctrine.

(f.) "Dialogus, quod unus sit Christus," on the unity of person in Christ; — "Adversus blasphemias Nestorii contradictionum libri V; " — "Apologeticus pro XII capitibus adv. orient. episcopos; " — "Liber contra Theodoretum pro XII capitibus; " — "Explanatio XII capitum " : — in all of which St. Cyril defends and vindicates his own doctrine laid down in his celebrated Anathematisms, against the misinterpretations of his opponents.

## II. *Exegetical.*

(a.) "De adoratione et cultu in spiritu et veritate," in 17 books; an allegorical exposition of the Pentateuch in reference to Christ and the Church, adoration in spirit being, as he maintains, prefigured in the Old Testament.

(b.) " Dicta elegantia " (γλαφυρά, *i. e.*, polished, elegant) chiefly allegorical explanations of select passages from the Pentateuch, in 13 books. This, as well as the preceding work, is rich in ideas and moderate in the use of allegorical interpretation.

(c.) Commentaries on most of the Psalms, the 12 minor Prophets, Isaias, Matthew (a fragment), Luke, John (in 12 books, of which 10 are complete and 2 in fragments), the Epistles of St. Paul to the Romans, Corinthians, and Ephesians.

## III. *Homiletical and Practical.*

(a.) Twenty-nine sermons for Easter, in which he either discusses matters relative to Christian life, or touches upon the burning questions of the day, or impugns the position of Jews and Gentiles.

(b.) " Diversæ homiliæ," amongst which are those delivered by St. Cyril at Ephesus on the Incarnation, the heresy and conduct of Nestorius, and on the Mother of God (θεοτόκος).

(c.) A severe sermon against the Eunuchs, and 3 discourses upon the Alexandrian martyrs Cyrus and John.

(d.) Seventy letters, which, for the most part, have reference to the dogma of the Incarnation and the Nestorian controversy, but also to matters of discipline. Many of them form extensive treatises, and some are of such dogmatic importance that they were adopted by the entire Church as rule of faith.

Other works ascribed to St. Cyril are either doubtful, as the 6 homilies " De quibusdam vitæ Christi

mysteriis," or spurious, as the treatise " De sancta et
vivifica Trinitate," and the sixteen homilies on Le-
viticus and nineteen on Jeremias. Many of his works
are entirely lost, or extant only in fragments, as
" Liber contra Synusiastas," " Sermo de fide," " Liber contra Pelagianos," "Commentarius in Matthæum, Lucam et in Epistolam ad Hebræos."

3. The chief merit of St. Cyril's writings is his
enunciation and explanation of the orthodox doctrine
as to the two natures in Christ. He stands in the
same position to Nestorianism as Athanasius does to
Arianism. The expression "physical union" (ἔνωσις
φυσική) employed by him, and misinterpreted by his
adversaries, only meant the hypostatic union; that is,
the real union of both natures of Christ in *one person*,
not *one nature*, in opposition to the " moral union "
(συνάφεια) of Nestorius. Cyril continually uses the
word φύσις, instead of ὑπόστασις, for person. His
doctrine is briefly and definitely expressed in the 12
Anathematisms, as well as in the following passage
from his second letter to Nestorius : "The natures
indeed that are brought together into a true oneness
are different, but one Christ and Son arises out of
both ; not as if the difference of natures had been
taken away by the union, but rather exhibiting to us
the one Lord Jesus Christ and Son of the Godhead and
manhood, on account of the unspeakable and incom-
prehensible meeting of them unto unity." * The mis-

---

* "Ὅτι διάφοροι μὲν αἱ πρὸς ἑνότητα τὴν ἀληθινὴν
συναχθεῖσαι φύσεις, εἰς δὲ ἐξ ἀμφοτέρων Χριστὸς καὶ Υἱός·
οὐχ ὡς τῆς τῶν φύσεων διαφορᾶς ἀνῃρημένης διὰ τὴν
ἔνωσιν· ἀποτελεσασῶν δὲ μᾶλλον ἡμῖν τὸν ἕνα Κύριον Ἰησοῦν
Χριστὸν καὶ Υἱὸν θεότητός τε καὶ ἀνθρωπότητος, διὰ τῆς
ἀφράστου καὶ ἀπορ᾽ρήτου πρὸς ἑνότητα συνδρομῆς."

takes he had made at the beginning of his episcopate from over-zealousness, he repaired later on by his great love of peace, and by his wonderful labors in the interests of the Church. His sermons are generally not adorned with any rhetoric, and often a mere collection of Scripture passages and mystical expositions. The want of fluency and elegance in his style is compensated, especially in his apologetic and controversial works, by clearness and precision of thought and directness of expression, as well as by an admirable use of illustrations and comparisons. Cyril was styled by Prosper " Fidei catholicæ gloriosissimus defensor et constantissimus prædicator ; " by Pope Celestine I. " Vir apostolicus," and by Anastasius Sinaita " σφραγὶς τῶν πατέρων " on account of his perfect explanation and brilliant defense of the doctrine of the Trinity. The Greek Menologium sings of him : —

> " I praise Cyril, the friend of my Lord
> And the champion of the Lady ever Virgin." *

*Editions and Literature.* — *Migne*, S. gr. LXVIII–LXXVII.— *Ceillier* l. c. XIII, 241–407.— A number of St. Cyril's dogmatical and exegetical works have been edited by *P. E. Pusey*, Oxford 1868–1877 ; his Commentary on St. Luke, from an ancient Syriac version, by *R. Payne Smith*, Oxford, 2 vols. 8ᵛᵒ, 1859 ; and fragments of the same from a Nitrian MS. by *W. Wright*, London 1874. 4º. — *Kopallik*, Cyrill von Alexandrien. Mainz 1881. — *Kohlhofer*, S. Cyrillus Alexandrinus de sanctificatione. Wirceburgi 1866. — *Largent*, S. Cyrille d'Alexandrie et le concil d'Ephèse. Paris 1892.

---

* " Κύριλλον ὑμνῶ τοῦ Κυρίου μου φίλον,
　Καὶ Κυρίας πρόμαχον ἀειπαρθένου."

## § 78. *Theodoret, Bishop of Cyrus* (*d. 458*).

1. *Theodoret*, born about 390 at Antioch, educated together with Nestorius by the monks of a suburban monastery, and instructed in the sciences by Theodore of Mopsuestia, was distinguished no less by his virtuous life than by his learning. After the early death of his parents, he distributed his great possessions among the poor, and withdrew for several years into a monastery, where he devoted his time to study and practices of piety. At the age of twenty-five, he became a deacon of the church at Antioch, and, in 420, Bishop of Cyrus in Syria. He was an exemplary administrator of his diocese, and displayed great zeal in the conversion of heretics. He became, however, unfortunately entangled in the Nestorian controversy, opposing Cyril's Anathematisms chiefly on account of the expression " ἕνωσις φυσική," and siding with those who rejected the Third Œcumenical Council. But, after many troubles and vexations, he finally (435) reconciled himself with Cyril and the orthodox party, without, however, entirely breaking with Nestorius. When the Eutychian, or Monophysite sect at the Robber Synod of Ephesus (449), passed sentence of deposition upon him, he appealed to Pope Leo the Great, who acknowledged him as the lawful bishop of his Diocese. He took his seat at the Council of Chalcedon, in spite of the objections raised by those bishops who inclined to Monophysitism, and, after his solemn renunciation of Nestorius, was recognized by all the bishops as the rightful incumbent of his see. After this Council he lived peacefully in a monastery,

engaged in literary labors, governing his diocese till his death (458).

2. Theodoret was a most prolific and able writer. His works are as follows: —

## I. *Exegetical.*

These consist partly in expositions of difficult passages of such sacred books as the Pentateuch, Kings, Paralipomenon; partly in commentaries on the Psalms, Canticle of Canticles, all the Prophets, and St. Paul's Epistles. The writer's clear and pregnant exposition of the literal sense of Scripture is excellent.

## II. *Historical.*

A History of the Church, from 324–428, in 5 books, beautifully written and supported by many important documents.

A History of Monasticism, full of the most edifying and wonderful incidents from the lives of thirty ascetics, chiefly of Simon Stylites.

A History of Heretics, from Simon Magus to Eutyches, in five books, in which he describes the origin, nature and development of the heresies, and explains the opposing Catholic doctrines.

## III. *Dogmatical.*

(a.) " Græcarum affectionum curatio," in 12 books, a cure for Greek (heathen) maladies, or the knowledge of Gospel truth hidden in pagan philosophy. The author contrasts the doctrines of pagan and Christian philosophy on such fundamental questions as the origin of the world, matter and spirit, the nature of man, etc.

(b.) "Mendicus vel polymorphus," directed against the Eutychians, and showing that the divine nature of the Logos underwent no change in consequence of the Incarnation, that there was no confusion of natures in Christ, and that the divinity of the Son was incapable of suffering.

(c.) "Orationes de providentia," perhaps the best treatise ever written on this subject.

(d.) "Reprehensio XII capitum Cyrilli," in 5 books, written in a severe style.

## IV. *About 180 Letters.*

Of these some are controversial; others, letters of condolence or ordinary friendly intercourse; others again are written for feast days and other special occasions; but the same elegance of language characterizes them all.

Some of Theodoret's works are completely lost, as the "Opus mysticum," in 12 books; "Libri de theologia et incarnatione," and others; some are lost in part, as "Pentalogium de incarnatione" against Cyril and the Council of Ephesus. — "VII Dialogi adversus Anomœos, Macedonianos et Apollinaristas," "XXVII libri s. sermones de diversis hæresibus," "Liber asceticus," and others are spurious.

3. Theodoret ranks as the most solid commentator of the Greek Church. He imitates St. Chrysostom in skillfully blending allegorical and historical matter.

But in matters of dogma he was not always on the orthodox side. For example, he repudiated the doctrine of the procession of the Holy Ghost from the Son, and, in opposition to the Council of Ephesus, defended the Nestorian heresy, till 450, when he

assented to the teaching of the Church upon the unity
of person in two natures, and pronounced, at the
Council of Chalcedon (451), anathema upon Nestorius
and all who refused to the holy Virgin Mary the title of
Mother of God, and divided the only begotten Son
into two persons. He died in the communion of the
Church. Many of his books were anathematized at
the Fifth Œcumenical Council, chiefly those written
against Cyril. Theodoret was learned, eloquent, and
generous, but sensitive and imperious. His style is
pure, clear, and graceful. Joannes Euchaita praises
him as "a divine man, a great master, and a high
column of orthodoxy." *

*Editions and Literature.* — *Migne*, S. gr. LXXX –
LXXXIV. — *Ceillier* l. c. XIV, 32–267. — Separate
edition of his "Græcarum affectionum curatio" by
*T. Gaisford*, Oxford 1839. 8ᵛᵒ; and of his Church History by the same, Oxford 1854. 8ᵛᵒ. — *Specht*,
Theodor von Mopsuestia und Theodoret von Cyrus.
München 1871. — *Kihn*, Bedeutung der antiochenischen Exegetenschule. 1866. — *Ph. Hergenröther*,
Die antiochenische Schule, p. 42. sq.— *Bertram*, Theo-
doreti episc. Cyr. doctrina christologica ex ejus
operibus composita. Hildesiæ 1883.


§ 79. *St. Isidore of Pelusium (d. about 440).*

1. *St. Isidore* was born at Alexandria about 370.
He appears to have been a lawyer before he consecrated
himself to the monastic life and the study of the Holy
Scriptures. His profound knowledge and love of

---

* " Ὡς ἄνδρα θεῖον, ὡς διδάσκαλον μέγαν,
Ὡς ἀκράδαντον ὀρθοδοξίας στῦλον."

dogma, as well as his method of interpretation, together with other circumstances, would point to the fact that he was probably taught, among others, by St. John Chrysostom. In consideration of his excellent personal qualities, he was elected Abbot of the monks who dwelt on a mountain near Pelusium, and whom he guided by word and example in the way of perfection. His strict asceticism, refined education, and profound erudition, earned for him a reputation far and wide, not only among the clergy, but also among all classes of the laity. He used his great influence for the good of the Church, everywhere upholding the orthodox faith and giving salutary counsels. He admonished the Emperor Theodosius II. to maintain order at the Council of Ephesus, warned Cyril of Alexandria against the proceedings of his crafty uncle Theophilus, and addressed earnest remonstrances even to bishops, a proceeding by which he naturally made some enemies. At the Council of Ephesus, he occupied the position of a mediator between the two extreme parties. Having labored and suffered much for the faith, he died in 440 in the odor of sanctity.

2. Of St. Isidore's writings there are extant 2012 Epistles, in 5 books, generally brief, but written with grace, spirit, and unction, and containing excellent counsels and principles, grave admonitions and rebukes, as well as information on dogmatical and exegetical subjects. His " Liber contra Græcos sive gentiles," and his " Tractatus brevis, quod non sit Fatum," treating of divine Providence and of the vanity of believing in blind fate, are contained in his long letter to the Sophist Arpokras (l. III, ep. 154).

3. Isidore was in great repute amongst his con-

temporaries and later writers for his solid piety and humility, noble peace-loving disposition, and indefatigable labors. He shows elevation of mind in dogmatic subjects, great earnestness in ascetics, and critical talent in matters of exegesis. While holding the same hermeneutical principles as St. Chrysostom and Theodoret, he yet strives to blend the allegorical with the historical sense, but disclaims forced methods of exposition, as doing more harm than good. He derives the authority of Holy Scripture from its divine inspiration. To him the words of the Old and New Testament are the " divine oracles " [τὰ θεῖα χρήσματα] ; the Gospel, " the divine and all-surpassing message" [κήρυγμα θεῖον καὶ ὑπερφυές, l. IV, ep. 30] ; the Apostles, " the messengers filled with divine wisdom " [οἱ ἀπόστολοι τῆς θείας ἐμπεπλησμένοι σοφίας, l. II, ep. 345] ; and he exhorts a friend " not to despise the sweet hearing of the divine Scriptures " [μὴ καταφρόνει, ὦ φίλος, τῆς μελισταγοῦς ἀκροάσεως τῶν θείων γραφῶν, l. IV, ep. 208]. Besides Holy Scripture, he also acknowledged tradition as a source of divine revelation. " It is necessary to take the proofs from the judgment of the sound, and to follow the holy Synod of Nicea without adding or detracting from it. For that Synod, being divinely inspired, proposed the true dogma." * Photius says that " he is a rule and pattern worthy of imitation, both in his learning and in holy ascetical behavior." †

---

* "Χρὴ ἀπὸ τῆς τῶν ὑγιαινόντων κρίσεως λαμβάνειν τὰς ἀποδείξεις· καὶ τῇ ἁγίᾳ συνόδῳ τῇ συγκρηθείσῃ κατὰ Νικαίαν ἀκολουθεῖν, μήτε προστιθέντας, μήτε ἀφαιροῦντας. Ἐκείνη γὰρ θεόθεν ἐμπνευθεῖσα τἀληθὲς ἐδογμάτισεν."

† "Ὅς ὥσπερ λόγων, οὕτω δὲ καὶ ἱερατικῆς καὶ ἀσκητικῆς πολιτείας κανών ἐστιν χρηματίζειν ἀξιόχρεως." Ep. II, 44.

*Editions and Literature.* — *Migne*, S. gr. LXXVIII, 9–1674. — *Ceillier* l. c. XIII, 600–640. — *Kihn*, in Wetzer and Welte's Kirchenlex. VI. (2 Aufl.) 964 sq. — *Bober*, De arte hermeneutica S. Isidori Pelusiotæ. Cracoviæ 1878. — *Bouvy*, De S. Isidoro Pelusiota libri III. Nemausi 1885.

### § 80. *St. Nilus, the Elder* (*d. after 440*).

1. *St. Nilus*, the year of whose birth and death is unknown, sprang from a wealthy family of Ancyra in Galatia. He became Governor of Constantinople, married, and had two sons, but resolved to renounce the world. With the consent of his wife he retired toward the close of the fourth century to the hermits of Mount Sinai, where he devoted himself to a strictly ascetical life, in the company of his son Theodulus. Here he displayed great activity, writing letters of admonition and warning to persons of all ranks, whether clerical or lay, and combating the errors of heathens, Gnostics, Manichæans, and Arians. With noble freedom, also, he pleaded with the Emperor Arcadius for the banished St. John Chrysostom.

By the incursion of the Arabs, A. D. 410, he and his son were driven from their solitude; his son having been taken captive and sold, came ultimately into the hands of the Bishop of Eleusa in Palestine, from whom both father and son received holy orders, and then returned once more to Mount Sinai, where Nilus died, not before 440.

2. The works of St. Nilus may be divided into three classes: —

### I. *Monastical.*

(a.) " Narrationes," seven accounts of the invasion

of Mt. Sinai by the Saracens, the massacre of the monks, and the experiences of himself and his son.

(b.) " Oratio in Albianum," a panegyric.

(c.) " Tractatus de monastica exercitatione," in 75 chapters, on the monastic life and the duties of superiors and monks.

(d.) "Tractatus de voluntaria paupertate," in 67 chapters.

(e.) " De monachorum præstantia," upon the advantages of eremitical life in the desert.

(f.) "Tractatus ad Eulogium monachum," in 34 chapters; instructions on piety.

(g.) " Institutio ad monachos," a short exhortation.

## II. *Moral and Ascetical.*

(a.) " Peristeria ad Agathium monachum," on avoiding sin and practicing virtue after the example of the pious Peristeria.

(b.) " Tractatus de oratione," in 153 chapters, short, but pithy.

(c.) " De octo spiritibus malitiæ," in 19 chapters, excellent instructions on the deadly sins.

(d.) " De vitiis, quæ opposita sunt virtutibus," in 4 chapters.

(e.) "De diversis malignis cogitationibus," in 27 chapters, on temptations and the means of resisting them.

(f.) On Luke xxii, 36.

(g.) Ninety-nine " Sententiæ " and 147 " Capita parænetica; " short, spiritual rules, calculated to lift up the mind from perishable to imperishable things.

## III. *Letters.*

Four books, containing 1061 letters, which, in matter and form, resemble those of St. Isidore of Pelusium.

They are, however, not all genuine. Many are mere extracts from his other writings. His "Liber adversus gentiles" and "Liber de compunctione" are lost. The "Tractatus moralis," "Sermo dogmaticus de Trinitate," and others, are supposititious. There is also much uncertainty with regard to the authenticity of other works, and it is probable that very few of the letters exist in their original form.

3. Nilus is one of the most eminent writers on moral and ascetical subjects. Dupin calls his letters an immense storehouse of beautiful and profitable thoughts on all kinds of subjects. The chief characteristic of his writings is brevity and earnestness. Nilus severely condemns the irregularities of the monks, and impressively exhorts them to poverty, obedience, peace, and harmony. The Greek Menologium contains the following beautiful eulogy on him: "The Nile waters Egypt, but the great Nilus waters the whole earth by his word, even after his death." *

*Editions and Literature.*— Migne, S. gr. LXXIX.— Ceillier l. c. XIII, 146–193. — *Fessler*, Institut. patrol. II (1851), 592–614.

§ 81. *St. Mesrop. — Bishop Eznik. — St. Elishe, the Hermit.*

Of Armenian authors, we shall only mention three : —

I. (a.) *Mesrop*, trained from his youth in Greek literature, became secretary first to the Armenian Patriarch, Nerses, the Great, and afterwards to King

---

\* "Αἴγυπτον ἄρδει Νεῖλος, ἀλλὰ καὶ κτίσιν
Λόγῳ καταρδεῖ καὶ θανὼν Νεῖλος μέγας."

Weramshapuh. He renounced the pleasures of the royal court and retired to a monastery, where he led a very strict ascetical life and attained to an eminent degree of Christian knowledge and perfection. In order to widen the circle of his influence, he left his solitude and founded schools for the education of youth. He traversed Greater and Lesser Armenia, and other neighboring provinces in company with some of his disciples, with a view to stamp out the remains of paganism, to extirpate and prevent heresy, to diffuse Christian knowledge, and to further the monastic life. He invented the Armenian alphabet and translated with the help of other learned men the Bible into that language (408–410). His great services to the Church and his country earned for him the title of the " Apostle of Armenia." He died in the odor of sanctity in 441.

(b.) Besides his translation of the Bible, he composed penitential hymns for Lent, as well as a number of simple, popular exhortations, redolent with Gospel flavor ; these discourses were formerly ascribed to St. Gregory Illuminator.

In his literary labors, Mesrop looked to the subject-matter rather than to the style and form, so that, while his homilies abound in deep thoughts and impressive admonitions, the style is monotonous and commonplace.

II. (a.) *Eznik*, a disciple of St. Mesrop, was sent to Edessa in 425, to translate the works of the Syriac Fathers into Armenian. After a short stay in that city he went to Constantinople, where he continued to occupy himself with translations till after the Council of Ephesus, when he returned to his home, taking with him the decrees of that Council together with a long coveted manuscript of the Bible. Some think he became Bishop of Bagrevand. The year of his death, as also of his birth, is unknown.

(b.) His literary work consisted chiefly in the revision and completion of the Armenian translation of the Bible, and in the composition of a work entitled "Refutation of the Sects," in four books, namely, "The Heathen Sects," "The Persian Religion," "The Greek School of Philosophy," and "The Sect of Marcion." The small book of "Exhortations" and certain homilies are of doubtful authenticity.

(c.) Besides a knowledge of languages, such as Greek, Syriac, and Persian, Eznik possessed a keen and penetrating mind, considerable erudition, and a remarkable gift for writing. His natural, simple, and clear style is considered a model of classical Armenian. His literary work and influence place him foremost among the greatest Armenian writers.

III. (a) *Elishe* (Elisæus), another disciple of Mesrop, was at one time secretary to St. Wardan, the commander of the Armenian army. Later on, he retired into solitude, first to South Armenia, then to the banks of Lake Wan, in order to shun intercourse with men. Here he ended his days in 480.

(b.) He wrote "The History of Wardan and the Armenian War," in a patriotic and enthusiastic strain; also commentaries on Genesis, on the books of Josue and the Judges; an explanation of the Pater noster; canons on the treatment of energumens, also "Words of Admonition to Hermits," in which he depicts the sufferings and persecutions of the Church and ardently exhorts the Armenian monks to a virtuous life. The authenticity of the homilies ascribed to him is doubtful, on account of the great difference of style.

(c.) Elishe's works are distinguished by the purity and elevation of his language, and from a theological point of view afford excellent testimony to the doctrines of the Trinity, Incarnation, duality of natures in Christ, the divine institution of the Church, the primacy of Peter, the Eucharist, and similar dogmas.

*Editions and Literature.* — Most of the Armenian literature has been edited and published during this century by the Mechitarist Congregation of St. Lazarus in Venice. — *Nirschl* l. c. §§ 239–250. — On two other Armenian writers, *Koriun*, Bishop of Georgia, and *Bishop Moses of Chorene*, see Kirchenlexikon V, 846, and VIII, 1955 (2 ed.) respectively. — Cf. *Bardenhewer*, § 90.

## § 82. *Dionysius, the Areopagite.*

Five celebrated writings have been handed down to us under this name:

(1.) "De divinis nominibus," in 13 chapters, an admirable explanation of the names by which God is called in Holy Scripture; treating also of the nature and origin of evil, the Trinity and Redemption.

(2.) "De cœlesti hierarchia," in 15 chapters, a theological treatise on the nature, names, office, and order of the angels, who form 9 choirs in 3 hierarchies.

(3.) "De ecclesiastica hierarchia," in 7 chapters, showing how the ecclesiastical hierarchy is a likeness of the heavenly hierarchy, embracing also 9 degrees in 3 orders, the first of which represents the divine mysteries (Sacraments), the second the ministers, and the third the receivers.

(4.) "De mystica theologia ad Timotheum," in

5 chapters, on union with God, the supreme object of our knowledge and love.

(5.) Ten "Epistolæ," which, for the most part, contain answers to dogmatical questions, or practical exhortations.

These valuable writings, whose origin is veiled in mystery, were, in the Middle Ages, without hesitation ascribed to Dionysius, the Areopagite, who had been converted by the preaching of the Apostle St. Paul, made first Bishop of Athens, and, according to Eusebius, died a martyr under Domitian. The MSS. bearing the name of Dionysius, the Areopagite, as well as the circumstance that their author speaks of the person of St. Paul with great admiration, and addresses the 10th letter to the "Theologian John, the Apostle and Evangelist in his banishment on the Isle of Patmos," etc., gave weight to the opinion of his authorship. But considering the difference of style; the use of theological terms belonging to the 4th and 5th centuries (as ὑπόστασις for *person*); the admixture of Neo-Platonic ideas and formulas; the minute description of the fully developed ecclesiastical liturgy and of monastic life, as well as the fact that these works are not mentioned by Eusebius, or any other ancient ecclesiastical author, and were not publicly referred to until the beginning of the sixth century by the Monophysites, whilst the Catholics objected to them as unknown:—considering all this, it is plain that these works could not have been written by Dionysius, the disciple of the Apostles. The theory, likewise, that the author of these writings is identical with Dionysius, the Great, of Alexandria, and that his instructor Hierotheus was the same person as Origen, is just as untenable as the above mentioned, on account of the

many anachronisms involved in it. The same must
be said of the opinion according to which the author
was a certain priest, who taught theology, between
350 and 370, at the catechetical school of Alexandria,
(or Rinocolura?) and assumed the mystical name of
Areopagite. It is much more probable that the five
above named works were the composition of a priest
and monk trained in the Neo-Platonic school, in the
interval between the Councils of Ephesus and Chalcedon (431–451), and were by a well-meant, but
nevertheless blameworthy fraud (pia fraus), ascribed
to Dionysius, the Apostolic disciple.

The works themselves show that the author was a man
of great talent, depth, and subtlety, but humble and
pious withal; they quickly attained great celebrity,
were repeatedly translated into Latin, commented
upon by the most renowned theologians, and became
to the Scholastics of the Middle Ages an aid to their
speculations; to mystics, a light in contemplation, and
to ascetics, a guide on the threefold way of perfection,
viz. : the purgative, illuminative, and unitive way.

The fundamental doctrine of these writings is
Christian, but the particular explanations and expressions savor at times of the Neo-Platonic philosophy.
This may explain why two essentially different schools
of mystic theology have arisen from it, both claiming
to rest on the same foundation, viz., an idealistic and
a mystical Christian school.

The doctrine on sin and redemption is rendered
obscure by the mysterious language of the author, and
concerning the Incarnation there are some passages
that might be taken in a Monophysite sense. But his
exhortations to union with God are always most
impressive and fascinating.

"Dionysius" was also the author of the following seven treatises, now no longer extant: —

"De informationibus theologicis;" "De hymnis divinis;" "De symbolica theologia;" "De anima;" "De iis, quæ sub intellectum et sensum cadunt;" "De hierarchia legis," and "De justo divinoque judicio." These writings, together with the other four treatises, would form a complete system of theology. The following epigram refers to him: —

"Having obtained many rays of angelic wisdom,
Thou hast appeared to men like an intelligent star."

*Editions and Literature.* — *Migne*, S. gr. III, IV. — *Ceillier* l. c. XV, 362–388. — A separate edition of the two hierarchies, with English translation and notes, by *J. Colet* and *J. H. Lupton*, London 1869. 8vo. — Another translation by *J. Parker*, London 1894. 8vo. — *Hipler*, Dionysius der Areopagite, Regensburg 1861, and in Wetzer and Welte's Kirchenlexikon III (2. Aufl.) 1789. — *Nirschl*, Lehrbuch II, 131–148; and *Hist.-polit. Bl.*, 1883, pp. 173, 257. — *Ceslaus W. Schneider*, Areopagitica, Die Schriften des hl. Dionysius vom Areopag. Regensburg 1884. — *Fessler-Jungmann* l. c. §§ 121–122. — *Vidieu*, St. Denys l'Aréopagite, évêque d'Athènes et de Paris. Paris 1889. — *Bardenhewer* l. c. p. 284.

## CHAPTER II.

### LATIN FATHERS AND WRITERS.

§ 83. *St. Hilary, Bishop of Poitiers* (*d. about 366*).

1. *Hilary*, the scion of a noble family of Poitiers, was born between 320 and 325. He received his scientific education in his native town and in Bordeaux, where he more especially applied himself to the study of rhetoric. The more he saw of the profligate life of his fellow-citizens, the more his noble soul was filled with disgust and longed after the knowledge of truth. The perusal of Holy Scripture freed him from all the doubts which heathen philosophy had raised in his mind, and together with his wife and daughter he embraced Christianity in 350. On account of his holy life, both the clergy and people demanded his elevation to the bishopric of Poitiers, and he was consecrated shortly before 355. Thenceforth he led a life of continency, devoting himself entirely to his episcopal duties. His uncompromising opposition to Arianism, favored by the Emperor Constantius, caused him to be banished by that prince to Phrygia. But as his influence here seemed to be still more dreaded by the Arians, he was allowed, in 359, to return to his bishopric, where he continued, by word and writing, and especially by means of the synods he summoned, to combat Arianism with such success, that he caused the Gallican bishops completely to renounce it. True, he was not able to gain over Auxentius, Bishop of Milan, which city was the stronghold of Arianism, but he forced him to be more cautious. The latter years of his life were spent in quietude, occupied with exe-

getical labors.  He died at Poitiers, January 13th, 366.

2. Of his historical, controversial, dogmatical, and exegetical works, the following are preserved: —

(a.)  " De Synodis seu de fide Orientalium," in 92 chapters, an Eirenicon upon the Eastern symbols of faith, to the bishops of Gaul and Germany; and " Apologetica ad reprehensores libri de synodis responsa," a moderate apology of the same, of which only some fragments are now extant.

(b.)  " Libellus supplex I. ad imperatorem Constantium," a spirited petition for liberty of conscience and the recall of the exiled bishops from banishment.

(c.)  " Libellus supplex II. ad imperatorem Constantium," a petition for leave of an audience and of a disputation with Saturninus, his metropolitan, who favored the Arians; a defense of the Catholic faith, and a complaint about the general confusion caused by the severe treatment of the bishops.

(d.)  " Libellus contra imperatorem Constantium," an uncommonly severe indictment, published only after the death of the Emperor, in which he is accused of the meanest hypocrisy, styled an angel of Satan and Antichrist, and put on a level with Nero and Decius.

(e.)  " Libellus contra Auxentium," in which, as a warning to the Italian bishops against Auxentius, the deceit and duplicity of the latter are unmasked, and the intrigues of the Arians exposed in forcible and elegant language.

(f.)  " De Trinitate libri XII," the greatest and most important of Hilary's works, composed during his exile, in which he explains, proves, and vindicates, against the Arians and Sabellians, the doctrine of the eternal generation of the Son from the Father, and the unity of nature in both. Apart from frequent repetitions, the work is remarkable for completeness, thoroughness, solidity of reasoning, logical order, and well chosen style. It is the best work produced during the contest with Arianism.

(g.) "Commentarius in Evang. Matthæi," in which the allegorical interpretation prevails, and many beautiful thoughts and passages may be found.

(h.) "Commentarii in Psalmos," full of lofty thoughts, and impressing the doctrinal views of Hilary in short and pithy sentences.

(i.) "Tractatus de mysteriis," in 2 books, only lately discovered by Gamurrini, but unfortunately incomplete. Formerly it was considered to be a kind of liturgical instruction, or Sacramentary, but, in reality, it is an explanation of the "mysteries," i. e. of the typical persons and events of the Old Testament.

Other writings are either entirely lost, as his exposition of the Epistles of St. Paul; or almost entirely, as the "Liber hymnorum" (a collection of hymns), and a book of his own hymns.

The 15 "Fragmenta historica" are of doubtful authenticity; the "Epistola ad Augustinum," the "Metrum in Genesin," and the "Epistola ad Abram filiam" are spurious.

3. St. Hilary's chief glory lies in his treatment of the Incarnation. What Athanasius is to the East, St. Hilary is to the West. He has been unjustly accused of Docetism, since he expressly taught that Christ became truly man, that his divine nature was most intimately united to the human, that he really suffered and died. Nevertheless, there are some minor points of doctrine which, owing in part to the obscurity of language, present difficulties which can only be solved

by a comparison with other passages. The Council of Chalcedon classes St. Hilary among those Fathers " ex quorum doctrina exponendum est fidei de Incarnationis mysterio decretum."

According to Rufinus, he was "mitis natura et placidus." His language, though sometimes ambiguous and heavy, is yet full of power and dignity. He is the first real dogmatic writer, as well as the first Latin hymn poet. Venantius Fortunatus sings of him : —

> Et quia summus apex fidei, virtutis, honoris,
> Hilarius famæ radios iaculabat in orbem,
> Rite sacerdotii penetralia jura gubernans,
> Buccina terribilis, tuba legis, præco tonantis,
> Pulchrior electro, ter cocto ardentior auro, etc.
>
> ("De vita S. Martini," lib. I, 123–127.)

*Editions and Literature.* — *Migne*, S. lat. IX, X.— *Ceillier* l. c. V, 1–150 — *Fessler-Jungmann* l. c., §§ 95–98. — *Reinkens*, Hilarius von Poitiers. Schaffhausen 1864. — *Kayser*, Beiträge zur Geschichte der ältesten Kirchenhymnen I. (Paderborn 1881) 58–88. — *Hansen*, Vie de S. Hilaire, évêque de Poitiers. Luxembourg 1875. — *J. G. Cazenove*, St. Hilary of Poitiers and St. Martin of Tours. London 1883. 8ᵛᵒ.

§ 84. *St. Pacian, Bishop of Barcelona* (*d. about 390*).

1. *Pacian* was descended from a distinguished Spanish family. He married and had a son, Lucius Dexter, to whom St. Jerome dedicated his "Catalogus scriptorum ecclesiasticorum," and who rose under Honorius to the highest honors of the empire. Pacian afterwards renounced the world, embraced the ecclesiastical state, and was chosen Bishop of Barce-

lona in 360. He died in 390, at an advanced age, universally venerated for his virtue and eloquence.

2. Of his various writings, which, though brief, are valuable, we possess the following: —

(a) Three Letters to Sympronianus, a Novatian, who had asked him for an explanation and justification of the Catholic faith. In the first letter, of 7 chapters, Pacian gives the definition of the one true Church, explaining its nature; refutes the Novatian error on penance, and shows that the remission of sin by the priests is in accordance with the mercy of God, with Holy Scripture, and the wants of the human heart. In the second letter, of 8 chapters, he answers the objections raised against the first. In the third, a rather comprehensive letter of 25 chapters, he treats again of the Catholic doctrine on penance, and of the erroneous views of Novatian concerning it. In the first letter occurs the well-known saying: "Christianus mihi nomen, Catholicus cognomen."

(b) "Paraenesis ad poenitentiam," in 12 chapters, a kind of pastoral letter, treating of the different kinds of sin, and of sinners who refuse to confess their sins, or do penance for them if confessed; of the punishment of the impenitent and the reward of the penitent.

(c.) "Sermo de baptismo," in 7 chapters, an excellent and minute explanation of the sacrament of baptism, and its renewing and transforming power, as also of the obligations of the baptized.

"Cervulus," another work of St. Pacian, written against certain entertainments and disorderly customs at New Year's, is no longer extant.

3. Pacian united solid piety with great learning and eloquence. In exhorting to virtue, his words are full

of sweetness and unction, but in denouncing vice, his tone is severe and uncompromising. His diction is elegant and pure, his reasoning correct and conclusive, his thoughts are noble, and his mode of expression is pleasing. His writings are true masterpieces of their kind, and, on account of the important testimony they bear to the discipline of the Church, are among the most valuable writings of the fourth century. St. Jerome calls him " Episcopus castitate et eloquentia et tam vita quam sermone clarus " (De viris illustr. c. 106.)

*Editions and Literature.* — *Migne*, S. lat. XIII, 1051–1094. — *Ceillier* l. c. VI, 713–739. — *Gams*, Kirchengesch. von Spanien, Bd. II. Abth. 1, p. 318 sq.

## § 85. *St. Optatus, Bishop of Mileve (d. about 400).*

1. *Optatus* was Bishop of Mileve in Numidia, about the middle of the fourth century, and, like St. Augustine, a most strenuous opponent of the Donatists. Augustine calls him " a pastor of venerable memory and an ornament of the Church." Fulgentius puts him on a level with St. Augustine and St. Ambrose, and the Church venerates him as a saint. The particular details of his life are unknown.

2. About 370, St. Optatus wrote his famous work " De schismate Donatistarum," in 7 books, against Parmenianus, who had become Bishop of Carthage after the death of Donatus, and was endeavoring to spread abroad the erroneous doctrine of his predecessor, by means of a verbose but fascinating work, now lost. After a pleasing introduction, St. Optatus gives first an account of the origin and history of the Donatist sect, and then proves that the Catholic

Church alone has the marks of the true Church. The accusation of persecution he turns back upon the Donatists, and confutes their assertion, that sacraments administered by sinners (Catholics) are invalid. He next treats of the sacrament of baptism, and of the doctrine of the " opus operatum," and denounces the destruction of Catholic churches and the desecration of sacred vessels as impious outrages. The seventh book, which is regarded by some as unauthentic, is a supplement and partly a recapitulation of the preceding books, written with a view to reconcile those who had separated from the Church. The entire work is more of an eirenical than of a controversial character, and is prompted by the most ardent desire of reconciliation with the separated brethren.

3. The above work, though not very comprehensive, is yet quite important, both from a historical and dogmatical point of view. It gives short, clear, and accurate explanations of many fundamental doctrines of the Catholic faith, and contains very valuable ecclesiastical notices. His singular remark in the third book, " The State is not in the Church, but the Church in the State," is not to be taken as expressing a principle, but a fact, namely, the actual condition of things under Constantius and Julian. His style, though forcible and expressive, is not free from African harshness, and, on the whole, lacks polish. This, however, is no serious blemish.

St. Optatus is distinguished in the Roman Martyrology (June 4th), as " Episcopus doctrina et sanctitate conspicuus."

*Editions and Literature.* — *Migne*, S. lat. XI, 760–1506. — *Ziwsa* in Corp. script. eccl. lat. vol. XXVI.

Vindob. 1893. — *Ceillier* l. c. VI, 625–661. — *L. Duchesne*, Le dossier du Donatisme: Mélanges d'archéologie et d'histoire, tom. X. 1890.

§ 86. *Popes — St. Julius I. (d. 352), St. Damasus I. (d. 384), and St. Siricius (d. 398).*

I. *Julius*, a Roman by birth, was elected Pope on July 6th, 337, and died April 12th, 352. He had to guide the bark of Peter through a very tempestuous time, but did so with enlightened wisdom, admirable firmness, Apostolic zeal, and in the gentle spirit of the Gospel. He steadfastly upheld the cause of Athanasius against the Eusebians, held a Synod at Rome in 343, sent representatives to that of Sardica in 347, and of Milan in the same year, and adorned the city with several new basilicas. Of the letters ascribed to him, and still preserved, only two are authentic, namely, that to the Eusebians, and that to the people of Alexandria. The former is a valuable document, written with Apostolical dignity, power, and sweetness, and throws light upon the ecclesiastical condition of the times. The latter contains the Pope's heartfelt congratulation to the people of Alexandria on the return of their Patriarch, Athanasius, from exile, and on the fact that his innocence was at last recognized; and he assures them that Athanasius is worthy of every praise and of their continued affection.

II. *Damasus*, a Spaniard by descent, was born about 306. His early life was spent in the practice of piety and self-denial. He became Archdeacon of the Roman Church, and in 366 was raised, on the death of Pope Liberius, to the Chair of St. Peter, from which,

however, Ursinus, the Deacon, who had been chosen
by the opposite party, endeavored to oust him.    His
pontificate was greatly harassed by the intrigues of
that antipope, but proved, nevertheless, very rich in
blessings for the Church.    Damasus not only enforced
a stricter observance of the laws of the Church, but
also held two synods at Rome for the suppression of
Arianism, strove to uproot the heresies of the Apollinarists, Semi-Arians, and Macedonians, and by his
confirmation raised the Council of Constantinople
(381) to the dignity of an Œcumenical Synod.    Being a patron of art and learning, he found an intimate
friend in St. Jerome, whom he often consulted and
urged, both by word of mouth and by letter, to under-
take the Latin translation of the Bible.    He died
Dec. 10th, 384.

Among his writings the following deserve mention : —

(1.) His *letters*, both private and synodal, which
however are only partially preserved ; (2.) his metrical
*epitaphs* (epitaphia, tituli), and (3.) his *poems* (carmina), some shorter ones on martyrs and Saints, and a
longer one on the conversion and martyrdom of St.
Paul.    These poems are not classical in style, but are
valuable as proofs of the simple and child-like piety
of this Pope, as well as of the practice of the veneration and invocation of Saints in his time.

III. *Siricius*, a Roman, distinguished for learning,
piety, and zeal for religion, ascended the papal chair in
384, energetically combated the Manichæans and Priscillianists, restored Church discipline, and insisted upon
the strenuous observance of celibacy.    He left several
letters.    Of the seven extant, the most important are
the epistle to Himerius, Bishop of Tarragona, and two

letters to the bishops of Africa and Gaul. The first contains an answer to 15 questions of Himerius; the two others concern the denunciation of Jovinian, Bonosus, and Priscillian, and treat of the rights, duties, and life of bishops, clerics, monks, and nuns, the administration of the sacraments, the punishment of disorderly clerics, and the like. He died Nov. 26th, 398.

*Editions and Literature.* — (To I.) — *Migne,* S. lat. VIII, 858-994. — *Ceillier* l. c. IV, 484-501. — (To II.) *Migne,* S. lat. XIII, 109-442. — *Ceillier* l. c. VI, 455-477. — *Rade,* Damasus, Bischof von Rom. Freiburg 1882. — *Kayser* l. c. I, 89-126. — *Carini,* Epigrafia e paleografia del Papa Damaso. Roma 1887. — *Storti,* S. Damaso e la Bibbia. Roma 1887. — (To III) *Migne,* S. lat. XIII, 1132-1196. — *Ceillier* l. c. VIII, 162-182.

## § 87. *St. Ambrose, Bishop of Milan* (*d. 397*).

1. *St. Ambrose* was probably born at Treves, about 340. After the early death of his father, he went, with his mother, his brother Satyrus, and his sister Marcellina, to Rome, where by the study of Latin and Greek classics, philosophy, and rhetoric, he acquired an education in every way befitting his high position. He then studied jurisprudence and became a distinguished lawyer. The Emperor Valentinian I. appointed him sub-prefect of Liguria and Æmilia (in 370) and after the death of the Arian bishop Auxentius, the people, as if by inspiration, acclaimed him Bishop of Milan, though he was as yet only a catechumen. Eight days after his baptism, he was consecrated (on Dec. 7th, 374). In order to acquire the necessary theological knowledge, he began at once to study the Greek Fathers of the Church, as well as the works of

Philo, the Jew. Moreover, he distributed all his goods to the poor, led a life of poverty and incessant labor, discharging the duties of the pastoral office with Apostolic zeal. Though meek and condescending to all, he was inflexible whenever the rights or doctrines of the Church were at stake. In spite of the imperial will, he steadily refused to make any concession to the Arians, or to give up churches to them. He made the Emperor Theodosius submit to canonical penance, because of the massacre at Thessalonica. Being zealous also for the beauty and dignity of the divine worship, he made important liturgical regulations for his diocese, which are still observed at Milan at the present day. Finally, he introduced a peculiar kind of ecclesiastical music, called the Ambrosian, or solid chant (cantus Ambrosianus, seu firmus). He ended his life, so full of successful labors, on April 4th, 397.

2. In spite of his laborious and troublesome episcopate, St. Ambrose found time for an extraordinary amount of literary work. His writings may be divided into dogmatical, exegetical, moral-ascetical, sermons and letters.

### A. *Dogmatical.*

(a.) " Libri V de fide sive de Trinitate " (378), in which he proves the divinity of Christ against the Arians, and expounds the doctrine of the Trinity.

(b.) " Libri III de Spiritu Sancto " (380), in which he teaches the consubstantiality of the Holy Ghost.

(c.) "Liber de incarnationis dominicæ sacramento," in 10 chapters, a complement of the preceding writings against Arians and Apollinarists.

(d.) "Liber de mysteriis scil. sacramentis," in 9 chapters, an instruction for the newly-baptized upon the sacraments of baptism, confirmation, and the holy Eucharist.

(e.) "Libri II de poenitentia," written about 384, against the Novatians, and containing important testimonies on the power of the Church to remit sin, the necessity of confession, and the meritoriousness of good works.

(f.) "Libri II de excessu sive obitu fratris Satyri," the first book of which is a panegyric on the virtues of his brother Satyrus, while the second furnishes proof for the consoling doctrine of the resurrection.

### B. *Exegetical.*

(a.) "Hexaëmeron," in 6 books, almost entirely drawn from St. Basil, with additions from Origen; — "Enarrationes in Psalmos Davidis," viz.: I, XXXV— XL, XLIII, XLV, XLVII, XLVIII, LXI; — "Expositio in Psalmum CXVIII," in 22 excellent discourses; — "Expositio Evangelii sec. Lucam," in ten books.

(b.) Commentaries on particular passages, persons or events, as "De paradiso," "De Cain et Abel," "Liber de arca et Noe," "De Abraham," "De Isaac et anima," "De bono mortis" (with proofs for the immortality of the soul), "De fuga saeculi," "De Jacob et vita beata," "De Joseph patriarcha," "De benedictionibus patriarcharum" (the blessing of Jacob upon his sons), "De Elia et jejunio" (praise of fasting, mostly taken from Basil), "De Nabuthe Jezraelita" (against oppressors of the poor), "De Tobia" (containing the strongest denunciation of usury), "De interpellatione Job et David" (a discourse on the complaints of Job and David about the prosperity of the wicked and the misfortunes of the virtuous), and "Apologia prophetæ David ad Theodosium Augustum."

### C. *Moral and Ascetical.*

(1.) "Libri III de officiis ministrorum" (about 391), a counter-treatise to that of Cicero, and to pagan morality, with beautiful words of admonition to clerics.

(2.) "Libri III de virginibus ad Marcellinam (sororem suam)," on the dignity and nobility of virginity, and a supplement, "De virginitate," in 20 chapters.

(3.) "Liber de viduis," in 15 chapters, a recommendation of widowhood.

(4.) "Liber de institutione virginis sive de S. Mariæ virginitate perpetua," in 17 chapters, against Bonosus, who denied the perpetual virginity of the Blessed Virgin.

(5.) "Exhortatio virginitatis," in 14 chapters.

### D. *Sermons.*

The most noteworthy are: —

"Sermo contra Auxentium de basilicis tradendis;" "Sermo in translatione reliquiarum SS. Gervasii et Protasii;" "Consolatio de obitu Valentiniani;" "Oratio de obitu Theodosii." The last two are regarded as models of rhetoric.

### E. *Letters.*

There are 91 extant. They treat of subjects historical, dogmatical, moral, and Biblical, or are letters of friendship. They reveal the nobility of his character, his Christian zeal, piety, education, and learning, as well as his high authority.

### F. *Hymns*.

Of the many hymns ascribed to St. Ambrose, there are, according to the researches of Dreves, only 14 authentic; according to Kayser and Ihms, only 4, viz., " Deus creator omnium ; " " Aeterne rerum conditor ; " " Veni redemptor omnium," and " Jam surgit hora tertia."

The so-called Ambrosian Hymn, " Te Deum laudamus," was not composed either by St. Ambrose or St. Augustine, but has probably Nicetas, Bishop of Remesiana, for its author.*

The following works are more or less doubtful: " Altera apologia Davidis ; " " De sacramentis ; " " De lapsu virginis consecratæ ; " " Lex Dei sive mosaicarum et romanarum legum collatio ; " " Commentaria in epistolas beati Pauli " (Ambrosiaster), and " De excidio urbis Hierosolymitanæ." Many of his writings are lost ; many others ascribed to him are spurious.

3. Whereas in the treatment of dogmatic subjects, he follows closely in the wake of the Greek Doctors, especially St. Athanasius and St. Basil, in dealing with ethical subjects St. Ambrose uses his own independent judgment. In his book " De officiis," he shows how vastly superior is Christian morality over pagan, and how every state of life, especially the priestly, finds its pattern in the Gospel.

In his exegetical writings, the allegorical method prevails ; often it exceeds the due measure and

---

* See Revue Bénédictine, 1894, pp. 49–77.

degenerates into mere trifling. Nevertheless, even here we may find traces of that eloquence which shines forth chiefly in his sermons. His discourses are animated by genuine conviction and enthusiasm, his tone is winning and his expression agreeable, but at times indefinite and obscure. St. Ambrose greatly resembles St. Basil in his ideas of Church government, his love of learning, zeal for divine worship, and encouragement of monasticism, as also in his large-minded charity and severe asceticism. He kept up both official and friendly intercourse with nearly all the bishops of the East and West. St. Augustine, whose conversion was greatly owing to the power and unction of St. Ambrose's words, regards him as "Homo Dei catholicus et catholicæ veritatis adversus hæreticos usque ad periculum sanguinis defensor acerrimus" (Lib. de cura pro mort. ger. c. 17), and he further says of him : "Ejus pro catholica fide gratiam, constantiam, labores, pericula sive operibus, sive sermonibus, et ipse sum expertus, et mecum non dubitat prædicare orbis Romanus" (Lib. II contra Julian. c. 5).

*Editions and Literature.* — *Migne*, S. lat. XV–XVII. — *Ceillier* l. c. VII, 329–693. — *Hermant*, Vie de S. Ambroise. Paris 1678. — *Baunard*, Geschichte des hl. Ambrosius. Freiburg 1873. — *Locatelli*, Vita di S. Ambrogio. Milano 1875. — *Kayser* l. c. I, 127 sq., 435 sq. — *Förster*, Ambrosius, sein Leben und Wirken. Halle 1884. — *Kellner*, Der hl. Ambrosius als Erklärer des Alten Testamentes. Regensburg 1893. — *Dreves*, S. J., Ambrosius, "der Vater des Kirchengesanges." Freiburg 1893.

### § 88. *Rufinus, Presbyter of Aquileia* (*d. 410*).

1. *Tyrannius Rufinus* was born about 345 in the vicinity of Aquileia, and baptized in that town in 370. Here later, began his more intimate friendship with St. Jerome, whom he had known before. When the latter set out for the Orient (in 372), Rufinus, with the "elder" Melania, journeyed to Egypt, whither he felt attracted by the life of the hermits of the Nitrian desert, as well as by the lectures of Didymus, the Blind, of Alexandria. Six years later, he visited Palestine and was ordained priest in 390 by Bishop John of Jerusalem, who, like himself, was a warm admirer of Origen. In the dispute that arose between St. Epiphanius and John concerning Origen, Rufinus sided with the latter, while Jerome took the part of the former. On his return to his own country, in 398, Rufinus, while staying in Rome, translated Origen's work "$\Pi\epsilon\rho\grave{\iota}$ $\grave{\alpha}\rho\chi\tilde{\omega}\nu$" as well as the apology for him composed by Pamphilus and Eusebius. In this translation, Rufinus omitted or softened down much that was objectionable, but not enough. Moreover, by the encomiums bestowed upon Origen, he gave offense and provoked a painful controversy with St. Jerome, the friend of his early years. Being cited before Pope Anastasius I., Rufinus was able to escape excommunication only by making an orthodox profession of faith. From that time forward, he spent many years in Aquileia, engaged in literary labors and practices of piety, till the invasion of the Goths, about 408, obliged him once more to leave this city and to withdraw to the island of Sicily, where death overtook him in 410.

2. The works of Rufinus consist, for the most part, of translations — often very arbitrary — from Greek

books, such as those of Josephus Flavius, Origen, St. Basil, St. Gregory Nazianzen, Eusebius' Church History, etc.

The following are his own independent works: —

(a.) "Apologia adversus Hieronymum," in 2 books, a somewhat bitter self-defense, to which Jerome returned a sharp answer in 3 books.

(b.) "Apologia ad Anastasium Rom. urbis episcopum pro fide sua."

(c.) "De benedictionibus patriarcharum," in 2 books, an exposition of chapter xlix of Genesis, according to the historical, moral, and mystical sense.

(d.) "Expositio Symboli seu Commentarius in Symbolum Apostolorum," the best work of Rufinus, and one that testifies to his profound erudition, and is important for the history of dogma.

(e.) "Historia monachorum sive liber de vitis Patrum," the lives of 30 pious solitaries of the desert of Nitria, written in an attractive manner.

(f.) "Dissertatio de adulteratione librorum Origenis, sive epilogus in Apologeticum Pamphili."

(g.) "Historiæ eccl. libri duo," a very arbitrary translation of the Church History of Eusebius, and continuation of the same till the death of the Emperor Theodosius.

3. Rufinus was pious, learned, and an admirer of the monastic life. By means of his translations, he opened to the West the rich treasures of Eastern literature, and preserved to posterity many a writing of which the original text is lost. His constant aim at elegant writing, however, and his endeavor to save the orthodoxy of Origen, often led him to make arbitrary alterations and to take other liberties with his authors. Gennadius gives him this flattering testi-

mony: "Rufinus non minima pars fuit doctorum Ecclesiæ, et in transferendo de Græco in Latinum elegans ingenium habuit" (De script. eccl. c. XVII).

*Editions and Literature.* — *Migne*, S. lat. XXI. [His translations from the Greek are not in this volume, but must be sought in the works of the respective authors.] — *Ceillier* l. c. X, 1–65.

## § 89. *St. Jerome* (*d. 420*).

1. *Sophronius Eusebius Hieronymus* was born at Stridon, in Dalmatia, probably in the year 331, of highly respectable Christian parents, who gave him a sound though somewhat severe home education. For his literary training he went to Rome, where he had Donatus and Victorinus for masters in grammar and rhetoric. Here, also, he was baptized by Pope Liberius about 364, but had not strength enough, as he himself sorrowfully confesses, amidst the dangers of the great capital of the world, to preserve "the garment of Christ and of innocence" in its original spotlessness, but stained it on the "slippery path of youth." His theological studies he began at Treves and continued at Aquileia, where he enjoyed the company and intercourse of other distinguished men, as Rufinus, Nicetas, Chrysogonus, and others. In 372 he resolved to make his first journey to the East with some of his friends and companions. At Antioch he found the then celebrated interpreter of Holy Scripture, Apollinaris, whose school he frequented for a time. After recovery from a severe illness, Jerome retired from Antioch into the desert of Chalcis, where, under the direction of Malchus, a pious hermit, he led for the space of five years a life of rigorous asceticism, relieved

by literary work and the study of the Hebrew language. At the end of that period he returned once more to Antioch, where, in the midst of the Meletian troubles, and, as it appears, against his own will, he was raised to the priesthood about the year 379. A year later he went to Constantinople, in order to hear Gregory Nazianzen and to learn his method of interpreting the Sacred Scriptures. In 382 Pope Damasus called him to Rome to assist at a synod, convened for the purpose of ending the Meletian schism. During his two years' stay at Rome, he devoted his time and talent to the study of Holy Scripture.

At the special request of Pope Damasus, he began the great work of preparing a trustworthy Latin text of the Bible. By his lectures on Scripture interpretation he drew around him a large circle of enthusiastic pupils and friends, both men and women, among them the two widows, Marcella and Paula. His popularity, however, especially with the learned and devout female sex, created for him many enemies, who cast ridicule upon his conduct and spread abroad unworthy suspicions. After the death of Pope Damasus (in 384), he left Rome and went for the second time to the East, visiting the most celebrated places of Palestine for the benefit of his Biblical studies. Passing through Egypt, he listened to Didymus, the Blind, at Alexandria, and visited the monasteries in the Nitrian mountains. In 386 he returned to the Holy Land and established his permanent abode at Bethlehem, where he founded a monastery for men and another for women. There he passed his time in practices of piety, in Biblical studies, especially in completing his translation of the Bible, and lecturing on theological subjects. He also took an active part in the religious disputes of the day, especially the Pelagian and Origenistic controversies. He died in 420, and his body, at a later period, was taken to Rome.

2. The works of St. Jerome are as follows: —

## A. *Exegetical.*

(1.) " Bibliotheca divina," a name given to his Latin translation of the Old and New Testament, the result of fourteen years of painstaking labor, and, in spite of many inaccuracies, the best among all the old translations preserved to us.[*]

(2.) " Liber de nominibus hebraicis seu de interpretatione nominum hebraicorum," an improved translation of a similar work by Philo, the Jew, on proper names of the Old and New Testament.

(3.) " Liber de situ et nominibus locorum hebraicorum," a new and amended edition of a similar work by Eusebius, with corrections based upon his own experience.

(4.) " Liber hebraicarum quæstionum in Genesin," annotations to particular difficult passages in Genesis.

(5.) Some 70 Homilies, translated from the Greek of Origen.

(6.) His Commentaries on Ecclesiastes; all the Prophets (Jeremias only half); Gospel of St. Matthew; the Epistles of St. Paul to the Galatians, Ephesians, Titus and Philemon.

---

[*] The most important extant Ms. of this translation is the Codex Amiatinus in the Bibliotheca Laurentiana of Florence, written in England between 690–716, and offered to the Holy See by Abbott Ceolfrid. — See J. B. *de Rossi*, La Bibbia offerta da Ceolfrido Abbate al Sepolcro di S. Pietro. Roma 1887. 2°. [R.]

These Commentaries, in which the literal interpretation chiefly prevails, though not always free from shallowness, form a rich mine of important exegetical matter.

### B. *Controversial.*

(1.) " Apologia adversus Rufinum," in three books, and written in a style that betrays bitterness of feeling and personal irritation.

(2.) " Dialogus contra Luciferianos," who refused to communicate with those that fell away in the Arian persecutions.

(3.) " Liber adversus Helvidium " (about 383), in defense of the perpetual virginity of Our Lady, a book full of moral indignation.

(4.) " Libri duo adversus Jovinianum " (about 392), with the same object as the preceding.

(5.) " Liber contra Vigilantium " (about 406), a vehement and passionate defense of the veneration of martyrs and relics, of the poverty of monks, and the celibacy of clerics.

(6.) " Dialogus contra Pelagianos " (about 415), in three books, showing forth the necessity of grace, and how, without it, it is impossible for us to live free from sin.

(7.) " Liber contra Joannem Hierosolymitanum " (about 399), similar in style to his Apology against Rufinus.

### C. *Historical.*

(1.) " Chronicon Eusebii," a Latin translation of the Chronicle of Eusebius, with corrections and additions chiefly from Suetonius and Eutropius, and a continuation from 325 to 378.

(2.) " Liber de viris illustribus seu catalogus de

scriptoribus ecclesiasticis," one of the greatest and most learned monuments of antiquity, written for the purpose of meeting the objection of scoffing heathens, that Christianity was but the religion of the uneducated.

(3.) "Vita S. Pauli Eremitæ, S. Hilarionis et S. Malchi."

### D. *Letters.*

There have been preserved to us 116 letters of the Saint, treating of different subjects. Some are exegetical, or dogmatical, or moral and ascetical, while others are historical or merely letters of consolation and friendship. Most of them excite our interest and admiration, not only by their contents, but also by the classical form of language in which they are written. Many writings ascribed to him are spurious (see Migne XXX.), and some genuine ones have been lost. The "Commentarioli in Psalmos," supposed to be lost, have recently been edited by P. Morin, O. S. B. (4°. Maredsoli et Oxoniæ 1895).

3. St. Jerome was a man of iron energy, who never shrank from any difficulty. He is undoubtedly the most learned among the Western Fathers, and his writings, for variety and importance, stand pre-eminent in patristic literature.

Although his labors turned chiefly upon critical and exegetical questions, St. Jerome was yet not a mere student. With a holy zeal, which was the mainspring of all his work, he ever sought to instruct men in the duties of a Christian life, to exhort them to perfection, to console the afflicted, to assist virtue, to reprove vice, and to banish abuses. Unfortunately the impetuosity of his zeal carried him at times to the verge of passion, and his asceticism may seem to many too excessive or too external. But even these faults, if faults they were, must be attributed to his overflowing love of God and of His holy Church on earth. For the rest, the student of St. Jerome's works will not find it difficult to rectify some of the more extreme statements of the Saint, made in the heat of controversy, by other more sober and more accurate passages. For instance, when he says that a priest is the same as a bishop, "idem est presbyter quod et episcopus;" or again, What can a bishop do, except ordination, that a priest cannot do likewise: "Quid enim facit excepta ordinatione episcopus, quod presbyter non faciat?" His knowledge of Biblical languages has no parallel in Christian antiquity. As a writer, he well knew how to adapt the form to the matter; his style is forcible and dignified, short and clear, pure and trenchant. He knew how to render clear the obscure, how to touch the heart, and to draw his pictures to life. In his Biblical commentaries, the style is very simple, and often dry, but in some of his earlier and more hastily written works, it is pompous and verbose, and lacking in finish. Nevertheless, in point of style, he is the best author of his time and well deserves to share with Lactantius the name of the Christian Cicero. His characteristic qualities have been well summarized in St. Prosper's "Carmen de ingratis" (I, 55-60):—

> Tunc etiam Bethlemi præclari nominis hospes,
> Hebræo simul et Graio, Latioque venustus
> Eloquio, morum exemplum, mundique magister,
> Hieronymus, libris valde excellentibus hostem
> Dissecuit; noscique dedit, quo turbine veram
> Vellent exortæ lucem obscurare tenebræ.

*Editions and Literature.* — *Migne*, S. lat. XXII–
XXX. (reprint of Dom. Vallarsi, Venice 1768–1772,
with additions). — *Ceillier* l. c. X., 172–463. — *Col-
lombet*, Histoire de S. Jérome, sa vie, ses écrits et ses
doctrines. 2 vols. Paris 1844. — *Thierry*, S. Jérome,
la société chrétienne à Rome, et l'émigration romaine
en Terre-Sainte. 2 vols. 3e éd. Paris 1876. — *Zöck-
ler*, Hieronymus, sein Leben und Wirken. Gotha
1865. — A great number of St. Jerome's writings are
translated into English by *W. H. Fremantle*, in the
"Select Library of the Nicene and Post-Nicene
Fathers of the Christian Church," series 2, vol. VI.
New York 1893. — *E. L. Cutts*, St. Jerome. London
1878. 8$^{vo}$ (Fathers for English Readers). — *C. Martin*, Life of St. Jerome. London 1888. 8$^{vo}$.

### § 90. *St. Augustine, Bishop of Hippo (d. 430).*

1. *Aurelius Augustinus* was born at Tagaste in
Numidia on November 13th, 354. On him nature had
lavished her choicest gifts. He possessed a keen and
penetrating mind, great depth of soul, and a rich and
glowing imagination. Patricius, his father, was a
heathen nobleman, who became a Christian in his old
age and was baptized, but Monica, his mother,
was always a Christian. Under her immediate care
Augustine began his first studies in his native town
and at Carthage. But neither the watchfulness of his
pious mother nor the natural nobility of his own soul
were able to prevent him from being drawn into the
errors and dissolute habits common to the youths of
those days. He fell into the hands of the Manichees,
and readily imbibed their pernicious doctrines, which
he continued to hold and successfully propagate for

the space of nine years.    Yet all this time his soul was
deeply agitated, seeking for rest and finding it nowhere.
On the one hand the prevailing systems of philosophy
gave him no satisfaction, while on the other the Sacred
Scriptures and the Christian faith seemed tasteless and
repulsive to a soul swayed by sensuality and ambition.
At last he broke away from the sect of the Manichees,
but only to throw himself into the arms of the skeptics
of the Academy.    In the year 383, he went to Rome
to teach grammar and rhetoric, as he had done before
at Tagaste and Carthage, and a year later to Milan,
whither his mother and some companions followed
him.    Here from mere love of rhetoric he diligently
attended the sermons of St. Ambrose.    These, together
with the entreaties of his mother, and the earnest con-
versation with his friends, at last opened his heart to
the power of divine truth and grace.    He finally
renounced his career as a teacher of rhetoric, and
retired, about 386, with his mother and some friends
to a lonely villa ; where in the full enjoyment of a most
blessed peace of soul, he prepared himself by spiritual
entertainments and pious exercises for baptism, which,
together with his son Adeodatus and his friend Aly-
pius, he received at the hands of St. Ambrose, on the
eve of Easter 387.    He next desired to return with
his mother to Africa, but as she died at Ostia, he
resolved upon staying another year in Rome.    In 388,
however, he returned to his native country, where he
distributed his patrimony to the poor and retired to a
small country property near Tagaste, where he lived
like a monk, devoting his time to exercises of piety
and literary work.    Being accidentally at Hippo,
about 390, the people demanded that he should
be raised to the priesthood.    Angustine declined ;

but Bishop Valerius, overruling all his objections, decided to ordain him there and then. At the death of Valerius, Augustine succeeded him in the see of Hippo. His episcopate was one of untiring labors in every direction. He gave his time to incessant study, prayer, preaching, diocesan administration; he devoted the church revenues to the support of the clergy, the building of churches, relief of the poor, and led in his own house a community life with his clergy. By his letters and writings he exerted a powerful influence far and wide. The cause of the Church and of the orthodox faith found in him an ever ready champion. He refuted the errors of pagan religion and philosophy, the heresies of the Manicheans, Arians, Pelagians, and Donatists, and in the celebrated Colloquium at Carthage (411), at which 286 Catholic and 279 Donatist bishops assisted, he successfully ended the schism of the latter sect which had lasted a hundred years.

Augustine died on the 28th of August, 430, three months after the Vandals had begun to lay siege to the city. His body, the shroud of a mighty spirit, rests at Pavia.

2. His literary labors were simply astounding. His numerous and extensive writings embrace every department of philosophy and theology. Besides these, there are two which may be classed as introductory to all the rest.

### A. *Introductory.*

(1.) " Retractationes," in two books, written towards the end of his life (about 427), containing a revision of all his previous works, with many corrections and explanatory additions.

(2.) " Confessiones," in thirteen books, written

about 400, a most touching autobiography, interspersed with continuous religious reflections, wherein he describes the vicissitudes, errors, and struggles of his life, and the final victory of God's grace, which he never wearies of praising.

### B. *Philosophical.*

(1.) "Contra Academicos," in three books, written about 386, against those who held that it is impossible to know the truth.

(2.) "De vita beata," in four chapters, an eloquent and beautifully written treatise upon the thesis that a happy life consists in the knowledge of God alone: "Beatam vitam nonnisi in Dei cognitione consistere."

(3.) "De ordine," two books on the divine order and government of the world, in its relation to the existence of evil.

(4.) "Soliloquia," two books on the acquisition of truth concerning ourselves, God, the immortality of the soul, etc.

(5.) "De immortalitate animæ," the soul, being made for God, is immortal.

(6.) "De quantitate animæ," on the origin, immateriality, and nobility of the soul.

(7.) "De Magistro;" Christ, the only perfect teacher of mankind; an explanation of St. Matthew xxiii, 10.

(8.) "De musica," six books on music in general, meter, prosody, and rhythm. Music and poetry are means to raise the mind to God, the source of all art, all truth and beauty; but they are not an end in themselves.

(9.) "De dialectica, rhetorica, geometria, arithmetica, et philosophia;" these are unfinished.

## C. *Dogmatical.*

(1.) "De vera religione," a kind of philosophy of religion (written about 390), showing that true religion is not to be found with philosophers or heretics, but only in the Catholic Church; the way that leads to it is authority and reason.

(2.) "De fide et symbolo" (about 393), an explanation of the Apostles' Creed, for the instruction and confirmation of the newly baptized.

(3.) "De fide rerum quæ non videntur" (about 399); on the reasonableness and necessity of faith in revealed truth.

(4.) "Enchiridion ad Laurentium, sive de fide, spe et caritate" (about 421), an admirable abridgment of the Christian doctrine, and a truly golden work — "opus vere aureum."

(5.) "De agone christiano" (about 396), on how to overcome evil and preserve the faith.

(6.) "Liber de fide et operibus" (about 413), a refutation of the assertion that faith without works suffices for salvation.

(7.) "De Trinitate," in fifteen books (written between 400 and 416), a speculative dogmatical vindication of the doctrine of the Trinity, based upon Holy Scripture, Creation, and the nature of man.

(8.) "De civitate Dei," in twenty-two books (written between 413 and 427). This is the most finished work of the Saint, distinguished alike by richness and variety of matter, vastness of conception, and systematic manner of treatment. It consists of two parts, an apologetical-polemical (books I–X), and a dogmatical-philosophical (books XI–XXII). In the first he shows the groundlessness of the heathen complaints, that Christianity was the cause of the downfall of the Roman Empire, and exposes the inanity and impotency of the pagan religion and philosophy. In the second he treats of the kingdom of God in its world-embracing character, of its origin, growth, and consummation, at the same time giving a complete summary of the Christian doctrine.

### D. *Polemical.*

(a.) "De hæresibus ad Quodvultdeum" (about 429), a pithy and telling sketch, in eighty-eight chapters, of the heresies from Simon Magus to Pelagius.

(b.) Against the Manicheans: (1.) "De moribus ecclesiæ catholicæ et de moribus Manichæorum" (about 388), in two books, containing the best representation of his system of moral theology; (2.) "De utilitate credendi" (about 391), a treatise on the nature and authority of the Church; (3.) "De duabus animabus" (about 390); (4.) "De libero arbitrio," in three books; (5.) "De Genesi contra Manichæos," in two books (about 389); (6.) "Contra Faustum Manichæum," in thirty-three books (about 404); (7.) "Contra Adimantum Manichæi discipulum" (394); (8.) "Liber contra epistolam Manichæi, quam dicunt fundamenti" (about 396 or 397); (9.) "Acta seu disputatio contra Fortunatum Manichæum;" (10.) "De actis cum Felice Manichæo" (about 404) in two books; (11.) "Liber contra Secundinum" (about 405), which is the best work against the Manicheans, and gives the reasons why he abandoned the sect.

In all these works St. Augustine strives to combat the fundamental errors of the Manicheans, their doctrine of two principles (Dualism), the existence of two souls, the denial of human liberty. His explanations of the liberty of the human will are very acute.

(c.) Against the Donatists: (1.) "Psalmus contra partem Donati," written in verse (about 393), also called "Abecedarius;" (2.) "Contra Parmeniani epistolam," in three books (about 400); (3.) "De baptismo contra Donatistas," in seven books; (4.) "Contra litteras Petiliani," in three books (about 400-402); (5.) "Contra Cresconium grammaticum partis Donati," in four books (about 406); (6.) "Liber de unico baptismo contra Petilianum" (about 406-410); (7.) "Epistola ad catholicos sive de unitate ecclesiæ" (about 402); (8.) "Breviculus (liber) collationis cum Donatistis, Carthagine a. 411 habitæ;" (9.) "Liber ad Donatistas post collationem;" (10.) "Liber de gestis cum Emerito, Cæsariensi Donatistarum episcopo;" (11.) "Contra Gaudentium, Donatistarum episcopum," in two books (about 420).

In these and other writings not mentioned here, the Saint gives a thorough refutation of the chief errors of the Donatists, concerning the Church, baptism, the power of the keys, the relation of the civil power to freedom of worship and liberty of conscience, and other points.

(d.) Against the Pelagians: (1.) "De anima et ejus origine," in four books (about 419-420); (2.) "De peccatorum meritis et remissione sive de baptismo parvulorum ad Marcellinum," in three books (about 412); (3.) "De spiritu et littera ad Marcellinum, i. e., de lege et gratia," about the same time; (4.) "De natura et gratia" (about 415); (5.) "Epistola ad Eutropium et Paulum episcopos de perfectione justitiæ hominis" (about 415); (6.) "De

gestis Pelagii ad Aurelium " (about 417); (7.) "De
gratia Christi et de peccato originali," in two books
(about 418); (8.) "De nuptiis et concupiscentia,"
in two books (about 419); (9.) " Contra duas epistolas Pelagianorum," in four books (about 420);
(10.) "Contra Julianum Pelagianum," in six books
(about 421); (11.) "Opus imperfectum contra Julianum," in six books (about 428), a thorough refutation of Pelagianism, as well as a brilliant vindication
of the Catholic doctrine; (12.) " Liber de gratia et
libero arbitrio, ad monachos Adrumetinos " (about
427); (13.) "De correptione et gratia," about the
same time; (14.) "De prædestinatione sanctorum"
and (15.) "De dono perseverantiæ ; " these last two
books, written towards the end of his life, are a further explanation of the previous book, " De correptione et gratia."

(e.) Against the Arians: (1.) "Liber contra
sermonem Arianorum," a criticism on the Arian doctrines, of which an anonymous synopsis had been sent
to him (about 418); (2.) " Collatio cum Maximino,
Arianorum episcopo," and (3.) " Libri duo contra
Maximinum Arianorum episcopum," containing a
report of his public disputations with Maximinus at
Hippo, about 427 or 428, and a full answer to the
contentions of the Arian Bishop.

(f.) Other Controversial Writings: (1.) "De
divinatione dæmonum," explaining the difference
between the predictions of demons and those of the
prophets ; (2.) " Liber ad Orosium contra Priscillian-
istas et Origenistas; (3.) "Tractatus adversus Judæos," showing that the Jews had been justly rejected
by God.

### E. *Exegetical.*

His principal exegetical works are : —

(a.) " De doctrina christiana," in four books
(about 397), an excellent introduction to the study
and use of Holy Scripture, both from a hermeneutical
and homiletical point of view.

(b.) Commentaries to the Old Testament: (1.)
" De Genesi ad literam liber imperfectus " (about
393); (2.) " De Genesi ad literam," in twelve books
(from 401–415), much better than the preceding work;
(3.) "Locutionum et quæstionum in Heptateuchum
libri VII," i. e. five books of Moses, Josue, and Judges
(about 419), an explanation of Biblical expressions
and passages; (4.) " Enarrationes in psalmos," chiefly
in form of allocutions to the people.

(c.) Commentaries to the New Testament: (1.)
" De consensu Evangelistarum," in four books (about
400), a painstaking work written with a view to clear-
ing up alleged contradictions in the Gospels; (2.)
" Quæstiones evangelicæ," in two books (about
400), on passages from St. Matthew and St. Luke;
(3.) " De sermone Domini in monte secundum
Matthæum," in two books (about 393), containing
well-nigh the entire doctrine of Christian morals; (4.)
"Tractatus 124 in Joannem," and ten Homilies " in
Epist. I. Joannis " (about 416); (5.) " Expositio
quarundam (84) propositionum ex Ep. ad Rom."
(about 394), but not quite correct; (6.) " Expositio
inchoata epistolæ ad Rom. ; " (7.) " Expositio ep. ad
Galatas " (about 394).

### F. *Moral, Ascetical, Practical.*

(1.) " Speculum," beginning with the words " Quis

ignorat," a collection of moral sentences from Holy Scripture (about A. D. 428).

(2.) " Liber de mendacio" (about 394) and " Contra mendacium " (about 420). In both writings he shows that it is never lawful to tell a lie; the latter work is especially directed against the Priscillianists, who held that an external denial of the faith was lawful.

(3.) " Liber de patientia " (about 418), showing that true patience is the fruit of grace.

(4.) " Liber de continentia " (about 395), an exhortation to continency, a gift of God which we can only preserve by continuous struggle and humble prayer.

(5.) "Liber de bono conjugali " (about 400), on the honesty, unity, and indissolubility of marriage.

(6.) " Liber de s. virginitate," and " Liber de bono viduitatis," showing the superiority of the state of virginity and widowhood over that of marriage.

(7.) "De adulterinis conjugiis," in two books (about 419), showing that husbands or wives who have separated cannot marry again, because of the absolute indissolubility of Christian marriage.

(8.) " Liber de opere monachorum " (about 400), on the duty of labor for monks.

(9.) " De cura pro mortuis gerenda " (about 421), inculcating the necessity of giving honorable burial to the dead, and of succoring them by prayer, almsdeeds, and the Holy Sacrifice of Mass.

(10.) " Liber de catechizandis rudibus " (about 400), a method of instructing catechumens in the Christian doctrine.

## G. *Sermons, Letters, Answers.*

A great number of the Saint's sermons are preserved to us. They are divided into four classes: (1.) "Sermones de scripturis," dealing with passages, facts, and persons of both Testaments; (2.) "Sermones de tempore," on the ecclesiastical feasts; (3.) "Sermones de sanctis," panegyrics on the virtues of the Saints and exhortations to imitation; (4.) "Sermones de diversis," on various occasions.

His numerous letters, some of which form regular scientific treatises, are most important, and deal either with matters dogmatical, polemical, and moral, or are letters of sympathy and friendship.

Besides these, there are extant a great many answers to diverse questions on philosophy, dogma or Scripture. Not a few of his writings have been lost, and many have been ascribed to him which are either doubtful or spurious.

3. St. Augustine is undoubtedly one of the greatest bishops of ancient times, and one of the greatest Doctors of all times. St. Jerome, though more learned, lacked somewhat of the acuteness, originality, and creative power of mind so conspicuous in St. Augustine. Every question of philosophy or theology that agitated his time, Augustine included in the circle of his studies and investigations. But nowhere did his philosophical mind show to better advantage than in the speculative grasp of the dogmas of the Church, especially those of Christian anthropology and soteriology, or on such questions as the relation between God and man, the estrangement by sin, the reconciliation by grace. In all his speculations, faith leads the way, reason follows. The truths of faith must needs be in

accordance with the light of reason, and it is our duty
to show forth this agreement. "Ea, quæ fidei firmi-
tate jam tenes, etiam rationis luce conspicias." *

His thoroughly Catholic mind and principles find
expression in the well-known dicta on the authority of
the Church and the Roman See: "Evangelio non
crederem, nisi me commoveret Ecclesiæ auctoritas." †
And again, speaking of the Pelagian controversy:
"Jam de hac causa duo concilia missa sunt ad Sedem
Apostolicam; *inde rescripta venerunt, causa finita est;*
utinam aliquando et error finiatur." ‡   There have
been those who drew from his works the doctrine that
the natural man in his fallen condition has only the
liberty to sin and not to do good.   But this conclusion
is utterly wrong.  In his book "De civ. Dei," II, 19, he
expressly teaches that fallen man is able to perform acts
of natural virtue, but that he lacks the power of act-
ing supernaturally and meritoriously, because he does
not act from motives of faith.   If in speaking against
the Pelagians he strongly insists upon the irresisti-
bility of grace, we must remember that, against the
Manicheans, he, with equal force, insists upon the
liberty of the human will.   Divine grace works in us,
both with our co-operation and without it; disposing
and preparing the will to good resolves, and assisting
it in carrying them out.   "Quia *præparatur voluntas*
a Domino, ab illo petendum est, ut tantum velimus,
quantum sufficit, ut volendo faciamus.  Certum est
*nos velle,* cum volumus.  Sed ille facit, ut velimus
bonum." §   And as to will or not to will is the work

---

* Ep. 120 ad Consent. — Cf. de ordine, II. n. 26.

† Contra Ep. Manichæi c. 5.

‡ Sermo 131, n. 10.

§ De grat. et lib. arb. c. 16, n. 32.

of our own free will, so to consent or not consent to divine grace is likewise a free act of our will. " Consentire vocationi Dei vel ab ea discedere, propriæ voluntatis est." * It is the willing man whom God justifies, but still God's action comes in the first place, lest we should think it our own justice. " Quia ergo fecit te sine te, non te justificat sine te; ergo fecit nescientem, *justificat volentem*. Tamen ipse justificat, ne sit justitia tua." †

Those sentences wherein St. Augustine seems to affirm an absolute and unconditional predestination, may be harmonized with opposite statements, by considering the particular scope and occasion of the writings in which those statements are found, as well as by his general system of doctrine and the practical work of his life. His moral system culminates in the following propositions: The end of man is the beatific union with God. The only means of this union is charity, or supernatural love of God, which is the source of a virtuous life (in the present order of Providence). As regards Biblical exegesis, Augustine adopts partly the grammatical-historical, partly the allegorical-mystical interpretation; the former especially in his scientific commentaries, the latter in his popular homilies. He considers the first and surest rule of interpretation on the one hand the living faith of the Church; on the other, the two immortal truths: (1) that all Scripture is inspired, and (2) that there can be neither error nor falsehood in it. On these truths he insists at every opportunity. Apparent contradictions, he says, are due either to a faulty codex, or to an error of the

---

* Ibid., n. 5. † Serm. 169, n. 13.

translator, or to the defective knowledge of the reader.

Augustine was equally great as a *preacher*. His sermons, though lacking the eloquence of Chrysostom, are yet distinguished by pregnancy of expression, clever antithesis, severe logic, unadorned simplicity, and above all by inexhaustible richness and depth of thought and feeling. His character was a wonderful mixture of mind and heart, whence his tendency to mystic as well as to dialectical theology. His language gives proof of his inner force and energy, originality and vigor, but lacks at times ease and symmetry of style, and even purity of expression; often it is surcharged with a play on words, far-fetched allegories and artificial metaphors. St. Paulinus speaks of his writings in the following enthusiastic terms: "Hos igitur libros (Augustini) lectioni habeo, in his me oblecto, in his cibum capio, non illum qui perit, sed qui operatur vitæ æternæ substantiam. . . . O vere sal terræ, quo præcordia nostra, ne possint sæculi vanescere errore, condiuntur." (Ep. IV, 1.)

*Editions and Literature.* — *Migne*, S. lat. tom. XXXII–XLVI, 1845–1849, which edition was preceded by that of the brothers Gaume, 11 vols. Paris 1836–1839, both being reprints of the "Editio Maurina," 1679–1700. — Many of his works have been separately edited and also translated into modern languages. — *Weihrich*, S. Augustini Speculum, Vindob. 1887, in Corp. script. eccl. lat. vol. XII. — *Zycha*, De util. cred., ibid. vol. XXV. Vindob. 1891. — *Dombart*, De civ. Dei, 2 voll. 2 ed. Lips. 1877. — An English translation of select works of St. Augustine by *Clark*, Edinburgh 1871. — *Ph. Schaff*, Select Library of the Nicene and Post-Nic. Fathers of the Church

(Ser. I.) Buffalo 1886. — A new edition of the Confessions of St. Augustine (ten books), Oxford and London. James Parker and Co. 1876.— *M. H. Allies*, Leaves from St. Augustine, London 1886, 8ᵛᵒ. — The letters of St. Augustine (36 of them), by the same author. London 1890, 8ᵛᵒ. — The literature on St. Augustine and his doctrine is immense. — *Ceillier* l. c. XI, 1–754. — *Poujulat*, Histoire de St. Augustin, 3 vols. Paris 1846. — *Stöckl*, Geschichte der patrist. Philosophie, pp. 341–496. — *Bindemann*, Der heilige Augustinus. 3 Bde. Berlin 1864–1869. —*Rottmanner*, Der Augustinismus. München 1892. — *W. Cunningham*, St. Austin and his place in the history of Christian thought. London 1886. 8ᵛᵒ. — See also *H. H. Milman*, History of Christianity, vol. III. Bk. 3, chap. x.

## § 91. *Sulpicius Severus (d. about 410)*.

1. *Sulpicius Severus*, the descendant of a noble and distinguished family of Aquitaine, was born about 363. He studied jurisprudence at Bordeaux, and, in course of time, became a brilliant lawyer. By his success in the profession, as well as by his marriage with the daughter of an illustrious house, he greatly increased his wordly means and prospects. But, after the early death of his wife, following the advice of his pious grandmother, Bassula, and of his friends Paulinus and St. Martin of Tours, he renounced the world and retired into solitude, regardless of the ridicule of his former friends. There he spent the rest of his life in literary labors and exercises of piety, and especially in the restoration and adornment of churches. He had a great veneration for St. Martin, the holy

Bishop of Tours, and often visited him to seek his advice in important matters. He died at Marseilles,
probably about 410. Whether he was a priest is
uncertain.

2. He wrote the following works : —

(a.) " Historia sacra sive Chronicorum libri duo,"
a short but elegantly written history of the Jewish
people and the Christian Church up to the year 400,
in which the author gives special attention and treatment to Priscillianism ; but the book is not quite free
from errors.

(b.) " Vita S. Martini Turonensis," a biography of
the holy Bishop and wonder-worker, St. Martin, written in the strain of a panegyric, and liable to the
charge of credulity on the part of the author.

(c.) " Dialogi tres," the first of which is a pleasing
description of the life and virtues of the Eastern
monks, while the second and third form a complement
to the life of St. Martin.

(d.) 3 " Epistolæ : ad Eusebium, ad Aurelium dia-
conum et ad Bassulam ; " the latter relating to the
last incidents of St. Martin's life and his burial. Also
two epistles " ad Claudiam sororem suam," one " de
ultimo judicio," and one " de virginitate." Other
letters ascribed to him are not authentic ; several are
lost.

3. Sulpicius Severus was conspicuous for his learning and for his humility, piety, and love of poverty.
He has been called " the Christian Sallust," on
account of the conciseness and purity of his style ;
and " the Palm of Eloquence," on account of his
fluency of language. The " Vita S. Martini " and
the " Dialogi " are particularly marked by beauty of
style. St. Paulinus of Nola extols the virtues of Sul-

picius Severus in the following verses, which he sent
him for a basilica he had built : —

" Dives opum Christo, pauper sibi, pulchra Severus
    Culmina sacratis fontibus instituit.
Corpore, mente, fide castissimus incola Christi
    Condidit ista Deo tecta Severus ovans.
Totus et ipse Dei templum viget hospite Christo,
    Gaudentemque humili corde gerit Dominum," etc.
                              [Epist. XXXII, n. 3 et 5.]

*Editions and Literature.* — *Migne*, S. lat. XX, 80–
248. — *Halm*, Sulp. Sev. opp., in Corp. script. eccl.
lat. vol. I. Vindob. 1866. — *Ceillier* l. c. X, 635–660.

### § 92. *St. Paulinus, Bishop of Nola (d. 431).*

1. *Pontius Meropius Anicius Paulinus*, the descendant of a rich senatorial family of Aquitaine, was
born at Bordeaux in 353, or 354. He was instructed
in poetry and rhetoric by Ausonius, and, being taken
to Rome by his tutor, he there acquired such fame as
an advocate that in the year 378 he was raised to
consular rank. Later on he traveled much, and thus
came into contact with the most eminent men of his
day. Following an abuse widespread at that time, he
had long remained a mere catechumen, but fully
convinced of the vanity of all earthly honor and wealth,
he, in 389, received baptism, and despite the re-
proaches of parents, brothers, and friends, withdrew
to a small estate, and lived with his wife Therasia in
voluntary retirement. Ordained priest in 393, he
repaired to Milan, and thence through Rome to Nola,
where, with his saintly wife, he led a life of severe
asceticism, avoiding all but spiritual intercourse with
his friends. Revered by all for his holiness of life,

he was consecrated Bishop of Nola in 409. An ever-watchful shepherd, he shielded his flock from the corrupt errors of Pelagius, and, during the sorely troubled times of the Gothic and Vandal invasions, gave a splendid example of resignation under the most severe affliction. He died June 22d, 431.

2. Of his writings we possess the following: —

(a.) Fifty Epistles, wherein he either explains Christian dogmas, such as the Blessed Trinity and the Incarnation, or describes the beauty of Christian virtue, or recommends himself to the prayers of his friends, — Augustine, Sulpicius Severus, Rufinus, Eucherius, Pamachius, and others. His correspondence with Ausonius, who had tried to dissuade him from his new mode of life, is of especial interest.

(b.) Thirty-five Poems, including among other things, prayers to God, expositions of certain Psalms, a description of the life of St. John the Baptist, a panegyric on St. Felix of Nola, and a vindication of his own conversion. The "Epithalamium Juliani et Iae" describes in 120 distichs the celebration of a Christian marriage; the "Panegyricus de obitu Celsi" is a fine elegy on the early death of a child, while the "Poema ultimum," in 254 hexameters, forms a brilliant apology for Christianity against Jews and heathens. His best prose writings, "Liber de poenitentia," a panegyric written on the occasion of the death of the Emperor Theodosius, "De laude generali omnium martyrum," together with some others, have unfortunately not been preserved. The "Passio Sancti Genesii Arelatensis" is of doubtful authenticity.

3. St. Paulinus had a special veneration for the Saints, and both by speech and writing strove to

arouse a similar devotion in others. In his own life
he united severity with mildness and was extremely
charitable to the poor. Though not a profound
scholar, yet on account of his refined style, he has
been called " Cicero Christianus," and because of
the love and veneration felt for him by the most eminent of his contemporaries, he was called " Deliciæ
sui sæculi." As a poet he more than surpassed his
teacher, Ausonius. All the thoughts and impressions
of his refined mind were reproduced in verses of cor-
responding beauty.

St. Gregory of Tours bears this honorable testimony
to him : " Assumpto episcopatu semper se humilem
proferebat, quia sciebat, se apud Deum excelsum
futurum, si humilitatem sectatus fuisset . . . Erat vir
sanctus mirae prudentiæ et rhetoricis litteris erudi-
tus " [Lib. de glor. conf. c. 110.]

*Editions and Literature.* — *Migne*, S. lat. LXI. —
*Ceillier* l. c. X, 543–631. — *Buse*, Paulinus von Nola.
2 B[de]. Regensburg 1856. — *Fabre*, Étude sur Paulin de
Nole. Strasbourg 1862. — *Lagrange*, Gesch. des hl.
Paulinus von Nola. Mainz 1882 (2[e] éd. franç. Paris
1882).

## § 93. *John Cassian, Priest and Abbot, of Marseilles* (*d. about 435*).

1. *John Cassian* was born about 360, probably in
Gaul (or according to Gennadius, in Scythia), of
wealthy and pious parents. He received his early
education in a monastery at Bethlehem. In 390, he
went with his friend Germanus to Egypt, and lived for
seven years with the solitaries of the Nitrian desert.
After a short visit to Bethlehem, he returned to Egypt,
and then set out for Constantinople. There he was

ordained deacon by St. John Chrysostom, who, a second time condemned to exile, chose him to be the bearer of a letter to Pope Innocent I. The lamentable state of affairs in the Byzantine Church induced him to leave the East and withdraw into Southern Gaul, where he was ordained priest. In 415 he founded two monasteries at Marseilles, one for men and one for women, which served as models for similar institutions and as places of refuge for innocence and learning. Cassian died, rich in merits and ripe in years, about 435.

2. Of his writings the following are preserved : —

(a.) "De institutis Cœnobiorum," in 12 books, of which the first four contain the rules and minute prescriptions of the government that obtained in the Eastern monasteries, of the habit of monks, of psalmody, and the reception of novices; while the last eight treat of the method of combating eight deadly sins: "gastrimargia, fornicatio, philargyria, ira, tristitia, acedia, cenodoxia, superbia."

(b.) "Collationes Patrum in eremo commorantium," in 24 sections, including the instructions which Cassian and Germanus received from the most celebrated monks of the desert, respecting the scope, end, and practical means of the religious life ; instructions which from that time forward served for the guidance of the most enlightened ascetics and founders of religious orders. While his "Instituta" deal chiefly with the external rules and observances, the "Collationes " aim at regulating the internal life of the religious.

(c.) "De incarnatione Christi," in 7 books, written about 431, at the request of the Archdeacon of Rome, afterwards Pope Leo I., and in every respect a very valuable work.

3. In the 13th Collation, "De providentia Dei," Cassian, referring to the example of Zaccheus and the penitent thief, employed the Semipelagian saying: " The beginning of faith proceeds from ourselves, but its completion is from God." For this he was sharply reprimanded by Prosper, who reproached him " with having, by the influence of his learning, put a powerful weapon into the hands of the enemies of the doctrine of grace." Thus it came that Cassian was generally considered as " princeps Semipelagianorum," and this is why, notwithstanding his saintly life, he has never been canonized by the Church.*

His writings, marked by perspicuity of style, testify to their author's vast experience and profound learning, to his intimate knowledge of Holy Writ, and his burning zeal for Christian perfection and purity of doctrine.

During the Middle Ages, his two ascetical books were regarded as standard works for the monastic life. Gennadius says of him: " Scripsit experientia magistrante plano et librato sermone, et ut apertius dicam, sensu verba inveniens et actione linguam movens, res omnium monachorum professioni necessarias " [De script. eccl. cap. 61.]

*Editions and Literature.* — *Migne,* S. lat. XLIX–L, 372. — *Petschenig,* Cassiani opp., in Corp. script. eccl. lat. vol. XIII et XVII. Vindob. 1886 et 1888. — *Ceillier* l. c. XIII, 37–146.— *Lombard,* Jean Cassien, sa vie, ses écrits, sa doctrine. Strasb. 1863.

---

* The opinion of the author may require some modification. In an article by Pohle in the Kirchenlexicon (art. Cassian), it is stated that in many places and from times immemorial his feast has been kept as that of a saint, and moreover that the authority of the Holy See is not altogether wanting. (R.)

§ 94. *St. Prosper of Aquitaine.* (*d. about 463*).

1. *Prosper*, the precise year of whose birth and death is uncertain, though but a layman, was an admirable and pious theologian. He had been led by the evils of his time to the practice of a devout life.

A warm admirer of the great Bishop of Hippo, especially in his teachings on grace, he was the occasion of St. Augustine writing his two books on "The Predestination of the Elect," and "The Gift of Perseverance;" and he himself, both before and after St. Augustine's death, took up the pen against the Pelagians and Semipelagians. In 431 he traveled to Rome and complained to Pope Celestine, that certain misguided priests of Marseilles were teaching erroneous doctrines on the subject of grace. Hereupon the Pope wrote a letter of rebuke to the bishops of Gaul and commended in terms of praise the doctrine of St. Augustine. According to Gennadius, Prosper was afterwards summoned to Rome and became secretary to Pope Leo I. He died about 463 in the odor of sanctity.

2. Of his works the following are preserved: —

### A. *Dogmatical.*

(a.) "Epistolæ duæ ad Augustinum et ad Rufinum de gratia et libero arbitrio," an account of the Semipelagian doctrines prevailing in Southern Gaul, with a refutation of them.

(b.) "Responsiones pro Augustino ad Capitula obiectionum Gallorum calumniantium," a defense of Augustine's doctrine on predestination, with an explanation of the writer's own view.

(c.) "Responsiones pro Augustini doctrina ad

Capitula obiectionum Vincentianarum;" written with the same design as the last mentioned, but contains a still clearer and more precise exposition of his doctrine, and lays greater stress on God's foreknowledge in the matter of predestination.

(d.) "Responsiones pro Augustino ad Excerpta Genuensium," an explanation of passages from St. Augustine's books on predestination and the gift of perseverance.

(e.) "Liber de gratia Dei et libero arbitrio contra Collatorem, i. e. Collationum auctorem Cassianum." This is Prosper's most important work, wherein, as his principal thesis, he defends that nature can only be the cause of natural goodness, but that salvation, being a supernatural work, must begin with a supernatural principle, i. e. with grace.

(f.) "Carmen de ingratis," a didactic poem in hexameter verse, written with great skill against the ungrateful enemies of divine grace, i. e. the Pelagians and Semipelagians.

## B. *Moral.*

(a.) "Liber sententiarum ex operibus S. Augustini delibatarum," 392 sentences, gathered from the works of St. Augustine and forming a kind of compendium of his theology.

(b.) "Liber Epigrammatum ex sententiis S. Augustini," 106 epigrams in distichs.

## C. *Other Writings.*

(a.) "Expositio Psalmorum 100–150," an extract from St. Augustine's Commentary on the Psalms.

(b.) "Chronicon integrum," a compendium of the Chronicle of Eusebius and Jerome, and a continuation of the same from 425 till the taking of Rome by Genseric (455).

### D. *Doubtful or Spurious.*

" Confessio quæ dicitur Prosperi epistola ad Deme-triadem, sive de humilitate," and " Poema conjugis ad uxorem," are doubtful. " De vita contempla-tiva," " Liber de promissionibus et prædictionibus Dei," and " De vocatione omnium gentium " are spurious.

3. The short compendium of the teachings of St. Augustine on grace and predestination which Prosper has left us, is most important, and is stamped with the public approval of the Church. It supplies clear and precise definitions of the doctrine of original sin, the free will of fallen nature, justification, merits, and pre-destination. To a firm grasp of his subject and solid reasoning, Prosper joined elegance of dic-tion. He ranks indeed as the best disciple of St. Augustine, whose severer views, or modes of express-ing the doctrine of predestination, he toned down, by making predestination dependent on God's foreknowl-edge of man's supernatural merits. Tritheim says of him : " Prosperum nostrum in divinis scripturis eru-ditissimum et in sæcularibus nobiliter doctum, car-mine excellentem et prosa, eloquio dissertum, sensu profundum, ingenio subtilem, assertione nervosum, vita et conversatione sanctissimum apparuisse " (De script. eccl.)

*Editions and Literature.* — *Migne*, S. lat. LI. 9–868. — *Ceillier* l. c. XIV, 518–601. — *Nirschl*, Lehrb. III, 144–154. — *Wörter*, Prosper über Gnade und Freiheit. Freiburg 1867.

§ 95. *St. Vincent of Lerins* (*d. about 450*).

1. *Vincent,* a native of Gaul, after pursuing for a time a worldly career, felt at last greatly attracted towards the monastic state and the religious life. He entered the monastery which St. Honoratus had founded on the Island of Lerins, and there became a monk and priest, and one of the most renowned scholars of his day. Undisturbed by the outside world, he spent the rest of his life until his death (about 450) in quiet study and contemplation.

2. His one great work is the celebrated " Commonitorium pro Catholicæ fidei antiquitate et universitate adversus profanas omnium hæreticorum novitates," written about 434, under the pseudonym of " Peregrinus," — called by Baronius " aureum plane opusculum ; " by Bellarmin, " parvum mole, sed virtute maximum ; " by Mabillon, " perenne contra omnes hæreses documentum."

It is a dogmatico-polemical treatise, of which, however, only the first part, comprising chapters I–XXVIII, is complete ; the latter part, with the exception of five chapters, having been lost. In the first part of the work, St. Vincent lays down a critical rule for distinguishing Catholic truth from heresy or error, while in the second part he endeavors to apply and illustrate the rule in a practical manner.

3. This work, written in a clear style, gives an exposition of the rule of faith. Vincent shows us how Holy Scripture and tradition are the groundwork of Christian belief. Owing to the profound meaning of Holy Writ and its liability to various and contradictory interpretations, it is necessary to hold fast to the tradition of the Church, i. e. " Quod semper, quod

ubique, quod ab omnibus creditum est." The true
witnesses of ecclesiastical tradition are the Holy
Fathers, and, therefore, Holy Writ must be interpreted
in accordance with their testimony.* Progress in the
knowledge of revealed truth is not only possible for
the individual as well as for the whole Church, but
also necessary, provided it be progress and not alteration of the faith. Though the "Commonitorium"
seems to be directed against the severer views of St.
Augustine in the question of grace, it affords no just
cause for suspecting the author of Semipelagian lean-
ings. Pope Benedict XIV at least would pronounce
no judgment on the subject.†

The Roman Martyrology commemorates St. Vincent as "Presbyter doctrina et sanctitate conspicuus."
His style, though forcible and concise, is yet fluent
and suited to his subject.

*Editions and Literature.* — *Migne*, S. Lat. L, 625–
686. — *Ceillier* l. c. XIII, 564–584. — *Elpelt*, Vincenz
von Lerin, sein Leben und seine Lehre. Breslau
1840. — *Hefele* in the Tübinger Quartalschr. (1854)
pp. 83–126. — An English translation of the Com-
monitory together with notes exists in "Nicene and
Post-Nicene Fathers" (Parker & Co.), but both
translation and notes, as is obvious, will require cau-
tion and careful control.

---

* For the full sense and meaning of the Vincentian canon,
the student should consult *Franzelin*, De Div. Tradit. et
Scriptura. Thesis XXIV.

† See *Hurter*, Opusc. PP. Tom. IX, in a note to chapters
XXVI–XXVII.

§ 96. *St. Eucherius, Bishop of Lyons* (*d. about 449*).

1. *St. Eucherius* was descended from an illustrious
Lyonese family, and on account of his education and
learning, was raised to senatorial rank. He was married and lived happily with his noble and pious wife,
Galla, and their two sons and two daughters. Forsak-
ing, however, his high position, he traveled to the
Thebaid, and, on his return, became, with his wife's
consent, a monk at Lerins, where his two sons, Salo-
nius and Veranius, had received their education.
Simultaneously Galla and her daughters assumed the
religious veil. After a short time, seeking still greater
facility for a contemplative life, Eucherius went to the
neighboring and more lonesome isle of Lero (Ste.
Marguerite). But the fame of his virtue so spread
abroad that, about 434, much against his will, he was
chosen Bishop of Lyons. During his episcopate he
built many churches, founded various institutions, and
greatly encouraged the monastic life. In 441, he
attended as metropolitan the Synod of Orange, and
continued to labor assiduously for the good of the
Church until his death, about 449. He was a man
well versed in sacred learning, mighty in word, and
rich in good works.

2. The following of his writings are deserving of
special mention: —

(a.) " Epistola paraenetica ad Valerianum de con-
temptu mundi et saecularis philosophiae," in which he
demonstrates that the world presents its votaries only
with counterfeit pleasures, that its honors, applause,
and assemblies are empty show and veritable slavery,
deluding those who are blinded by their passions.

(b.) " Libellus de laude eremi ad Hilarium Lirinensem," written in praise of solitude in general, and of Lerins, its spirit, and the holiness of its monks in particular, and addressed to Hilary, afterwards Bishop of Arles. This and the preceding work are very able productions, and distinguished for elegance and purity of language.

(c.) "Institutionum libri II ad Salonium filium," the first of which, in the form of questions and answers, explains difficult passages of the Old and New Testaments, while the second supplies an explanation of some Hebrew, Greek, and Latin words and names occurring in Scripture.

(d.) "Liber formularum spiritualis intelligentiæ ad Veranium filium," a typical or spiritual interpretation of certain words and sentences of Holy Scripture.

(e.) "Sermones et homiliæ," extant only in fragments, amongst which the "Decem homiliæ," and the "Exhortatio ad monachos" deserve special notice. The "Historia passionis SS. Mauritii et sociorum, Agaunensium martyrum legionis Thebaicæ" is incorrectly ascribed by some to Bishop Eucherius of Lyons. A letter, "Ad Philonem," and a Commentary on Genesis and the Books of Kings, are spurious.

3. Eucherius was a man of acute mind, extensive knowledge, and great eloquence. His style is flowing and pleasant, clear, lofty, and refined. He enjoyed the veneration and esteem of all the great men of his time; for his noble qualities proclaimed him a worthy successor of St. Irenæus. Claudianus Mamertus, Bishop of Vienne, calls him "maturus animi, terræ despuens, cœli appetens, humilis spiritu, ardens merito, ac perinde ingenii subtilissimus, scientiæ plenus, eloquii profluus, magnorum sui sæculi pontifex longe maximus," and speaks of his eloquence in these

words: "Sic Isocratis schematibus modulata, structa, picturataque est oratio, ut nusquam frigeat aut ineptiat; sic arguta, ut interim nervosa, sic elaborata, ut tamen dilucida, sic nova, sed ut tædio careat affectationis; sic festiva, ut nihilo secius gravis ac seria; sic rhetorica, ut γνησίως tamen christiana," etc. (De statu animæ).

*Editions and Literature.* — *Migne* S. lat. L, 686–1212. — Eucherii Lugdunensis opp. omnia. Pars I, ed. *Wotke* (Vindob. 1894) in Corp. script. eccl. lat. vol. XXXI. — *Ceillier* l. c. XIII, 539–564. — *Gouilloud*, Saint Eucher et l'église de Lyon au 5me siècle. Lyon 1881. — *Stolle*, Das Martyrium der thebaischen Legion. Breslau 1891.

## § 97. *St. Hilary, Archbishop of Arles* (d. 449).

1. *Hilary*, born about 401, in Gaul, received an education befitting his distinguished birth, and made great progress in all branches of human knowledge, particularly in rhetoric and philosophy. After spending most of his youth in worldly pursuits, he resolved, after a hard struggle, to follow the advice of a relative (afterwards Bishop Honoratus of Arles) and enter the religious state. He sold his goods and distributed the proceeds amongst the poorer monasteries, and then, leaving the land of his birth, repaired to the isle of Lerins, where, as a monk, he was soon distinguished for his love of prayer and self-denial. When Honoratus became Bishop of Arles, Hilary, yielding to his constant entreaties, followed him thither. However, he soon returned to his beloved solitude, but on the death of Honoratus he was elected to the vacant see. As Bishop, he lived with

all the strictness of a monk; his charity towards the poor was extraordinary, and, in preaching, his zeal was almost excessive. He founded a seminary for the training of his clergy, held numerous synods, and put in force most excellent disciplinary enactments. Ever ready to encourage those aspiring to perfection, he founded new monasteries and frequently visited the various monastic institutes. When Leo the Great overruled his decision as to the deposition of Chelidonius, Bishop of Besançon, St. Hilary, though deeply grieved, submitted to the papal judgment. Worn out by his extraordinary austerities and by the immense labors of a zealous episcopate, he died prematurely on May 5th, 449.

2. Of his writings only the following are extant: —

(a.) " Vita S. Honorati, Episc. Arelat." Properly speaking, this is not a life of St. Honoratus, but a discourse delivered on the anniversary of his death.

(b.) "Epistola ad Eucherium Episc. Lugdunensem."

The following are doubtful: " Narratio de miraculo S. Genesii; " " Carmen in natali Machabaeorum ; " " Metrum in Genesin: " on the creation of the world till the deluge in hexameter verse. Other writings, as the homilies for all the feasts of the ecclesiastical year, an explanation of the Symbolum, and numerous letters have been lost. The " Carmen de Providentia" is spurious.

3. Hilary possessed an extensive knowledge of Holy Scripture; he also had a deep love of poverty and wonderful charity for the poor. He was an excellent and graceful teacher, pre-eminently endowed with the talent of adapting his instructions to the needs and capacities of his hearers. Although he is ranked by

Prosper amongst the opponents of St. Augustine's doctrine on predestination, he must on no account be regarded as a Semipelagian. The reputation of his sanctity, however, was slightly tarnished by a zeal that was overbearing and almost violent.

An epitaph in the church of St. Honoratus contains the following praise of the Saint: —

" Spernit opes, dum quærit opes, mortalia mutans,
Perpetuum cœlum donis terrestribus emit:
Gemma sacerdotum, plebisque orbisque magister,
Rustica quin etiam pro Christo munia sumens,
Servile obsequium non dedignatus adire,
Officio vixit minimus, sed culmine summus," etc.

*Editions and Literature.* — *Migne*, S. lat. L, 1214-1292. — *Ceillier* l. c. XIII, 523-538.

## § 98. Salvian, Priest, of Marseilles (d. about 490).

1. *Salvian*, born of heathen parents at Cologne, or Treves, towards the end of the 4th century, married the pagan daughter of Hypatius. Both he and his wife, however, greatly to the indignation of their parents, became Christians. Later on they made a mutual vow of chastity, and Salvian himself embraced the monastic state at Lerins. Having (about 428) been ordained priest at Marseilles, he undertook the education of the two sons of Eucherius, and trained them with so much ability that they were afterwards raised to the episcopacy, and Salvian himself was styled "Master and Teacher of Bishops." Like a new Jeremias, he bewailed and denounced the prevailing vices of the age as the sources of public misfortune and of the divine displeasure. He labored most successfully and to an advanced age both in word and deed, and enjoyed the

esteem and friendship of the most distinguished men of the Church of Gaul. He died about 490.

2. Of his numerous works the following are preserved: —

(a.) "De gubernatione Dei libri VIII," in which, after proving by Biblical examples, that God directs the destinies of nations and of men, he meets the objection that Christians and good men are less fortunate than pagans and sinners. He points out and paints at times too forcibly the general moral corruption of the Roman Empire, calling for the vengeance of God.

(b.) "Ad ecclesiam vel adversus avaritiam libri IV," in which, under the assumed name of Timotheus, he inveighs, with great eloquence, but much tedious repetition, against the vice of avarice, and calls upon the rich to practice the duty of almsgiving.

(c.) "Epistolae IX," written for the most part to friends, on subjects of private interest. The fourth of these, written to effect a reconciliation with his wife's parents, who for seven years had continued in their resentment, is a singular monument of Christian eloquence and filial tenderness. His homilies as well as his other writings and letters, many of which are quoted by Gennadius, have been lost.

3. Salvian's writings, though generally too diffuse in style, are yet distinguished by elegance and ease of expression; they contain, also, passages of great power and maxims of noble beauty. His arguments are skillfully developed, his expositions and demonstrations are clear, and his appeals are strikingly effective. "Humana et divina litteratura instructus, scripsit Salvianus scholastico et aperto sermone multa " (Gennadius, De vir. illust. c. 67.)

*Editions and Literature.* — *Migne*, S. lat. LIII, 9–238.—*Pauly*, Salv. Massil. opp., in Corp. script. lat. vol. VIII. Vindob. 1883. — *Ceillier* l. c. XV, 46-81. — *Zschimmer*, Salvian und seine Schriften. Halle 1875.

### § 99. *St. Leo, the Great, Pope* (*d. 461*).

1. *Leo*, surnamed the Great, was descended from a distinguished Tuscan family and born in Rome about the year 400.

We know nothing of the events of his life previous to the time of his diaconate. He was, however, certainly held in high esteem during the pontificate of Celestine I. (422–432) and Sixtus III. (432–440), and was employed in affairs of the utmost importance, such as the official examination of Semipelagianism. Elected Pope on the death of Sixtus, he ascended the Chair of Peter in a stormy time. He proved to be one of the most able of pontiffs, and in his continued and widespread labors, pre-eminently exemplified the truth that the papal primacy is the groundwork of the unity of the Church. His extraordinary solicitude as Chief Shepherd of Christ's flock, showed itself in his strenuous maintenance of ecclesiastical discipline, in his earnest exhortations addressed by letter to the bishops of Mauritania, Egypt, and Sicily, and in his vigorous opposition to Anastasius, Metropolitan of Thessalonica, and Hilary of Arles. He zealously suppressed Manichæism, Pelagianism, and Monophysitism. The latter heresy having, under the protection of the Emperor Theodosius II. and a powerful court party, occasioned fresh disputes and serious disturbances in the Eastern Church, St. Leo, with a view to its

suppression, summoned, in 451, a General Council at
Chalcedon, at which his famous dogmatical letter to
Flavian on the two natures in Christ was accepted by
the assembled Fathers with the joyful acclamation:
"This is the faith of the Fathers! the faith of the
Apostles! Thus we all believe! Peter has spoken
through Leo." And when the Monophysites, even
after the General Council, continued their intrigues
and caused new divisions in Alexandria, Pope Leo
sought by every means in his power to restore order
and unity in that troubled Church. Finally, by sav-
ing old Rome from the destruction with which it was
menaced by the Huns under Attila (452), and again
by Genseric (455), he not only added honor and pres-
tige to the papacy, but also showed forth its importance from a political point of view. The labors of
his glorious pontificate were only ended by his death,
April 11, 461.

2. The works of St. Leo consist of 96 sermons and
143 letters.

## A. *Sermons.*

(a.) "Sermones de festis Domini et Sanctorum,"
in which an admirable exposition is given of the great
mysteries of Our Lord's life, beautifully combining
both dogmatic and moral teaching.

(b.) "Sermones de jejunio," on the reasons for,
and the advantage and method of fasting.

(c.) "Sermones varii," as, for instance, 6 "de
collectis," i. e., on alms-giving; 5 "de natali ipsius,"
in which occur the famous passages on the primacy
and the dignity of the priesthood. These sermons are
nearly all quite short but very profound, and are

marked by a graceful, clear, and flowing style; they are among the finest specimens of patristic eloquence.

## B. *Letters.*

(a.) Dogmatical, which for the most part, expound and prove the truth of the mystery of the Incarnation. Amongst them (28.) is the celebrated "Epistola ad Flavianum episcopum Constantinop. contra Eutychis perfidiam et hæresin," which the Fourth Œcumenical Council of Chalcedon accepted as a rule of faith.

(b.) Historical, having mostly reference to the Robber-synod (Latrocinium) of Ephesus in 449 and the Council of Chalcedon in 451.

(c.) Letters bearing on ecclesiastical discipline and the constitution of the Church.

(d.) Letters which chiefly treat of the time of celebrating Easter.

Many of his letters have been lost; of others, fragments only are extant. Several sermons and treatises ascribed to him are of doubtful authenticity. The " Sacramentarium Leoninum," the most ancient form of the Roman Missal, though bearing traces of the spirit and style of St. Leo, was nevertheless probably the work of a private individual of the sixth century.

The following are certainly spurious: "De vocatione gentium," "Epistola ad Demetriadem virginem," and "Capitula sive præteritorum sedis apostolicæ episcoporum auctoritas."

3. By his writings, which are as remarkable for elegance of style as for loftiness of conception, richness of thought, and purity of doctrine, Leo, with a more than earthly wisdom, defended and explained the doctrines of the Church, especially those that were

assailed by unbelievers and heretics. The clearness, depth, and precision of his dogmatic judgments prove at once his high mental endowments and the vast extent of his theological knowledge.

His thoughts bear the stamp of truth, and his language is so beautiful and dignified that it cannot fail to attract and impress the reader. To him we are indebted not only for the admirable exposition of the mystery of the Incarnation and the two natures of Christ's one person, but also for other equally fundamental doctrines of the Catholic Church, as, for instance, the authority and inerrancy in faith of the Roman Church. He says: "Per beatissimum Petrum, Apostolorum principem, sacrosancta ecclesia romana tenet super omnes totius mundi ecclesias principatum" (Epist. 65, c. 2); "Soliditas illius fidei, quæ in Apostolorum principe est laudata, perpetua est" (Serm. 2, c. 2); "Per tot sæcula docente Spiritu Sancto hæresis nulla ecclesiam romanam violavit" (Serm. 96, c. 3). Again, on the primacy of St. Peter and its continuation in his successors, he says: "Primus est in apostolica dignitate" (Serm. 4, c. 2); "Soliditas illa, quam de Petra Christo etiam ipse Petra factus accepit, in suos quoque se transfudit heredes" (Serm. 5, c. 4); "Cujus (Petri) dignitas etiam in indigno herede non deficit" (Serm. 3, c. 4).

The clear assertion of the authority of the Apostolic See, as well as its universal acknowledgment at the time of St. Leo, is a historical fact which compensates to some extent for subsequent events, such as the decline and disappearance of patristic literature, the almost complete cessation of great councils, and the continual and increasing troubles of the Church. The Greek Menology thus commemorates him: "Leo

admirabili virtute animi, sapientia et sanctitate prædi-
tus, Romanæ Ecclesiæ pontifex, præclarissimis mon-
umentis virtutem suam, præcipue autem rectam fidem
testatam reliquit," and Pope Sergius I. extols his
merits in the following inscription with a manifest
allusion to his name: —

> " Commovet e tumulo, quod gesserat ipse superstes,
>    Insidians ne lupus vastet ovile Dei
>  Rugiit, et pavida stupuerunt corda ferarum,
>    Pastorisque sui jussu sequuntur oves."

*Editions and Literature.* — *Migne*, S. lat. LIV-
LVI. — *Ceillier* l. c. XIV, 316–517. — *Arendt*, Leo
d. Gr. Mainz 1835. — *Saint-Chéron*, L'histoire du
pontificat de S. Léon. 2 vols. Paris 1845. — *Amelli*,
San Leone Magno. 2 ed. Monte Cassino 1890. —
*Grisar*, in Wetzer und Welte's Kirchenlex. VII (2.
Aufl.) 1746–1767. — *Kuhn*, Die Christologie Leos
des Grossen. Würzburg 1894. — Select Sermons and
Letters of St. Leo may be found in *Hurter*, Opusc.
PP., tom. XIV, XXV, XXVI. — *W. Bright* also published, with English translation and notes, select
sermons of St. Leo the Great on the Incarnation,
together with his 28th epistle. (2 ed. London 1886.
8$^{vo}$.)

§ 100. *St. Peter Chrysologus, Archbishop of Ravenna*
(*d. about 450*).

1. *Peter*, surnamed, on account of his eloquence,
Chrysologus, was born about 405 at Imola, and baptized by Bishop Cornelius, from whom he also received
his ecclesiastical training and ordination to the diaconate. After studying the spirit of asceticism in a

monastery, he was consecrated Bishop of Ravenna by Pope Sixtus III., in 433. By his ever watchful solicitude, his untiring practice of prayer, and his constant fidelity to the duties of his office, he was a shining pattern of the Good Shepherd. His method of life was that of an ordinary priest, and he labored successfully in converting the pagans, as well as in combating the Manichæan, Novatian, Pelagian, and Nestorian errors. By word and example he encouraged the practice of Christian virtue and in his sermons freely denounced prevailing vices, and exhorted the faithful to avert, by works of penance, the divine chastisement. The Archimandrite Eutyches, who was trying to find supporters for his new heresy in the West, he entreated to submit to the authority of the Pope, "because through him St. Peter, who continues to sit in the Chair of Rome, makes known the true faith to the sincere enquirer." St. Chrysologus was on intimate terms with Pope Leo. He died and was buried about 450 at Imola.

2. Besides his affectionate letter to Eutyches, exhorting him to obey the Roman Pontiff, we possess 176 of St. Chrysologus' sermons; of these, some treat of Biblical events, others of moral and dogmatic questions, and others again were written for feasts of Our Lord and the Saints. His sermons on Biblical or dogmatic subjects are remarkable for conciseness of style and richness of thought; his moral discourses have almost always a doctrinal basis, and his sermons for festivals are generally very elevated in tone. All that he wrote bears the impress of a thorough ecclesiastical spirit.

3. In most of his shorter discourses, St. Peter expressly recommends frequent communion, prayer,

fasting, and alms-deeds, and emphatically denounces pagan customs, particularly those of New Year's day. These sermons abound in brilliant epigrams, as, "Voluptas nescit expleri" (Serm. 2). "Plus vigilare plus vivere est" (Serm. 24). "Ebrietas in alio crimen est, in sacerdote sacrilegium" (Serm. 26). "Da, homo, Deo tantum, quantum carni vitiisque tribuistia" (Serm. 114). "Vitia non nosse felicitatis est, nosse periculi, vicisse virtutis est" (Serm. 116). The holy Bishop Adolphus of Metz, in one of his sermons, calls St. Chrysologus "Beatissimus et apostolicus auceps, qui animas juvenum volantes calamo divini sermonis attingit" (Serm. 107). The style of St. Peter Chrysologus is very uneven; sometimes sweet and pleasant, at other times grave and dry; occasionally also obscure and overladen with antitheses.

*Editions and Literature.* — *Migne*, S. lat. LII, 9–680. — *Ceillier* l. c. XIV, 11–29. — *Dapper*, Der hl. Petrus Chrysologus. Köln 1867.— *Stablewski*, Petrus von Ravenna. Posen 1871.— *Looshorn*, Petrus Chrysologus und seine Schriften, in the Innsbruck Theol. Zeitschr. 1879, pp. 238 sq.


§ 101. *Christian Poets.*

Amongst the Latin Christian poets of this period, there are three who deserve special notice, Juvencus, Aurelius Prudentius, and Sedulius.

1. *Juvencus*, whose full name in the older books is Gaius Vettius Aquilinus Juvencus, was descended from an illustrious Spanish family. Of his life and education we only know that he became a priest and was a contemporary of Hosius of Cordova, and that during the reign of Constantine (325–337), he devoted his poetical

talent to the cause of the Christian faith.    In order to make the Christian doctrines more attractive to the intellectual class of pagans, he clothed them in the poetical garb of Virgil.

Among his works we may mention : —

(a.) " Evangeliorum libri IV," a kind of Gospel harmony (historia evangelica), wherein the author, followingly closely the text of the Itala, describes in flowing hexameters the life of Our Lord.

(b.) A metrical rendering of the Heptateuch (" Liber ad Genesin," in 1441 verses ; " Metrum ad Exodum," in 1392 verses ; " in Josue," in 586 verses ; " ad Le-viticum, Numeros, Deuteronomium," in 1204 verses), has been ascribed to him ; but modern critics are inclined to attribute it to a later author, a certain Cyprian, who lived in Gaul at the beginning of the 5th century.  The poems " De laudibus Domini " and " Triumphus Christi heroicus " are of doubtful authenticity, and " De mysteriis " is spurious.

Venantius Fortunatus praises him in these words : —

"Primus enim docili distinguens ordine carmen
Majestatis opus metri canit arte Juvencus.
Hinc quoque conspicui radiavit lingua Seduli."
(De vita S. Martini, lib. I.)

Tritheim calls him " vir nobilis, atque doctissimus philosophus, poeta, rhetor et theologus insignis et non minus conversatione quam scientia Scripturarum Ecclesiæ venerabilis " (De script. eccl.).

2. *Aurelius Prudentius Clemens* was born in 348 of a noble family at Saragossa in Spain.    After a child-hood passed, as it seems, under a somewhat severe discipline (" ætas prima crepantibus flevit sub feru-lis "), he devoted himself to the study of rhetoric,

anɑ embraced the career of an advocate, which, however, according to his own sorrowful avowal, he disgraced by sophistical deceptions and shameful excesses.

> " Mox docuit toga
> Infectum vitiis falsa loqui non sine crimine.
> Tum lasciva protervitas
> Et luxus petulans (heu pudet et piget)
> Fœdavit juvenem nequitiæ sordibus ac luto."
>
> (Præf. v. 8-12.)

His talents and ability won for him the favor of the Emperor Theodosius, who twice gave him the post of Governor and afterwards a high military position.

> " Bis legum moderamine
> Frenos nobilium reximus urbium,
> Jus civile bonis reddidimus, terruimus reos.
> Tandem militiæ gradu
> Evectum pietas principis extulit,
> Assumptum propius stare jubens ordine proximo."
>
> (Præf. v. 16-21.)

It was at the very time when his fortunes were at their highest, that he experienced a fierce inward struggle between virtue and vice. As in the case of so many other great men of those turbulent (4th and 5th) centuries, the conviction of the vanity of all earthly honor and pleasure suddenly forced itself upon him, and virtue triumphed.

Accordingly, in the 57th year of his age, he resigned his high offices, and going to Rome, visited many of the martyrs' tombs. On his return, he consecrated the rest of his life to the special service of God, and, in complete retirement, devoted himself to an ascetic life. He exercised his poetical talents for the promotion of God's glory and the defense of the Church. He died probably about the year 410.

He composed the following poems with Greek titles: —

(1.) " Cathemerinum sive liber hymnorum quotidianorum," twelve hymns, destined some for the different hours and regular exercises of the day; some for other occasions, feasts, and seasons.

(2.) " Apotheosis," a didactic poem in 1084 hexameters, in praise of the mysteries of the Trinity and Incarnation, against the Patripassionists, Sabellians, and Jews.

(3.) " Hamartigenia sive Carmen de origine peccatorum," directed against the Marcionites and Manichæans and containing a magnificent picture of the universal corruption of all nature after the fall.

(4.) " Psychomachia seu de pugna animæ," a kind of dramatic play in 915 hexameters, in which the combat between virtue and vice and the ultimate victory of virtue are represented by striking symbolical figures.

(5.) " Contra Symmachum," in 2 books, consisting of a prologue and 1799 hexameters, and containing a powerful attack upon pagan superstitions with a brilliant apology of Christianity.

(6.) " Peristephanon sive de coronis," 14 hymns in praise of 31 martyrs, written in various meters, full of feeling and pathos.

(7.) " Dittochæon," in 49 strophes, consisting of 4 hexameters each, describing various Biblical events and persons, viz.: 24 from the Old and 25 from the New Testament. The scope of the poem was perhaps to explain the mural decoration of some church. Though not above all doubt as to its authenticity, it is of considerable archæological importance. All these poems are distinguished for variety and wide range of ecclesiastical subjects, and are marked not merely by a very flowing style, but also by real poetical genius. Prudentius holds the foremost place amongst early Christian poets, and has not unjustly been called the " Christian Virgil." The Church has partially adopted 14 of his hymns for her Divine Office. Venantius Fortunatus sings of him: —

"Martyribus piis sacra hæc donaria mittens
    Prudens prudentes Prudentius immolat actus."

3. *Coelius Sedulius*, of whose birth and life little is known for certain, devoted himself for some time to the study of the profane sciences, especially philosophy. Failing to find satisfaction either in these, or in the sinful pleasures of the world, he yielded to the voice of divine grace, and, encouraged by Macedonius, a virtuous priest, turned his heart toward the study of the "divine science." In course of time he became a priest, and, according to some accounts, an Antistes, or Bishop, and rendered himself justly famous for his beautiful religious poems. He flourished in the middle of the 5th century.

Among his poems are: —

(1.) " Carmen paschale sive mirabilia divina," in 5 books, describing the miracles wrought by God under the old law and by Christ in the new. This magnificent poem was afterwards turned into very indifferent prose by Sedulius himself, under the name of " Opus paschale."

(2.) "Elegia sive collatio veteris et novi testamenti," in 55 distichs, showing how the types of the Old Testament have been fulfilled in the New.

(3.) "Hymnus abecedarius," in 23 alphabetical strophes, describing the birth, life, and death of Christ.

The hymn " De Verbi incarnatione," written in a style borrowed from Virgil, is undoubtedly spurious.

Sedulius devoted his great poetical talents exclusively to religious subjects, and is not without reason called " Poeta Christianissimus." His style is a clever and successful imitation of that of Virgil. The two hymns adopted in the Roman Breviary " A solis ortus cardine," and "Hostis Herodes impie " are taken from the "Abecedarius." Venantius Fortunatus sings of him: —

" Quod tonat Ambrosius, Hieronymus atque coruscat,
    Sive Augustinus fonte fluente rigat:
    Sedulius dulcis, quod Orosius edit acutus." . . . .

*Editions and Literature.* — (To 1.) *Migne*, S. lat. XIX, 9–388. — *Huemer*, in Corp. script. eccl. lat. vol. XXIV. Vindob. 1891. — *Gams*, Kirchengesch. von Spanien, Bd. II. Abth. 1, pp. 326. sq. — The Latin Heptateuch . . . critically reviewed by *John B. Mayor*, London 1889. 8vo. — (To 2.) — *Migne*, S. lat. LIX, 567–1078, et LX, 9–596. — *Brockhaus*, Aurel. Prudentius. Leipzig 1872. — *Gams*, l. c. pp. 337 sq. — *Kayser*, l. c. I, 249 sq. — *Rösler*, Der katholische Dichter Aurel. Prudentius. Freiburg 1886. — *Manitius*, Geschichte der christl.-lat. Poesie. Stuttgart 1891. pp. 61 sq. — English translations from Prudentius by *F. St. John Thackeray*, London 1890. 8vo. — (To 3.) — *Migne*, S. lat. XIX, 433–794. — *Huemer*, Opp. omnia, in Corp. script. eccl. lat. vol. X. Vindob. 1885. — *Idem*, De Sedulii vita et scriptis commentatio. Vindob. 1878. — *Kayser*, l. c. I, pp. 337 sq.

## FOURTH EPOCH.

## DECLINE OF PATRISTIC LITERATURE.

### FROM 461 TILL ABOUT 700.

### § 102. *Causes of Decline.*

The universal decline of patristic literature during the period we have now to consider was due to a two-fold cause: first, the untoward political events of the time, and, second, the internal troubles that afflicted the Church.

As regards the first of these causes, we may recall in the West the constant incursions of barbarian hordes, and in the East, the rise and growth of Islamism with its seductive flattery of the sensual passions. The interior troubles of the Church arose from the unbridled fanaticism of the various sects, together with the despotic interference of the Greek Emperors in matters of faith and ecclesiastical discipline. Such were the causes that worked together for the extinction of Christian literature among the Greeks and Romans. It is, therefore, not surprising that only a few Fathers of the Church or ecclesiastical writers are found in this period, who have combated the remnants of the great heresies, and endeavored to revive and diffuse the Christian spirit. Nor again will it surprise if, with few exceptions, there is little originality in the writings we have now to consider. Their authors for the most part merely drew from the works of the earlier Fathers, and contented themselves with collecting together and adapting the results of their research and reading to the general want.

# CHAPTER I.

## GREEK FATHERS AND WRITERS.

§ 103. *St. John Climacus, Abbot* (*d. about 600*).

1. *John,* who from his most celebrated work (*Κλίμαξ = scala*) is surnamed Climacus, but whose time and place of birth are unknown, was evidently endowed with splendid talents, by the careful use of which he soon began to acquire a rich store of knowledge. At the age of sixteen he renounced the honors of the world and entered the monastery of Mount Sinai. After the death of his teacher, Martyrius, he lived for forty years as an anchorite in a lonely cave at the foot of the mountain, spending his time in rigid penance, prayer, contemplation, the study of Holy Scripture and the writings of the Fathers. Having ever edified his brethren by willing submission to others, they made him at the age of 70 their abbot, and venerated him almost as a second Moses. But after a few years, he resigned his dignity and chose as his successor his brother George, a man of great experience in the ways of spiritual life. He then returned to his solitary cell, in which he ended a long and holy life about the year 600.

2. The following two works of St. John are extant: (a.) "Scala paradisi" (*Κλίμαξ παραδείσου*) i. e. the Ladder of Paradise. Under the figure of a ladder consisting of thirty steps, the author gives a most ingenious description, first of the way of perfection, from its inception till its end in the union with God and the attainment of perfect peace; secondly, of the origin, process, and manner of combating sin.

(b.) "Liber ad Pastorem," i. e. the Book for the Shepherd, in which he shows how the superior of a monastery must be a shepherd, pilot, physician, teacher, and pattern of his subjects, and how he has to govern his monastery and regulate his intercourse with each individual member.

3. These two works, composed at the request of a friend of the same name and superior of a monastery, bear witness to the author's solid piety and also to his spiritual discernment and wide experience in the interior life. They contain excellent advice, the " Scala " for individual religious, the " Ad pastorem " for superiors ; and on this account have always been highly appreciated in monastic institutions. Concise in style, they are rich in thought, but the meaning of not a few passages is far from obvious.

The following verse of a hymn has reference to his constant endeavor to show forth the heights of God by his ascetical life and his study of the inspired Word :

> Πάτερ Ἰωάννη ὅσιε,
> διὰ παντὸς τοῦ Θεοῦ
> τὰς ὑψώσεις ἔφερες
> μελετῶν πραχτιχώματα,
> τὰ θεόπνευστα λόγια, χ. τ. λ.

*Editions and Literature.* — *Migne*, S. gr. LXXXVIII, 579–1248.— *Ceillier* l. c. XVII, 569–596.

§ 104. *St. Sophronius, Patriarch of Jerusalem* (*d. 638*).

1. *Sophronius* was born at Damascus in 560. He frequented the most celebrated schools and showed a

marked predilection for the study of rhetoric and philosophy. At Alexandria he embraced the religious state, and accompanied by his friend John Moschus, a monk, journeyed through Upper Egypt, Palestine, Cyprus, and Asia Minor to Samos, and thence through the islands of the Archipelago to Rome. Here Moschus, after composing his "Pratum spirituale," which he dedicated to Sophronius, died. The Saint took the dead body of his friend back to Jerusalem. On his arrival in the Holy City he learned that the Emperor Heraclius was endeavoring to effect the return of the Monophysites to the Church by sacrificing the true doctrine that in Christ there existed two natures, and, therefore, also two wills and two distinct operations of the will. Whereupon he hastened to Alexandria and Constantinople, in order to dissuade the Patriarchs Cyrus and Sergius from accepting the proposed formula of union. His zealous efforts met with no success, but in the year 634 he was himself installed Patriarch of Jerusalem, and forthwith held a synod of the bishops under his jurisdiction. The synodal decisions and decrees, which stated in the most lucid terms the doctrine of the Church concerning the existence of two natures, and, therefore, of two wills in Christ, were forwarded not only to the two Patriarchs already mentioned, but also to Pope Honorius at Rome, whom Sophronius urged to take energetic measures against the Monothelites. The Pope, however (deceived by a wily letter from Sergius), thought the controversy prejudicial to the interests of the Church and prohibited any further discussion on the subject of Christ's two wills. Far from terminating the dispute, this decision fanned it to a greater flame, for Honorius himself spoke in his letter of one will in

Christ. Unfortunately, Sophronius was no longer able to take part in the defense of the orthodox faith. In 637, Jerusalem, after sustaining a protracted siege, was taken by the Saracens. Under the strain of anxious solicitude for the future, and of grief for the loss of the Holy Places, his physical strength gave way. He departed this life a few months after the capitulation of the city in the fourth year of his patriarchate.

2. The following of his works are preserved: —

(a.) "Epistola synodica," in which he gives a minute account of all the errors which up to his time had been rejected by the Church, especially those concerning the mysteries of the Blessed Trinity, the Incarnation, the two natures and unity of person in Christ. He next proceeds to state in clear, accurate, and emphatic terms the teaching of the Church as regards the two wills in Christ and their operation. This important work was examined and approved, as expressing the genuine doctrine of the Church, by the Sixth General Council in 680.

(b.) "Orationes," 9 sermons for feasts, the best and most important of which is that on Our Lady's Annunciation, wherein the preacher, with great eloquence, discourses on the mystery of the Trinity, the fall of man, and the dignity of Mary as the Virgin Mother of God.

(c.) "De peccatorum confessione," an instruction to confessors on their twofold capacity of judges and physicians of souls.

(d.) "Laus SS. martyrum Cyri et Joannis," containing an interesting account of their martyrdom, burial, and the translation of their bodies, as well as of the miracles wrought at their intercession.

(e.) "Vita Mariæ Egyptiæ," a history of her

life and conversion, according to the account of Zozi-
mus, a pious monk, who, a year before she died, met
the Saint in the wilderness and administered to her
the Blessed Sacrament, and, after her death, gave
her Christian burial.

(f.) " Anacreontica," 23 poems on saintly persons
or great events, marked by depth of thought and tender
piety.

(g.) "Triodium," 234 odes on Christ, the Redemption, the Cross, the Resurrection, Ascension, and
other subjects, all full of beautiful reflections, acts of
prayer, thanksgiving, and repentance.

(h.) " Commentarius liturgicus," a short but very
beautiful historical-mystical explanation of the Greek
liturgy.

(i.) Troparium horarum," hymns for the first, sixth,
and ninth hour of the day, in praise of the Holy Trinity.

The little work " De laboribus, certaminibus et peregrinationibus SS. Petri et Pauli," is spurious.

3. Sophronius was the pattern of a true shepherd in
his diocese and an ornament of the whole Church. All
his works, which, however, require still further critical
examination, are pregnant with the spirit of piety and
reveal a deeply religious mind. His synodal letters
prove him to have been an acute, learned, and orthodox theologian ; and the character of his sacred poetry,
both as to matter and form, shows that he was a divinely gifted singer of God and his Virgin Mother.
The " vitae epitome " in the Menologium concludes
with the following sentence : " Hæc illius vivendi ratio,
qua se Deo probavit, alios erudivit, Christi linguam
vicariam exhibuit, commissumque sibi gregem rexit et
intra triennium pontificatus beata potitus pace ad
Dominum est translatus."

*Editions and Literature.*—*Migne*, S. gr. LXXXVII,
3116–4014. — *Ceillier* l. c. XVII, 615–621. — *Nirschl*,
Lehrbuch III, 580 sq.

§ 105. *St. Maximus, Abbot and Confessor* (*d. 662*).

1. *Maximus* was born in 580 of a distinguished
family of Constantinople. He eagerly pursued the
study of rhetoric and philosophy, and his talents and
learning gained for him the post of First Secretary to
the Emperor Heraclius. Disgusted, however, with the
venomous intrigues of the heretics at court, and attracted by love of solitude, he, in 630, embraced the
religious state. He was made Abbot of the monastery of Chrysopolis, but soon gave up this position. In the year 633 he repaired to Alexandria,
where he joined Sophronius in his contest with the
Monothelites. Later, Maximus journeyed to Rome
and thence to Carthage. Here in the year 645 he
held a disputation with the Monothelite Patriarch
Pyrrhus, and so ably vindicated the true faith
that, in the following year, Pyrrhus accompanied
him to Rome, and, after making an-orthodox profession of faith, was received into communion with the
Church, but shortly after relapsed again at Ravenna.
It was Maximus who persuaded Pope Martin at a
synod held in the Lateran (649) to lay the originators
and promoters of Monothelitism under anathema. In
consequence of this bold act, both Martin and Maximus were seized by order of the Emperor Constans
and taken to Constantinople. Pope Martin soon died
(655), from the ill-treatment to which he was sub-
jected. Maximus, remaining constant in the profession of the orthodox faith, was deprived of all he

possessed and banished to Bizya in Thrace. But stoutly refusing even then to accept the imperial edict called Typos, he was dragged from place to place, and after much ill-treatment, brought back to Constantinople, where he was anathametized by a synod, and then by order of the city prefect, beaten with rods, deprived of his tongue and right hand, and in this mutilated state led through the streets of the city. Finally he was banished to Lazika on the Black Sea, where he died on the day he had foretold, Aug. 13, 662.

2. Of the many and various works of St. Maximus, the following deserve special mention : —

(a.) " Quæstiones in locos Scripturae difficiles," an allegorical and occasionally obscure exposition of difficult passages of the Old Testament, with many mystical reflections.

(b.) " Quaestiones, interrogationes et responsiones," shorter and clearer than the preceding.

(c.) " Expositio in Psalmum LIX," entirely allegorical.

(d.) " Liber asceticus," a clear and simple instruction, in form of a dialogue, upon the chief duties of the spiritual life, as based upon the love of God and the renunciation of worldly desires.

(e.) 400 "Capita de caritate," a well written explanation of the manifold ways in which the love of God may be practised.

(f.) 200 " Capita ad theologiam Deique filii in carne dispensationem spectantia," a kind of handbook on the doctrines of faith and morals.

(g.) 500 " Diversa capita ad theologiam et œconomiam spectantia deque virtute ac vitio," a treatise on mystical theology, clearly written and full of profound thought.

(h.) "Opuscula theologica et polemica," treating of various theological subjects, particularly directed against the Ekthesis of the Emperor Heraclius.

(i.) "Disputatio adversus Pyrrhum," an excellent defense of the Catholic doctrine of the twofold will of Christ, with a confutation of the Monothelites.

(j.) "Mystagogia," an explanation of the ceremonies of the sacred liturgy.

(k.) 71 "Capita theologica sive sermones selecti," gleanings chiefly from Holy Scripture, but including some also from ecclesiastical and profane authors.

(l.) 243 "Capita alia," moral and ascetical.

(m.) "Orationis dominicæ brevis expositio," very good.

(n.) "De variis difficilibus locis SS. Dionysii et Gregorii Theologi." St. Maximus assumed that the celebrated work which passes under the name of Dionysius, the Areopagite, was written by that author, whom he consequently praises as "a holy revealer of divine mysteries."

(o.) "De anima," on the nature and properties of the soul.

(p.) Commentaries upon St. Luke xviii, 2 sq.; vi, 29, and St. John xx, 17.

(q.) Forty-five letters to bishops, abbots, monks, and priests, upon dogmatic, moral, ascetical, philosophical, and personal subjects.

Many writings of St. Maximus have been lost and some are not yet published. Three hymns, an ecclesiastical calendar, and five dialogues on the Trinity are spurious.

3. St. Maximus was in his time one of the greatest theologians and one of the most profound mystical writers of the Greek Church. His steadfast ortho-

doxy, his keen dialectics, and his contemplative turn of mind made him one of the principal forerunners of the Scholastic and mystical schools of the Middle Ages, and exercised a lasting influence upon them. His explanation of the relation between faith and science, between theology and philosophy, is excellent. But his chief efforts were directed to the confutation of the Monothelite and Monophysite heresies. He was an able disputant and expressed himself freely and powerfully. As to his style, it is clear in subjects moral, but obscure in mystical themes, and often diffuse in his controversial writings.

An ode thus celebrates his praise: —

> Having stored in thy heart, O Saint!
> The treasures of heavenly wisdom,
> Thou hast by means of the same
> Enriched the world with thy doctrines.*

*Editions and Literature.* — *Migne*, S. gr. XC, XCI. — *Ceillier* l. c. xvii, 689–708. — *Boll.* Acta S. August. III, 97–132. — *Hefele*, Conciliengeschichte III (2 Aufl.) 189–247.

§ 106. *St. Anastasius Sinaita, Priest and Monk (d. after 700)*

1. *St. Anastasius* was a priest and monk in the celebrated monastery on Mount Sinai, whence his surname.

---

> \* Τῆς ἀνωτάτου σοφίας
> τοὺς θησαυροὺς κτησάμενος
> ἐν τῇ καρδίᾳ, ὅσιε,
> δι᾿ αὐτῆς ἐπλούτισας
> τὸν κόσμον τοῖς δόγμασιν.

Here he passed the main portion of his life from 640 to 700. At times, however, he would leave his solitude, and traverse Egypt and Syria, and hold, wherever an opportunity offered itself, disputations with heretics (Monophysites and Monothelites). He also wrote in defense of the orthodox doctrine of the Church. He lived to an advanced age, but the precise dates of his death and his birth are unknown.

2. Of the many writings attributed to him, the following are extant: —

(a.) "Viæ Dux" ('Οδηγός = Guide), in twenty-four chapters; a guide for defending the Catholic doctrine against various sects, particularly that of the Monophysites. Except for a few repetitions, the work keeps well within its scope and gives us an interesting insight into the religious contests of the time.

(b.) One hundred and fifty-four questions and answers on various points of dogma, morals, ascetics, and Holy Scripture.

(c.) Questions on the Hexaëmeron, in twelve books, treating of the six days of creation, the Sabbath, the two trees and four rivers of Paradise, Adam and Eve, the creation and sin of Eve, the consequences of the fall, the clothing of our first parents and their ejection from Paradise, and concluding with an eloquent panegyric on the Church. Apart from a number of inept allegorical interpretations, the work has many good points and gives evidence of the author's great love of Christ and His Church.

(d.) A sermon on Holy Mass and the forgiveness of sins.

(e.) Two discourses on Psalm VI., an earnest exhortation to penance.

(f.) A discourse on Genesis i, 26, against the Monothelites.

(g.) A profitable discourse on the departed, wherein the author puts his words of exhortation and warning into the mouth of a dying man addressing those present at his bedside.

(h.) Discourses of the Holy Fathers, or a collection of such passages of their writings as prove the dogmas of faith, particularly those of the Trinity and Incarnation.

(i.) An exposition of the faith, very short and clear.

Many of his writings mentioned in his " Guide," are lost. The " Disputatio adversus Judæos " is spurious.

3. Anastasius Sinaita, who must not be confounded with the Patriarch of Antioch, who died in 599, or with his successor, Anastasius the Younger, was one of the most learned men and writers of his time, a pillar of the Church, a valiant champion against heresy, and a profound mystical writer. His truly Apostolical labors in a time of great trouble, earned for him the name of the "New Moses." His method of interpreting Holy Writ was chiefly allegorical. His writings are a source of fruitful ideas. Ceillier remarks upon his style: " Les discours qui nous restent de lui ont du feu, de l'onction et de l'élégance " (l. c. XVII, 458.)

Editions and Literature. — Migne, S. gr. LXXXIX, 9–1288. — Ceillier l. c. XVII, 430–458. — J. B. Kumpfmüller, De Anastasio Sinaita. Ratisb. 1865.


§ 107. St. John Damascene (d. before 754).

1. St. John was (probably) born toward the end of the 7th century, at Damascus, where his father, though

a Christian, held a high position under the government
of the Saracen ruler of the province.  His education
was entrusted to a learned and pious monk of the name
of Cosmas, under whose tuition John quickly advanced in learning and virtue.  On the death of his
father, he succeeded to his office and position, which
he soon, however, abandoned, in order to retire to the
monastery of St. Sabas in Jerusalem and there devote
himself exclusively to study and the service of
the Church.  Ordained priest, he most courageously
defended the veneration of holy images, first during
the reign and persecution of Leo the Isaurian, and
later, during the reign of Constantine Copronymus,
who pursued him with unrelenting hatred.  For this
good work he was highly commended by the Second
Œcumenical Council of Nice, in 787.  The date of
his death is unknown, but may probably be fixed at
about 754.

His numerous works may be classified as dogmatical, controversial, moral, exegetical, homiletical, and
hymnological.


A.  *Dogmatical.*

(a.)  "Fons scientiae" ($\Pi\eta\gamma\grave{\eta}\ \gamma\nu\acute{\omega}\sigma\epsilon\omega\varsigma$), consisting
of three main parts, the first of which is introductory
and explains, in 68 chapters (capita philosophica),
some of the fundamental notions of philosophy,
such as "being, essence, substance, hypostasis,"
etc.  The second part, "De hæresibus," is historical, describing and explaining 103 heresies.  The
third part, "Expositio accurata fidei orthodoxæ,"
is dogmatical, systematically explaining and proving the various dogmas from Scripture and tradi-

tion. This part, consisting of four books in 100 chapters, contains the whole treasure of Greek theology, and was ever considered by the Greeks as their standard work. The theologians of the Middle Ages, too, made large use of it, and it formed the groundwork and pattern for Peter Lombard's "Books of Sentences." The first book treats of the nature and attributes of God; the second, of the spiritual and material creation (cosmogony and anthropology); the third, of the Incarnation of the Logos and of the work of Redemption (Christology and soteriology); and the fourth, of the glory of the God-man, of baptism and the Eucharist, of sin and of the last things.

(b.) "De sancta Trinitate," treating of the doctrine of the Trinity and the Divine Word, as well as the sinlessness and integrity of the Mother of God.

(c.) "Libellus de recta sententia," in which St. John freely and joyfully declares his entire submission to the decrees of the six general councils.

(d.) "Expositio et declaratio fidei," an explanation of the creed.

(e.) "De hymno trisagio," showing that the hymn "Sanctus Deus, sanctus fortis, sanctus immortalis," refers not to the Son alone, but to the entire Trinity.

Of his controversial writings, directed against the Manichæas, Monophysites, Monothelites, Nestorians, and Mohammedans, the most important and authoritative are three discourses against the Iconoclasts ("Adv. eos, qui sacras imagines abjiciunt"). In these St. John cites many witnesses and facts from Holy Scripture, the Fathers, the councils of the Church, and conclusively proves the lawfulness, utility, and fitness of venerating holy images.

## B. *Moral.*

(a.) " De sanctis jejuniis."
(b.) " De octo vitiis."
(c.) " De virtutibus et vitiis."

## C. *Exegetical.*

To these belong his commentary on the Pauline epistles, mainly drawn from the homilies of St. Chrysostom and the commentaries of Theodoret of Cyrus and Cyril of Alexandria. Also an alphabetically arranged " Repertorium " on matters of faith and morals, drawn from parallel passages of Holy Scripture and the Fathers.

## D. *Homiletical.*

Of the 13 homilies extant, there are three, " In dormitionem beatæ Mariæ semper virginis," which are important, because in them we find, for the first time, a complete assertion of the Church's tradition concerning the assumption of Mary's body into Heaven. Two homilies on Mary's birth are of doubtful authenticity; two on the Annunciation are spurious.

## E. *Hymnological.*

The subjects of his hymns are generally the mysteries of Our Lord's life, such as his birth, manifestation, resurrection, transfiguration, and ascension; or, also, the lives and virtues of different Saints. All his hymns end with a verse of praise and prayer to the Mother of God. His poetry is often marred by an excess of artificiality.

The " Passion of St. Artemius " is doubtful.

The following are spurious: " De confessione ; " " De iis qui in fide dormierunt ; " " De azymis ; " " De SS. corpore et sanguine Domini ; " " Oratio de sanctis et venerandis imaginibus ; " and the Vita Barlaam et Joasaph (cf. § 44, No. 2 a.).

3. St. John Damascene was not an original writer. His chief effort was to collect and arrange all that he thought best in the works of his predecessors, his principal source of authority being St. Gregory of Nazianzen. Nevertheless, on account of his learning and holiness, he has always been held in high estimation by the Greek and Latin Churches. As a sacred poet, the Greeks place him in the first rank. His writings combine loftiness of thought with natural grace and elegance of diction. With St. John closes the line of the great representatives of Greek theology. The spring of the latter seems to have run dry and spent itself in him.

The Greek Menology eulogizes him thus : —

> What shall we call thee, O Saint?
> John the Theologian, or David the singer?
> Harp of the Divine Spirit or magic flute?
> Who dost rejoice the Church's assemblies by thy
>     sweet sounds . . . .
> Plead for the salvation of our souls . . . *

*Editions and Literature.* — *Migne,* S. gr. XCIV —

---

\* Τί σε ὀνομάσομεν, ἅγιε;

θεολόγον Ἰωάννην, ἢ Δαβὶδ τὸν μελῳδόν;

πνευματέμφορον κιθάραν, ἢ αὐλὸν σημαντικόν;

εὐφραίνων Ἐκκλησίας τὰ συστήματα τοῖς μελιρ᾿ρύτοις

σου φθέγμασι καταγλαΐζων τὰ πέρατα· ἱκέτευε τοῦ

σωθῆναι τὰς ψυχὰς ἡμῶν, κ. τ. λ.

XCVI. — *Ceillier* 1. c. XVIII, 110–165. — *Perrier*,
Jean Damascène, sa vie et ses écrits.    Strasb. 1863. —
*Grundlehner*, Joh.   Damascenus.    Utrecht 1876. —
*Langen*, Johannes von Damaskus.    Gotha 1879.

---

## CHAPTER II.

### Latin Fathers and Writers.

§ 108. *St. Fulgentius, Bishop of Ruspe* (*d. 533*).

1. *Fulgentius* was born in 467, or 468, at Telepte,
a town in North Africa, and carefully educated by his
widowed mother Mariana.   His noble character as
well as his knowledge and administrative talent earned
for him, though still young, the high position of pro-
curator of his native city.   A change came over
him after reading St. Augustine's exposition of the
36th Psalm.   He now resolved to renounce his vast
possessions, and, in spite of his mother's tears,
retired to a monastery to lead an ascetic life.   Being
driven away from his monastery by the Arians, at
whose hands he suffered inhuman treatment, he wandered about foreign countries, but in 500 returned
once more to his native city, where he built a new
monastery, received the priesthood, and soon after, in
508, in spite of his reluctance, was consecrated Bishop
of Ruspe.   This step involved direct opposition to
King Thrasamund, who had prohibited any further
appointments to the Catholic bishoprics, and in consequence, Fulgentius and sixty other bishops were
banished to Sardinia, where he founded a monastery
under the rule of St. Augustine.   Twelve years later,

Thrasamund recalled him to Carthage, but exiled him once more in 520, at the instigation of the Arian bishops. The death of Thrasamund and the accession to the throne of Hilderic opened the way for the return of the banished bishops to their sees. Amidst the joyful acclamations of the people, Fulgentius re-entered his episcopal city, and from that time forward lived peacefully, devoting himself with fidelity and zeal to the welfare of his flock. He died in 533, after an earnest preparation for death and the patient endurance of a painful malady for two months.

2. His writings consist of treatises, letters, and sermons.

## A. *Treatises.*

(a.) "Ad Monimum libri III," in which he treats (1) of the twofold predestination, i. e. of the good to glory and of the wicked to punishment; (2) of the oblation of sacrifice; the mission of the Holy Ghost; and the meaning of I. Cor. vii, 25; (3) of the true meaning of the Gospel text: "Et Verbum erat apud Deum."

(b.) "Liber contra Arianos," in answer to the ten questions addressed to him by King Thrasamund on the Catholic doctrine of the Logos and the Holy Spirit.

(c.) "Ad Thrasamundum regem Vandalorum libri III," wherein, in answer to further objections of the King, he shows that in the one person of Christ, there are united two complete natures, the divine and human; that the divine nature is unlimited and immense, while the human nature of Christ is circumscribed by space and time, and that in this human nature the Son of God has suffered.

(d.) "Liber de Trinitate ad Felicem Notarium," a short but excellent instruction, in three chapters, on how to refute the Arian objections against the divinity of the Logos and of the Holy Ghost.

(e.) "Contra sermonem Fastidiosi Ariani," in twenty-two chapters, in which the author shows that though there is but one inseparable divine nature in three divine persons, it does not follow that the divine nature, as such, but only the person of the Logos, has become incarnate.

(f.) "De remissione peccatorum libri II," wherein he treats of the question whether divine omnipotence could pardon a sinner even after this life, either before or after the general judgment, and answers emphatically in the negative.

(g.) "De Incarnatione Filii Dei et vilium animalium auctore," in which he explains that, though the divine nature is common to all three divine persons, yet it is proper to the Son alone to be begotten from eternity of the Father, and to be born in time of Mary. Furthermore, that God made all things good, even the vilest animals, and that these only changed in consequence of the sin of man.

(h.) "De veritate praedestinationis et gratiae Dei libri III." Closely adhering to the doctrine of St. Augustine, the author affirms in these books the absolute necessity of preventing grace, the reality of our free-will, the wounds and weakness inflicted on it by sin, and healed again by divine grace; and, finally, the predestination to eternal life.

(i.) "De fide sive de regula verae fidei ad Petrum," is an excellent compendium of dogmatic theology.

### B. *Letters.*

There are thirteen letters extant, the first seven of which deal with moral questions as, Debitum conjugale et votum continentiæ conjugum, the rights and duties of married persons; virginitas, renunciation of the world and true penance. The rest consist of doctrinal discussions on the Logos, the Trinity, the Incarnation, grace, etc.

### C. *Sermons.*

Of the many sermons formerly ascribed to St. Fulgentius, only nine are genuine. Of these, some are on the feasts of Our Lord and the Saints, others deal with Biblical and moral subjects.

Several of his writings, letters and discourses, have been wholly or in part lost. The following are spurious: "Liber de prædestinatione et gratia," a sermon "In Purificatione B. M. V.," and "De S. Vincentio."

3. St. Fulgentius was an intrepid and indefatigable defender of the Catholic cause against Arians, Monophysites, and Semipelagians, and has made his name immortal in the Church. A perfect pattern of a bishop, an admired preacher, and one of the greatest theologians of his time, he may be justly called a second Augustine (alter Augustinus). Possessing much acuteness of mind and great power and precision of language, he was able to treat the most difficult questions in an easy and clear manner. While closely following the doctrine of St. Augustine on predestination, he yet refrained from pushing it to extremes. His style reflects the rigor of his mind and the meekness of his heart; and though at times verbose and in-

clined to repetition, it never fails to attract and captivate the reader.

His reasoning is thorough and concise, and his conclusions chiefly based upon the authority of Scripture or tradition. Ceillier speaks thus of him: " La vertu et le savoir de S. Fulgence le rendirent également la gloire et l'ornement de l'église d'Afrique. Vrai disciple de S. Augustin, il ne se contenta point d'en épouser les sentiments, il en imita la conduite. Son style est moins pur et moins châtié que celui de son maître; mais il est net et facile " (l. c. XVI, 139).

*Editions and Literature.* — *Migne*, S. lat. LXV, 103–1020. — *Ceillier* l. c. XVI, 1–140. — *Nirschl* Lehrbuch III, 370–385.

## § 109. *St. Ennodius, Bishop of Pavia (d. 521).*

1. *Magnus Felix Ennodius,* the descendant of a noble but impoverished family, was born in 473 at Arles (or, according to others, at Milan). After the premature death of his parents, he was left to the care of his aunt at Milan, who provided for his education. He loved the study of rhetoric, but tried his talents especially in poetry, and the least success in that line enraptured him beyond measure. His aunt, who seems to have destined him for the ecclesiastical state, committed him to a certain Servilius for instruction in the ecclesiastical disciplines. But she died before Ennodius had reached his seventeenth year, and had it not been for an offer of marriage from a wealthy and pious lady, he would have been left in extreme poverty. His new fortune, however, led him on the dangerous path of pleasure and enjoyment, until a serious illness roused him from his worldly slumber.

Having been restored to health by the intercession of St. Victor, he embraced the ecclesiastical state, and his devout wife assumed the religious veil. As a priest, he soon rose to high distinction. In the year 494, he accompanied Epiphanius, his bishop, to Burgundy. Eight years later, he was present with his successor, Maximus, at a synod in Rome, where he made such a splendid defense of the lawful Pope, Symmachus, against the accusations of the adhérents of the anti-pope Laurentius, that the Synod gave it its special approbation and ordered it to be preserved among its acts. After the death of Maximus, in 511, Ennodius became Bishop of Pavia. He stood in high favor with Pope Hormisdas, who sent him twice to the Emperor Anastasius at Constantinople to heal the rupture caused by the Monophysite troubles. Though his mission at the time proved unsuccessful, and only a source of humiliation for him, he yet lived long enough to see, under the Emperor Justin, the restoration of peace to the Church. He died soon after in 521.

2. Of his writings we possess the following: —

(a.) "Epistolarum libri IX," 296 verbose letters to Pope Symmachus, bishops, statesmen, and other persons.

(b.) "Opuscula miscella X," namely: —

(1.) "Panegyricus regi Ostgothorum Theodorico," somewhat too laudatory, but important from a historical point of view.

(2.) "Libellus apologeticus pro synodo IV. Romana (palmari)," in which Ennodius defends the conduct of the Synod, and affirms that the Pope is the visible representative of God on earth, and holds the supreme authority in the Church, to which all bishops are subject.

(3.) "Vita S. Epiphanii," written with great sympathy and piety.

(4.) "Vita S. Antonii," who was a disciple of St. Severinus, the Apostle of Noricum.

(5.) "Eucharisticum de vita sua," a thanksgiving for his cure and for other gifts of God, a kind of autobiography.

(6.) "Paraenesis didascalica," an exhortation to virtue and knowledge, written partly in prose and partly in verse.

(7.) "Praeceptum de cellulanis sive syncellis." Priests and deacons should only employ near relatives as female servants in their household.

(8.) "Petitorium," attestation of the manumission of a slave, drawn up at the request of his former master.

(9.) "Benedictiones duae cerei paschalis."

(c.) "Dictiones," twenty-eight discourses on profane and spiritual subjects, almost all masterpieces of rhetoric.

(d.) "Carmina sive poemata," 171 poems on sacred and profane subjects, together with epigrams and epitaphs.

3. Ennodius was an important man in his time, highly esteemed by his contemporaries, and, after his death, numbered among the Saints. Although everything he wrote is marred by the pompous and bombastic style of the period, he yet takes a high place among the poets and orators of his age. His works display considerable talent and learning, great love of knowledge and a zeal for religion and the Church. The lives of Epiphanius and Antonius, as well as the Panegyricus on Theodoric, are valuable contributions to the history of that changeful age, and many of his

hymns are remarkable for poetical beauty. Sirmond
writes of him: "Ennodius ea ingenii fama floruit et
doctrina, ut non solum in pretio essent, quæ sua
sponte scriberet, sed amicorum quoque, quos impen-
sissime coluit, rogatu in dictandis aliorum nomine
orationibus, epistolis, epitaphiis, ac diversarum rerum
epigrammatis assiduam operam dare cogeretur" (In
vita Ennod.).

*Editions and Literature.* — *Migne*, S. lat. LXIII. —
*Hartel*, M. F. Ennodii opp., in Corp. script. eccl. lat.
vol. vi. Vindob. 1882. — *Ceillier* l. c. XV. 413–433. —
*Magani*, Ennodio. 3 vols. Pavia 1886.


§ 110. *Boethius, Senator and Roman Patrician*
(*d. 525*).

1. *Boethius Anicius Manlius Torquatus Severinus*,
a scion of the famous race of the Anicians, was born
in 480 at Rome. He studied in that city and acquired
an extraordinary proficiency in Greek philosophy and
literature. The distinction of his birth, his marvelous
erudition, his probity and nobility of character, gained
him the dignity of Roman Senator and the high favor
of the Gothic King Theodoric. And, indeed, much
of the success and glory of Theodoric's reign was due
to the combined wisdom and skill of Boethius and his
friend Cassiodorius. However, his success, as well as
his rigorous justice, aroused the envy and hatred of
some of the courtiers, who accused him of treasonable
designs, and of plotting with the Emperor of Constantinople for shaking off the yoke of the Goths.
Theodoric, believing these unproved accusations, dis-
missed him from his office, stripped him of his wealth,
and sent him to a prison at Pavia, where, after a long

and painful imprisonment, and without a trial, he was beheaded in 525.

His friend, Pope John, and his father-in-law, the noble Senator Symmachus, met with the same fate.

2. The writings of Boethius are partly theological and partly philosophical.

## A. *Theological.*

(a.) " Brevis fidei christianæ complexio."

(b.) "De Trinitate sive quomodo Trinitas unus Deus ac non tres dii."

(c) "Utrum Pater et Filius et Spiritus Sanctus de divinitate substantialiter prædicentur."

(d.) "Liber de persona et duabus naturis (in Christo)" against Nestorianism and Eutychianism.

(e.) "Quomodo substantiæ in eo, quod sint, bonæ sint, cum non sint substantialia bona."

The authenticity of these theological tracts has been often disputed. But the style of writing as well as the manuscripts bearing his name and the testimony of his friend Cassiodorius, seem to leave no room for any reasonable doubt.

## B. *Philosophical.*

(a.) Translations of the Isagoge of Porphyrius, and of Aristotle's Categoriae, Logica, Topica, and Perihermeneias, as well as of the two books of Euclid's Geometry.

(b.) "Commentarii in Topica Ciceronis."

(c.) Commentary on the two books "De institutione mathematica" by Nicomachus.

(d.) "De musica libri V."

(e.) "De syllogismo categorico et hypothetico;" "De rhetoricae cognitione;" "Liber de divisione," etc.

(f.) "De consolatione philosophiæ libri V." This is the best and most celebrated work of Boethius, written during his imprisonment. Philosophy is represented as appearing to him in the form of a female figure, consoling him in his misfortune. The enjoyment of earthly goods, she says, cannot give true happiness, neither can their loss bring misery to the wise. True happiness can only be found in God, who is the highest good and the end of all things; the happiness of the wicked on earth is but apparent: divine Providence watches over and directs the ways of the just towards final happiness, while the wicked are reserved for eternal punishment; man's freedom of will is compatible with God's fore-knowledge. — The work is arranged with consummate art and elegantly written. It was highly esteemed and widely read in the Middle Ages.*

3. Boethius was formerly venerated as a Confessor of the faith and even as a martyr for Catholic truth. In modern times, however, the question has been raised whether he was even a Christian, for, it has been urged, in his chief writings there occurs no specifically Christian passage, nor even a single allusion to Christ. This argument, however, is far from convincing. For, on the other side, it may be urged that the whole bent of his mind, his way of viewing earthly things, the purity of his moral principles, as well as his earnest advocacy and maintenance of them in his "Consolation," — all show that Boethius was a Christian philosopher, and even if he is not a martyr, he is, to quote the opinion of Pope Leo

---

* Our own King Alfred, the Great, translated it into Anglo-Saxon. (R.)

XIII, "worthy of veneration." His writings are marked by purity of style, elevation of thought, and happiness of expression. His translations and commentaries on philosophical and mathematical works were used as text-books in the monastic schools of the Middle Ages. The following epitaph is written over his tomb: —

> Maeonia et latina lingua clarissimus, et qui
> Consul eram, hic perii missus in exilium.
> Et quia mors rapuit, probitas me vexit ad auras,
> Et nunc fama viget maxima, vivit opus.

*Editions and Literature.* — *Migne*, S. lat. LXIII–LXIV. — *Ceillier* l. c. XV, 555–593. — *Suttner*, Boethius, der letzte Römer. Eichstätt 1852. — *Nirschl*, Lehrbuch III, 401 sq. — *Biraghi*, Boezio, filosofo, teologo, martire. Milano 1865. — *Hildebrand*, Boethius und seine Stellung zum Christenthum. Regensburg 1885.

## § 111. *Cassiodorius, Statesman and Abbot* (*d. about 570*).

1. *Magnus Aurelius Cassiodorius* was born of a noble family about 477 and received an education that would qualify him for any public office in the State, So great were his talents and his integrity of character, that, when little more than twenty years of age, he obtained the high post of Quæstor and Secretary to King Theodoric, and, later on, of Minister, Præfectus prætorio, Life-senator and Consul of Rome. His policy of establishing friendly relations between the Roman and Gothic subjects of the Empire was skillfully carried out and contributed greatly to the peace, justice, and glory of Theodoric's reign.

After the death of that monarch he still continued at the head of affairs with the same vigor and wisdom, till the year 539, when, in consequence of the increasing troubles of the kingdom and the feebleness of its rulers, he resigned his office and retired to a monastery, which he had founded on his patrimonial estate, at Vivarium, intending to consecrate his declining years to the service of God and to study. He became Abbot of the monastery, and began to lay the foundations of a work that was even more important and had more lasting consequences than his previous political labors. He established a library of considerable size and encouraged his monks not only to till the fields, but also to transcribe the ancient classics and translate works of Greek theology. He himself wrote numerous philosophical and theological works, and strove by word and example to encourage both piety and learning in his community. Having accomplished his great purpose and set everything in working order, he resigned his office of Abbot and lived as an ordinary religious, till he died in the odor of sanctity in the year 570.

2. The following of his works are extant: —

(a.) "Variarum scil. epistolarum et formularum libri XII," a collection of royal and ministerial rescripts, very important for the history of that period.

(b.) "Chronicon," from the creation of the world to A. D. 519, compiled, for the most part, from the writings of Eusebius, Jerome, Livy, and others.

(c.) "De Getarum sine Gothorum origine et rebus gestis libri XII," of which only a small part is extant.

(d.) "De anima sive de ratione animæ," in 12 chapters, dealing with the nature, faculties, and condition of the soul after its departure from the body.

This is a clever work, and it may be considered to mark the point of the author's transition from profane to sacred writings.

(e.) "Commentarius de oratione et de octo partibus orationis," giving the rudiments of rhetoric.

(f.) "De orthographia," written at the request of his monks.

(g.) "Expositio in psalterium sive psalmorum librum," a commentary on the Psalms, much used during the Middle Ages, with an excellent introduction on prophecy, the division of the Psalms, and the rhetoric of Holy Scripture.

(h.) "Complexiones in epistolas et acta Apostolorum et Apocalypsin."

(i.) "Historia ecclesiastica tripartita," a compilation from the ecclesiastical histories of Socrates, Sozomen, and Theodoret.

(j.) "Institutiones divinarum et sæcularium litterarum," in two books. The first, in thirty-three chapters, gives excellent instructions on the method of studying theology, particularly Holy Scripture and the Fathers, and concludes by earnestly exhorting the monks to the love of study. The second, in seven chapters, explains the nature and scope of the various branches of the Trivium and Quadrivium. The whole work constitutes a kind of encyclopedia of sacred and profane knowledge and was used as a regular textbook in the schools of the Middle Ages.

3. Extensive as were his literary labors, Cassiodorius did not attempt any complete exposition of the doctrines of the Church; nevertheless, he added to the resources of theology by his writings on Holy Scripture. He must certainly be considered one of the most learned writers and theologians as well

as one of the most influential statesmen of his
time. Yet his chief merit in the eyes of posterity is
that, in his own writings, he gave a more scientific
direction to the activity of the monks and provided
the required instruction therefor. In founding schools
and libraries he set an example which was zealously followed, first by the Benedictines, and later on by other
orders. By collecting and preserving many gems of
ancient literature, Cassiodorius earned the lasting gratitude of the literary world. His style is not so refined
and elegant as that of Boethius, but the variety and
richness of his language fully sustain his reputation
for great eloquence. Hincmar of Rheims calls him
" Virum acerrimi ingenii et insignis eruditionis ; "
and Baronius, " Virum doctissimum et æque sanctissimum, decus Romanæ nobilitatis."

*Editions and Literature. — Migne*, S. lat. LXIX —
LXX. — *Ceillier* l. c. XVI, 374-462. — *A. Franz*,
Cassiodorius Senator. Breslau 1872. — *Th. Mommsen*
has edited several of Cassiodorius' works, and there
exists also an English translation of the Variarum
Epistolarum libri XII by *Th. Hodgkin*, London 1886.


§ 112. *St. Cœsarius, Archbishop of Arles (d. 542).*

1. *St. Cœsarius* was born of pious parents, about
470, at Chalons sur Saône, and studied for the priesthood at the monastery of Lerins. As his health became
enfeebled by the austerity of his life, the Abbot of
Lerins sent him to Arles, where, in 499, he was ordained priest by his relative, Bishop Æonius, whom
he succeeded in 502. As Bishop, he exercised a truly
Apostolic ministry by preaching, by attending to the
sick and prisoners of war, by promoting the divine

service, ecclesiastical discipline and monastic observance. Owing to the false accusation of some unscrupulous priests, among them his own secretary,
Cæsarius was, in 505, driven into exile, by Alaric,
King of the Visigoths, but recalled again as soon as the
King became convinced of his innocence. Somewhat
later, he was likewise accused of disloyalty to Theodoric, King of the Ostrogoths, but he completely
cleared himself of the charge. Pope Symmachus took
advantage of his presence at Rome to confer upon him
the pallium. Cæsarius held synods at Agde (506),
Epaon (517), Arles (524), and at Carpentras (527),
in which many important disciplinary decrees were
enacted. He also presided over the Synods of Orange
(529), and Valence (529), which reasserted against
the Semipelagians the Catholic doctrine of "gratia
præveniens, prædestinatio, libertas arbitrii," etc.
After thus laboring continuously and successfully
for a period of 40 years, Cæsarius died in the year
542.

2. The following of his works are extant, though
not yet gathered in a complete edition.

(a.) "Homiliæ," allegorical expositions of passages from the Old and New Testament.

(b.) "Sermones," on the feasts of Our Lord, on
matters of faith and morals, such as judgment and
penance, divine service, preaching, etc., or, again, discourses on various occasions and exhortations to
monks.

(c.) "Epistolæ tres;" two "ad Cæsariam abbatissam," and one "ad Oratoriam abbatissam," pointing out what are the duties and requirements of the
monastic life.

(d.) "Regulæ ad virgines et ad monachos." It is

noteworthy that in one of these rules even the nuns are commanded to copy books.

(e.) "Testamentum Cæsarii," in which he commends his monastery to the care of his successor.

(f.) "Liber de gratia et libero arbitrio," against the Semipelagians.

3. St. Cæsarius had a great veneration for St. Augustine, and, like him, drew his wisdom chiefly from the Holy Scriptures, on which he continually meditated. Among his writings, which have a practical rather than a speculative tendency, we must assign the first place to his sermons, which are simple and easy, yet full of life, power, and thought. The subjects are chiefly moral, but whether he treats of moral or dogmatic matters, his doctrine is always pure and orthodox.

We may quote the words of Ceillier: "Tout plaît dans les écrits de S. Césaire. Le stile en est uni, net et simple ; les pensées nobles, mais d'un tour aisé ; les raisonnements solides et concluants, les exemples persuasifs et toujours à la portée de ceux pour qui il écrivait" (l. c. XVI, 282).

*Editions and Literature.* — *Migne,* S. lat. LXVII, 997–1166. — *Ceillier* l. c. XVI, 226–284. — *Trischaud,* Histoire de S. Césaire, archevêque d'Arles. Arles 1853. — *Villevieille,* Histoire de S. Césaire. Aix-en-Provence 1884. — *Arnold,* Cäsarius von Arles und die gallische Kirche seiner Zeit. Leipzig 1894.

§ 113. *St. Benedict, Abbot and Founder of a Religious Order* (*d. 543*).

1. *St. Benedict* was born of a distinguished family at Nursia, in the year 480. For his higher education he

was sent to Rome. But the example and life of his school-fellows was such as to inspire him with horror and with fear for the salvation of his soul. For this reason, whatever other attractions for learning and piety the great capital of the world may have exercised upon his youth, he sacrificed them all. His soul yearned after God, and to His divine service he wished to consecrate himself and his life. In his twentieth year, he bade farewell to the city and retired to a wild and deserted spot at Subiaco, where, after the manner of the Egyptian hermits, he spent three years in prayer, mortification, and waging war with the powers of darkness. His retreat, however, was discovered by shepherds, and the fame of his sanctity soon spread abroad. In consequence, he was chosen superior of the monastery of Vicovaro. But finding the monks there quite incorrigible and even hostile, he soon abandoned the post and returned to his solitude. But it was solitude no longer. Men from everywhere, seeking his spiritual guidance, flocked to him in such numbers that in a short time he was able to establish and fill twelve monasteries.

For thirty-five years St. Benedict lived and labored at Subiaco, laying the first foundations of that wonderful Order and rearing that extraordinary race of men and women which is known in the history of the Church and civilization as "the Benedictines."

Owing to the senseless enmity and vexation of a neighboring priest, the Saint at last left Subiaco and went with a few of his companions to Monte Cassino, with its temple and grove of Apollo. The latter he destroyed and built in its place the famous monastery, which was ever after looked upon as the real cradle of his Order, because here he is said to have drawn up the Rule in its present form. Having converted the people of the neighborhood to the faith of Christ, he ended a life, grand in its moral beauty and rich in divine favors and blessings, on March 21st, 543, in his 63d year. He was not a priest, but was, as Mabillon states, according to a constant Benedictine tradition, a deacon.

2. Of the writings ascribed to him, the " Regula S. Benedicti " is certainly genuine, and has come down to us almost as it left his hands. It was explained and commented upon by many of the most pious and learned men, as St. Benedict of Aniane, the saintly Abbot Smaragdus, the monk Hildemar, Abbot Tritheim, Cardinal John Turrecremata, and the famous biblical scholar, Augustine Calmet. It ever was and still is the " Magna Charta " of the Benedictine Order and all its various branches. As a legislative code adapted to the requirements of human nature, it is in truth a masterpiece, and, taken in its entirety, provides a perfectly arranged method of life. In the 73 chapters of which it is composed, nothing needful or suitable for the right government of a monastery, or for the observance of a truly monastic life, is omitted. We subjoin a brief analysis of its contents.

CHAPTER I. Introduction, with an impressive exhortation to self-renunciation and generous following of Christ. Various kinds of monks.

II–IV. On the Proper Government of Monasteries.

V–VII. On the Requirements for a Life of Perfection.

While there cannot be any reasonable doubt as to the authenticity of the " Regula," the same cannot be said of the " Epistle " of St. Benedict to his disciple St. Maurus. Other writings ascribed to him by some, as the " Sermo in Placidum " and the " Epistola ad Remigium," are certainly of later origin.

3. St. Benedict was, in truth, " et gratia et nomine *benedictus*," one of the most favored saints of God. In founding his order, he gave the Church one of the noblest, most venerable and useful of its institutions, one, also, that has proved of immense importance to the world, by teaching the barbarians the arts of civilization, by the education of youth, and the preservation and diffusion of learning. His rule, written in the latinitas vulgaris of the time, and distinguished for clearness, prudence, and moderation, has earned for its author the honorable title of " Patriarch of the Monks of the West." St. Gregory, the Great, describes it as " discretione præcipuam, sermone luculentam." Nicholas of S. Germano closed his commentary on the Rule with the words: " Ut rosa flos florum, sic est liber iste librorum."

*Editions and Literature.* — *Migne*, S. lat. LXVI,
125–941. — *Ceillier* l. c. XVI, 284–311. —*Schmidt*,
O. S. B., Vita et Regula S. Benedicti, una cum expo-
sitione Regulæ a Hildemaro edita. Ratisb. 1880. —
*Woelfflin*, Benedicti Regula monachorum. Lipsiae
1895. — An English translation of the Rule, with explanatory notes, exists, by a monk of St. Benedict's
Abbey, Fort Augustus (London, Burns & Oates,
1886). — *Tosti*, Della vita di San Benedetto. Monte-
cassino 1892 ; translated into English by *W. R. Canon
Woods*, O. S. B., with a Preface by Bishop Hedley,
O. S. B., of Newport. London 1896. — See also *Montalembert*, The Monks of the West, vol. II, Bk. 4. —
*Brandes*, Leben Benedicts, Regel und Erklärung der-
selben ; 3 vols. Einsiedeln 1856–1858. — *Lechner*,
Leben des hl. Benedict. Regensburg 1859.

§ 114. *St. Gregory, Bishop of Tours* (*d. 594*).

1. *St. Gregory*, whose original name was Gregorius
Florentius, was born at Clermont, in the Province of
Auvergne, in the year 539. Having lost his father at
an early age, his uncle Gallus, Bishop of his native
city, took charge of his first education. After the
death of Gallus, St. Avitus, his successor in the see,
instructed him in ecclesiastical discipline and ordained
him deacon. Suffering from a bodily infirmity, he
went on a pilgrimage to the shrine of St. Martin, to
whom he had a great devotion, and sought his intercession. His prayer was heard. Twelve years later,
on the death of Euphronius, Bishop of Tours (573),
Gregory, being then thirty-four years of age, was
chosen both by clergy and people as his successor. It
was, however, only at the instance of King Sigebert of
Austrasia that he submitted to the election. He dis-

charged the duties of his episcopate in a spirit of great self-sacrifice, and extended the field of his labors even beyond the boundaries of his diocese.

Chilperic I., brother of Sigebert and king of Neustria, who desired to get the city of Tours into his own possession, showed him much ill-will, and the Saint suffered greatly by the false accusation of Queen Fridegonde. But never for an instant would he swerve from the just and honorable position he had taken, and in an assembly of bishops fully exculpated himself from the charges brought against him. He was most zealous for the purity of the orthodox faith and for the worthy celebration of the divine service. He held several disputations with Arians and Jews, he repaired many ruined churches, entirely rebuilt his cathedral and the church of St. Martin, and, despite his many and varied occupations, found time for literary work. The great anxieties and fatiguing labors which the episcopal office in so troublesome a time involved, brought his holy career all too soon to a close, on November 17th, 594.

2. He wrote the following works: —

(a.) "Historia Francorum," in 10 books. After a compendious account of the history of the world from its creation down to A. D. 400, the author proceeds to dwell at great length upon events from both the sacred and profane history of the Franks, thus providing us with our chief source of information as to the first beginnings of the Frankish Church and monarchy.

(b.) "De gloria martyrum," in 107 chapters, in which he relates the miracles of the martyrs of Gaul.

(c.) "De passione, virtutibus et gloria S. Juliani martyris," in fifty chapters, a continuation of the previous work.

(d.) " De gloria sive miraculis beatorum confessorum," in 112 chapters; a narration of wonderful events in the lives of the Frankish saints, with the greater number of whom Gregory had been personally acquainted.

(e.) "De miraculis S. Martini episcopi," in four books, showing how miracles prove the truth of the Catholic faith and help to strengthen our belief.

(f.) "De vitis Patrum," or "De vita quorumdam religiosorum," in twenty chapters, an interesting and instructive sketch of the wonderful lives and miracles of many saints who lived in or near Tours.

(g.) "De cursibus ecclesiasticis," an astronomical arrangement of ecclesiastical offices and lessons.

(h.) "Passio septem dormientium apud Ephesum," which the Saint with the help of a Syrian, translated into Latin.

3. St. Gregory of Tours was a learned and shrewd historian and a most exemplary bishop. By his History of the Franks he has rescued from oblivion the history of the infant Frankish Church and monarchy, and by his hagiography, the wonderful lives and deeds of many saints. Though his writings are open to the charge of credulity on the part of the author, and are not altogether free from errors, yet he was ever desirous of presenting a plain and accurate account of the events he describes. That all might understand, he used the simple and popular style of expression (lingua rustica), which often departs from the purity of the Latin language and constitutes, in reality, the transition-stage between Latin and French. This simple, natural, and unstudied style gives to his narratives a charm which effectively compensates for what might otherwise be considered a weak and defective style.

*Editions and Literature.* — *Migne*, S. lat. LXXI. —
*Arndt* et *Krusch*, Gregorii Turon. opp. 4°. Hannov.
1884–1885. — *Ceillier* l. c. XVII, 1–65. — *Löbell*,
Gregor von Tours und seine Zeit. 2 Aufl. Leipzig
1869. — *Ranke*, Weltgeschichte IV, 2, p. 328–368.

### § 115. *Venantius Fortunatus, Bishop of Poitiers* (*d. about 602*).

1. *Venantius Honorius Clementianus Fortunatus*
was born about 530 in a village near Treviso (Tarvis-
ium), in Northern Italy, and studied grammar,
rhetoric, and poetry with great success. He had no
taste for philosophy and theology, and but little for
jurisprudence. The great heroes of Christian literature were quite unknown to him. The following inci-
dent brought about a change in his life. Having been
cured of a painful distemper in the eye by anointing it
with oil from the lamp burning before the consecrated
altar of St. Martin of Tours, he made a vow to visit
the tomb of the great wonder-worker. About the year
565, he crossed the Alps and journeyed towards
Tours through the lovely and to him most attractive
provinces of the Rhine and Moselle. It was the
journey of a gay poet rather than of a devout pilgrim,
for his bright and amiable disposition and his talent
for improvising verses made him a welcome guest with
the wise and great at whose houses he rested. Thus he
came to be present at the nuptials of King Sigebert of
Austrasia and Brunhilda, and commemorated the event
by a happy poem. For nearly two years he remained
at the Austrasian court, in spite of the uncouth songs
and wild carousals that were customary there, and when
at last he made a new start for Tours, Sigebert provided

him with everything necessary for the journey. He visited every person of consequence, by whose estates he passed and repaid their ready hospitality by still readier poetical adulation. At last he reached Tours and there fulfilled his vow. After gaining the friendship of Bishop Euphronius and his nephew, he started in the gayest spirits on a tour through Southern Gaul, but a turning-point in his hitherto merry life occurred at Poitiers, where he visited two saintly nuns, Radegundis, widow of Clotaire II., King of the Franks, and her former attendant Agnes. At the earnest request of these two ladies, Fortunatus decided to make Poitiers his permanent place of residence, and after acquiring the requisite knowledge, was ordained priest and served as chaplain and secretary to the Royal Nun. The life of seclusion from the world pleased him daily more and more. Nevertheless, he kept up an active correspondence with St. Gregory of Tours and other men of high standing in Gaul. His name began to be held in great honor, and, in 599, on the death of Bishop Plato, he was nominated to the see of Poitiers, but died after a short episcopate, in the odor of sanctity.

2. The following of his works are extant: —

(a.) "Miscellanea, libri XI," a collection of more than 300 poems, mostly written for special occasions, and upon various subjects of either a spiritual or secular character; they comprise panegyrics, epigrams, epitaphs, epistles, and elegies. The tenth book begins with an "Expositio orationis dominicæ," and the eleventh with an "Expositio symboli."

(b.) "De vita S. Martini," an heroic poem, in four books, containing 2,243 hexameters.

(c.) "Libelli tres sive Carmen elegiacum de excidio

Thuringiæ," in which he strikingly describes Queen
Radegundis' grief over the ruin of her native country.

(d.) "Vitæ sanctorum;" the lives of 13 holy
bishops, written in plain prose, and a very detailed
life of Queen Radegundis.

His "Vita S. Saturnini" and many hymns for liturgical feasts are lost.

3. Fortunatus was indisputably a born poet. His
poems for special occasions display sportive gaiety,
charming simplicity, and attractive liveliness. He is
always original. His religious poems are distinguished
by deep piety, a surprising richness of ideas, and brilliancy of imagination, — merits which fully counter-
balance certain errors in prosody and grammar that
are to be found in them. Some hymns, such as:
"Vexilla regis prodeunt," "Crux fidelis, inter omnes
arbor nobilis una," . . . "Quem terra, pontus, sidera," and others, have been considered worthy
of insertion in the Office and liturgy of the Church.
The style of his prose writings, however, is heavy,
awkward and bombastic.

An epitaph on Fortunatus runs thus: —

> "Hac quoque præsenti præsul requiescit in aula,
>    Fortunatus enim vir, decus Ecclesiæ;
> Plurima qui fecit sanctorum carmina metro,
>    Concelebrans sanctos laudibus hymnidicis;
> Qui sermone fuit nitidus, sensuque fidelis,
>    Ingenio callidus, promptus et ore suo."

*Editions and Literature.* — *Migne*, S. lat.
LXXXVIII, 9-596. — *Leo* et *Krusch*, Opera Venan-
tii. 4°. Berol. 1881–1885. — *Ceillier* l. c. XVII, 84–
105. — *Kayser*, Beitr. etc. I. 386, sq. — *Hamelin*,
De vita et operibus Ven. Fortunati. Rennes 1873. —

*Caron*, Le poète Fortunat et son temps. Amiens 1884. — *Nisard*, Le poète Fortunat. Paris 1890. — *Kaulen*, in Wetzer and Welte's Kirchenlex. IV (2. Aufl.), 1628 sq.

## § 116. *St. Gregory, the Great, Pope (d. 604).*

1. Pope *Gregory I.*, surnamed the Great, was descended from a Roman senatorial family, and was born in 540. By the influence of his pious mother Sylvia, he devoted himself to the study of jurisprudence and in a special way to the study of the Latin Fathers. In 570, the Emperor Justin (the Younger) made him Prætor of Rome. Gregory discharged the duties of his office under the most difficult circumstances with great dignity and to the entire satisfaction of the Roman people. But the glory of earthly dignities and honors had, in reality, less attraction for him than the noble example of Cassiodorius, Chancellor of State. He therefore resigned his position, sold his possessions, and, having erected with the proceeds seven Benedictine monasteries, six in Sicily and one in Rome, he became himself a monk, about 575. But his monastic solitude was of short duration. Pope Benedict I., requiring his services, ordained him Cardinal-deacon of the Roman Church; and Pope Pelagius II., in 578, sent him as legate (Apocrisiarius) to the Byzantine court. By his tact and skill he succeeded, not only in removing all causes of friction between Emperor and Pope, but also in reclaiming the Patriarch Eutychius from the erroneous opinions of Origen. On his return, in 584, he again withdrew to his monastery, of which he was made Abbot, but still continued to assist the Pope by his

counsels, especially in the renewed dispute about the Three Chapters. In the year 590, at the unanimous and express wish of the Roman Senate, clergy, and people, but contrary to his own inclination, he was raised to the Chair of St. Peter, at a time when the general condition of the world presented a very sorrowful picture. Plague and famine were reigning in Italy, the Lombards were ravaging the land with fire and sword, the whole of the civilized world was shaking in its very foundations. But, by his energy, prudence, and gentleness, St. Gregory arrested the tide of destruction and prepared the way for a new and better era. Conscious of the immense responsibility of his position, he incessantly labored to do justice to it in every direction. Many and great were the labors and blessings of his pontificate. He made a supreme effort to completely suppress the controversy on the Three Chapters; he maintained a firm and dignified attitude towards the Lombards and the Byzantine court; he burned with great zeal for the spread of the Gospel, and sent St. Augustine with his 40 monks to evangelize the heathen Anglo-Saxons; he was unweary in promoting the monastic life and the beauty of the liturgy and divine worship; by word and example he aided the diffusion of learning, raised the standard of ecclesiastical life, and restored ecclesiastical discipline in Italy, Illyria, and the East. Nor was his social activity less conspicuous; his heart went out to the oppressed, the slaves, the poor, the widows and orphans, whose condition he tried to soften and alleviate by every measure in his power. Worn out by his great and incessant labors during a most troublesome epoch of the Church, and in his later years by severe illness, he died on March 12th, 604.

2. The following of his works are preserved : —

(a.) " Expositio in beatum Job sive Moralium libri XXXV," a moral and allegorical exposition of the Book of Job, wherein St. Gregory supplies principles, rules, and precepts for every state of life. Those who love an interior life may still read it with great advantage.

(b.) 22 " Homiliæ in Ezechielem" and 40 " Homiliæ in Evangelia" and a sermon " De immortalitate." These are unequal in merit, but still very valuable.

(c.) " Liber regulæ pastoralis sive de cura pastorali," an admirable instruction on the office of teacher, priest, and pastor, showing: (1) " qualiter ad culmen regiminis quisque *venire* debeat," (2) " qualiter *vivat*," (3) " qualiter *doceat*," (4) " quanta consideratione *infirmitatem* suam quotidie *cognoscat*."

(d.) " Dialogorum libri IV de vita et miraculis Patrum italicorum et de æternitate animarum." Owing to the many extraordinary and almost incredible stories narrated in these books, the authenticity of the Dialogues has often been called in question, although the writer is constantly appealing to eye-witnesses as his authority. The second book contains the life of St. Benedict, Abbot and founder of the Benedictine Order.

(e.) " Registri epistolarum libri XIV sive rerum a Gregorio gestarum monumenta." This is a collection of some 848 undoubtedly genuine letters of the Saint on various subjects. They are a splendid memorial of his genius and work, and are most valuable for contemporary history.*

---

* Venerable Bede (Hist. Eccl. Gentis Angl. I, 27) mentions an answer of St. Gregory to a series of questions addressed to him by St. Augustine of Canterbury. But this answer (Registr. XI, 4), says Bardenhewer (l. c. § 99, 2) is now almost generally considered as not genuine. (R.)

(f.) "Sacramentarium Gregorianum," "Liber antiphonarius et responsialis." The first is a collection of prayers for use in the administration of the sacraments and at holy Mass; the second contains the liturgical chants of the divine service.

(g.) Many hymns, some of which are to be found in the Divine Office, are ascribed to him, but their authenticity is not certain.

The following are doubtful: "Expositio in librum I. Regum" and "Expositio super cantica canticorum;" and the following spurious: "Expositio in septem psalmos pœnitentiales," and "Concordia quorundam testimoniorum S. Scripturæ."

3. St. Gregory is justly called "the Great." He was a man of extraordinary erudition and piety, and his influence and work were immense. His knowledge was truly *sacred* knowledge, and almost entirely of a practical kind. He drew it chiefly from Holy Writ, which he used to consider as an "epistola omnipotentis Dei ad creaturam suam."[*] The holy Fathers, too, he held in great esteem, especially SS. Ambrose, Augustine, and Gregory of Nazianzen, and the four General Councils he revered as the holy Gospels.[†]

---

[*] It may be well to record another passage of his which shows how intense was his love of Holy Scripture. "Stude ergo, quæso, *et quotidie* creatoris tui verba meditare. *Disce cor Dei in verbis Dei*, ut ardentius ad æterna suspires" . . . (lib. IV, Ep. 31). (R.)

[†] This saying of St. Gregory refers, of course, to the effectual authority of both, not to the cause or reason of that authority. The words of Scripture have divine authority, because the Scripture is inspired and has God for its Author. The dogmatic decrees of General Councils have divine authority, not because they are inspired, but because of the infallible divine assistance promised to them. (R.)

St. Gregory was great, too, in his humility. When the Patriarch John of Constantinople claimed the title of "Œcumenical Bishop" (ἐπίσκοπος οἰκουμενικός), St. Gregory chose that of "Servus servorum Dei." Nothing but the perfect consciousness and assurance of his superior dignity and position as Vicar of Christ could give him, under those circumstances, the courage to act like his Lord and Master. "Quis dubitet Constantinopolitanam Ecclesiam Sedi apostolicæ esse subjectam?" (Epist. lib. IX, 12.)

Furthermore he was as clear-sighted as energetic in asserting the Catholic principle, that in matters of religious conviction and conversion, no physical force or violence can be used. He severely blamed the bishops of Arles and Marseilles for having forced the Jews to receive baptism: "Dum enim quispiam ad baptismatis fontem non prædicationis suavitate, sed necessitate pervenerit, ad pristinam superstitionem remeans inde deterius moritur, unde renatus esse videbatur" (Epist. lib. I, 47). His zeal for justice and the political freedom of the people is shown by the words: "Terrestre regnum cœlesti famuletur" (Epist. lib. III, 65). "Quidquid agitis (reges et imperatores!) prius quidem servata justitia, deinde custodita per omnia libertate agere debetis. Scriptum est: 'Quod tibi non vis fieri, vide ne ipse alteri feceris.' Libertatem ergo eorum qui vobis in discussionem commissi sunt ut vestram specialiter attendere debetis; et si ipsi a majoribus vestris injuriari libertatem vestram non vultis, subjectorum vestrorum honorando libertatem custodite" (Epist. lib. X, 51). Gregory was not only great as a theologian, but also as a statesman in matters temporal, who knew how to grapple with the most difficult problems, and seldom failed in bringing them to a happy issue. Abbot Trithemius thus speaks of him: "Erat vir in divinis scripturis eruditissimus et in sæcularibus litteris utique doctissimus, theologorum princeps, splendor philosophorum et rhetorum lumen; vita et conversatione integer atque sanctissimus."

From his writings the student may learn the true nature of sacred eloquence, the knowledge of Holy Scripture, reverence for ecclesiastical authority, love and zeal for God and justice, in fact everything that appertains to the requirements of a perfect shepherd of souls. Granted that his writings are not quite free from traces of the depraved taste of his time, still they are always full of the spirit of wisdom and the fear of the Lord, and possess an unction not always to be found even in the more ancient Fathers.

With St. Gregory closes the period of the old Græco-Roman ecclesiastical literature; * St. Isidore of Seville forming the transition to the new period.

*Editions and Literature.* — *Migne*, S. lat. LXXV–LXXIX. — The newest edition of the Registrum Epistolarum is by *Ewald*, continued by *Hartmann*. 2. tom. Berolini 1891–1895. — The book on the Pastoral Care has been brought out in many separate editions and translations. For King Alfred's West-Saxon Version, with English translation, Latin text, notes and introduction, by *H. Sweet*, London 1871, see " *Publications of the Early English Text Society*," vol. XLV and L. For the Vita S. Gregorii by Paulus Diaconus,

---

* The position and influence of this admirable and probably the greatest of all Popes has been faithfully expressed by a French writer when he says that "The Middle Ages were born on the same day as Gregory the Great." (R.)

and another by Joannes Diaconus, see *Migne* l. c.
The oldest "Vita S. Gregorii," however, according
to Ewald, was written in England at the beginning of
the 8th century, but has not yet been published.
(See *Bardenhewer* § 99, No. 5.) — *A. Snow*, St.
Gregory the Great: his work and his spirit. London
1892. 8ᵛᵒ. — See also a series of articles on St.
Gregory's pontificate in the *Civiltà Cattolica* for
1890–1891, vol. V–IX. — Also *Montalembert*, The
Monks of the West, vol. II, Bk. 5.

### § 117. *St. Isidore of Seville* (*d. 636*).

1. *St. Isidore* was born about 560 at Carthagena.
After the early death of his parents, he received his
education and training for the priesthood from his
brother Leander, Bishop of Seville. Endowed with
great mental gifts and a thirst for learning, he made
himself master, not only of the Latin, Greek, and
Hebrew languages, but of almost every other branch
of knowledge, so that he may be said to have possessed an almost universal erudition. He was thus
fully equipped for taking up the defense of the Nicene
faith against the Arian heresy, then prevalent among
the Visigoths. For this reason, too, he was unanimously chosen, in 600, by both clergy and people, as
successor to his deceased brother, St. Leander, in the
see of Seville. As bishop, he zealously strove to
repair the evils caused by Arianism, by promoting
Church discipline among clergy and people, and
stricter observance among the religious; by erecting
monasteries and establishing houses of education.
But for the extirpation of abuses and heresies (Monophysites acephali) and the restoration of ecclesias-

tical discipline, he trusted above all to the action and
influence of synods. He held and presided over a
synod at Seville, 619, and another at Toledo, 633.
Before his death, he divided his property amongst the
poor, and, girt with the symbol of penance, with ashes
strewn on his head, and pouring out his soul in touching prayer, he expired on April 4th, 636, lamented by
people and clergy alike.

2. The following works are extant: —

(a.) "Etymologiarum libri XX." This most extraordinary work is a compendium, or rather an encyclo-
pædia, of all the known branches of sacred and profane
knowledge, beginning with grammar and ending with
treatises on ships, houses, clothes, domestic and agri-
cultural implements. The name is derived from the
author's curious etymological explanations of the
various subjects.

(b.) "Differentiarum, sive de proprietate sermo-
num, libri II." The first book, " De differentia ver-
borum," is a kind of dictionary of synonyms; while
the second, " De differentia rerum," is an explanation
of philosophico-theological terms.

(c.) " Allegoriæ quædam sacræ Scripturæ." Examples of allegorical interpretation of Scripture.

(d.) " De ortu et obitu Patrum, qui in Scriptura
laudibus efferuntur," in eighty-six chapters.

(e.) " In libros V. et N. Testamenti proœmia," a
general and particular introduction to Holy Scripture.

(f.) " Liber numerorum qui in sanctis Scripturis
occurrunt," in twenty-seven chapters, on the mystical signification of the numbers 1–60 occurring in the
Bible.

(g.) " De V. et N. Testamento quæstiones XLI,"
with answers.

operum factus est mundo, et ideo jam sine fine regnat cum Christo."

As St. John Damascene is the last of the Greek Fathers, so St. Isidore may fitly be considered as closing the list of the Latin Fathers.

*Editions and Literature.* — Sti. Isidori Hispal. Episc. opera omnia, ed. a *Faustino Arevalo,* S. J. 7 vols. 4°. Romæ 1797–1803. — *Ceillier* l. c. XVII, 621-651. — *H. Florez,* Esp. sagrada IX, 216–236. 394–419. — *Bourret,* L'école chrétienne de Seville (Paris 1855), pp. 59–193. — *Gams,* Kirchengesch. von Spanien (Regensburg 1874). Bd. II, Abth. 2, p. 102–113.

# CHRONOLOGICAL INDEX

## OF ECCLESIASTICAL WRITERS.

### WITH A LIST OF THE PRINCIPAL EDITIONS OF THEIR WORKS.

#### I. APOSTOLIC FATHERS AND THEIR WRITINGS.

"DOCTRINE OF THE TWELVE APOSTLES," Διδαχὴ τῶν δώδεκα Ἀποστόλων, Ed. *Bryennios.* Constantinople 1883. *Funk,* Doctrina duodecim Apostolorum. Tubingæ 1887.

BARNABAS, d. 76. (?)
CLEMENT OF ROME, d. 101.
IGNATIUS OF ANTIOCH, d. 107. (?)
LETTER TO DIOGNET.
HERMAS, (d. ?)
POLYCARP, d. 166.
PAPIAS, d. 160. (?)

Patrum apostol. opera gr. et lat. ed. *Cotelerius et Clericus,* 2 fol. Par. 1672 et Amstel. 1724. 2 fol. — *Dressel,* Patr. apostol. opp. ed. II. Lipsiæ 1863. — *Gebhart, Harnack, Zahn,* Patr. apost. opp. ed. III. Lipsiæ 1877. — *Funk,* Patr. apost. opp. omnia. Editio post Hefelianam quartam sexta. Tubingæ 1887. — *Hilgenfeld,* Hermæ Pastor græce e cod. Sinaitico. Lips. 1881.

## II. Christian Apologists of the Second Century.

| | |
|---|---|
| Justin, the Martyr, d. 167. | Corpus apologetarum Christianorum sæculi II., ed. *Otto,* 9 vol. 8°. Jenæ 1847–1872. — Justini opp. omnia et Tatiani Oratio, ed. *Prud. Maranus* O. S. B. fol. Venet. 1747. — Tatiani Oratio ad Græcos, ed. *Schwartz* Lips. 1888. — Athenagoras ed. *Schwartz.* 1891. |
| Tatian, the Assyrian, d. about 180. | |
| Athenagoras, d. about 180. | |
| Melito of Sardes, d. about 180. | |
| Theophilus of Alexandria, d. about 186. | |
| Hermias, d. toward 200. | |

## III. Ecclesiastical Writers of the Third Century.

Irenæus, Bishop of Lyons, d. 202. — Opera gr. et lat. ed. *Massuet* O. S. B. fol. Venet. 1734. — *Stieren,* Lips. 1853. — *Harvey,* 2 tom. 8°. Cantabr. 1857.

Pantænus, d. about 200. — *Migne,* S. gr. tom. V, coll. 1327–1332.

Clement of Alexandria, d. about 215. — Opera omnia gr. et lat. ed. *Potter,* fol. Oxon. 1717. — Only Greek: *Klotz,* 4 vols. 8°. Lips. 1831–1834. — *Dindorf,* 4 vols. Oxon. 1869.

Gajus, d. about 220. — *Migne,* S. gr. tom. X, coll. 17–36.

Julius Africanus, d. about 232. — *Routh,* Reliquiæ sacræ, ed. II, tom. II, 221–509. Oxon. 1840.

Hippolyte, Martyr, d. about 235. — *De Lagarde,* Hippolyti Rom. quæ feruntur omnia græce. Lips. et Lond. 1858.

Tertullian, d. about 240. — Opp. omnia ed. *Semler et Schülz,* 6 vols. 8°. Halæ 1769 sq. — *Oehler,* 3 B<sup>de</sup>. 8°. Leipzig 1853–1854. — *Reifferscheid et Wissowa,* in Corp. script. eccl. lat. vol. XX, pars I. Vindob. 1890.

MINUCIUS FELIX, d. ( ? ) — *Oehler*, Leipzig 1849. — *Halm*, in Corp. script. eccl. lat. vol. II. Vindob. 1857.

CORNELIUS, POPE, d. 252. — Epistolæ Rom. Pontificum ed. *Coustant*, fol. Paris 1721. — *Migne*, S. lat. tom. III, coll. 697–888.

ALEXANDER, BISHOP OF JERUSALEM, d. 252.—*Routh* Reliqu. sacr. ed. II, tom. II, 159–179.

ORIGEN, d. 254. — Opp. omnia gr. et lat. ed. *De la Rue*, 4 fol. Paris 1733–1759.

STEPHEN, POPE, d. 257. — Epist. Rom. Pontif. ed. *Coustant*. — *Migne*, S. lat. tom. III, coll. 1016–1046.

CYPRIAN, BISHOP, d. 258. — Opp. omnia ed. *Balusius* et *Prud. Maranus*, fol. Paris 1726. — *Hartel*, in Corp. script. eccl. lat. III. Vindob. 1868–1871.

NOVATIAN, d. about 262. — Opp. ed. *Jackson*, Lond. 1728.

DIONYSIUS OF ALEXANDRIA, d. about 264. — Opp. omnia gr. et lat. ed. *Sim. de Magistris* fol. Romæ 1796.

FIRMILIAN, BISHOP OF CÆSAREA, d. 269. — *Migne*, S. lat. tom. III, coll. 1357–1418.

GREGORY THAUMATURGUS, d. 270. — Opp. omnia gr. et lat. ed. *Vossius*, 4°. Moguntiæ 1604.

ARCHELAUS OF CASCAR, d. about 282. — *Routh*, Reliqu. sacr. ed. II, tom. V, 1–206. Oxon. 1848.

IV. ECCLESIASTICAL WRITERS OF THE FOURTH CENTURY.

PAMPHILUS, d. 309. — *Migne*, S. gr. tom. X, coll. 1529–1558.

METHODIUS OF OLYMPUS, d. 312. — *Migne*, S. gr. tom. XVIII, coll. 9–408.

PETER OF ALEXANDRIA, d. 311. — *Migne*, S. gr. tom. XVIII, coll. 449–522. — *Routh*, Reliqu. sacr. IV, 19–82.

ARNOBIUS, d. after 325. — *Reifferscheid*, in Corp. script. eccl. lat. vol. IV. Vindob. 1875.

LACTANTIUS, d. about 330. — Opp. omnia ed. *Le Brun et Lenglet Dufresnoy*, 2 vols. 4°. Paris 1748; denuo *Brandt et Laubmann*, in Corp. script. eccl. lat. vol. XIX. Vindob. 1890.

JUVENCUS, d. after 337. — Opp. ed. *Arevalus*, 4°. Romæ 1792. — *Huemer*, in Corp. script. eccl. lat. vol. XXIV. Vindob. 1890. — *Marold*, Leipzig 1886.

EUSEBIUS OF CÆSAREA, d. about 340. — Opp. omnia ed. *Valesius, Vigerus, Montfaucon, Mai*. — *Migne*, S. gr. tom. XIX–XXIV Præp. et Demonstr. evang. et Hist. eccl., ed. *Dindorf*, 4 vols. 8°. Lipsiæ 1867–1871.

JULIUS, P., d. 352. — *Coustant* l. c. and *Migne*, S. lat. tom. VIII, coll. 858–994.

HILARY OF POITIERS, d. 366. — Opp. omnia, ed. *Coustant et Maffei*, 2 fol. Veronæ 1730. — *Zingerle*, Hilarii tractatus super psalmos in Corp. script. eccl. lat. vol. XXII. Vindob. 1890.

ATHANASIUS, THE GREAT, d. 373. — Opp. omnia, gr. et lat. ed. *Montfaucon et Justiniani*. 4 fol. Patavii 1777.

BASIL, THE GREAT, d. 379. — Opp. omnia gr. et lat. ed. *Garnerius O. S. B.*    Par. 1721–1730.

EPHRAEM, THE SYRIAN, d. after 379. — Opp. omnia gr. et lat. ed. *Sim. et Steph. Assemani*. 6 fol. Romæ 1732–1746. — S. Ephraemi Syri Hymni et Sermones. Edidit, latinitate donavit, variis lectionibus instruxit, notis et prolegomenis illustravit *Th. J. Lamy*, 3 vols. 4°. Mechlinæ 1882–1889.

OPTATUS OF MILEVE, d. after 384. — Ed. *Du Pin*, Paris 1700. — *Ziwsa*, in Corp. script. eccl. lat. vol. XXVI. Vindob. 1893.

DAMASUS, P., d. 384. — *Migne*, S. lat. tom. XIII, coll. 109–442. — *De Rossi*, in Bollettino di Archeologia christ. 1884. p. 7–31.

CYRIL OF JERUSALEM, d. 386. — Opp. omnia gr. et lat. ed. *Touttée* O. S. B. 2 vols. Munich 1848–1860.

MACARIUS, THE ELDER, d. 390. — *Migne*, S. gr. tom. XXXIV, coll. 1–968.

GREGORY OF NAZIANZEN, d. about 390. — Opp. omnia gr. et lat. ed. *Clemencet* O. S. B. 1778. — *Caillou*, 2 fol. Paris 1840.

PACIAN OF BARCELONA, d. about 391. — *Migne*, S. lat. tom. XIII, coll. 1051–1094.

DIODORUS OF TARSUS, d. about 392. — *Migne*, S. gr. tom. XXXIII. coll. 1546–1628.

DIDYMUS, THE BLIND, d. about 395. — *Migne*, S. gr. tom. XXXIX, coll. 131–1818.

GREGORY OF NYSSA, d. after 395. — Opp. omnia gr. et lat. ed. *Fronto Ducaeus*, S. J. 3 fol. Par. 1638.

SIRICIUS, P., d. 398. — *Migne*, S. lat. tom. XIII, coll. 1131–1196.

AMBROSE, d. 397. — Opp. omnia ed. *Du Frische et Le Nourry*. 2 fol. Paris 1686–1699; aucta et emend. apud *Migne*, S. lat. tom. XIV–XVII.

V. ECCLESIASTICAL WRITERS OF THE FIFTH CENTURY.

EPIPHANIUS, BISHOP OF SALAMIS, d. 403. — Opp. omnia gr. et lat. ed. *Patavius*, S. J. 2 fol. Paris 1622. — *Dindorf*, 5 vols. 8°. Lips. 1859–1862.

SULPICIUS SEVERUS, d. about 410. — *Hieronymus de Prato*. 2 vols. 4°. Veron. 1741. — *Halm*, in Corp. script. eccl. lat. vol. I. Vindob. 1866.

CHRYSOSTOM, d. 407. — Opp. omnia gr. et lat. ed. *Montfaucon*, 13 fol. Paris 1718–1728.

RUFINUS, PRESBYTER, d. 410. — Opp. incompl. ed. *Vallarsi*. fol. Veron. 1745.

PRUDENTIUS, d. 410. — Ed. *Arevalus*, 2 tom. 4°. Rome 1789. — *Obbarius*, Tubingæ, 1845. — *Dressel*, Lips. 1860.

SYNESIUS, d. 413. — Opp. omnia ed. *Petavius*, S. J. fol. Par. 1640. — *Krabinger*, Synesii Cyrenæi orationes et homiliarum fragmenta. Landesh. 1850. — *Druon*, Œuvres de Synesius. Paris 1878.

JEROME, d. 420. — Opp. omnia ed. *Vallarsi*, 11 tom. 4°. Veron. 1766–1772.

THEODORE OF MOPSUESTIA, d. 428. — *Migne*, S. gr. tom. LXVI, coll. 9–1020.

AUGUSTINE, d. 430. — Opp. omnia ed. *Blampin*, *Coustant* et alii, 11 fol. Paris 1679–1700. — De Civitate Dei ed. *Dombart*, 2 vols. 8°. Lips. 1863.

NILUS, MONK, d. after 440. — *Migne*, S. gr. tom. LXXIX.

PAULINUS OF NOLA, d. about 431. — Ed. *Le Brun*, 2 tom. 4°. Paris 1685.

ISIDORE OF PELUSIUM, d. 440. — *Migne*, S. gr. tom. LXXVIII.

JOHN CASSIAN, d. 435. — Opp. omnia ed. *Alardus Gazœus*, fol. Atrebati 1628; denuo *Petschenig*, in Corp. script. eccl. lat. voll. XIII et XVII, Vindob. 1886–1888.

DIONYSIUS, THE AREOPAGITE. — Opp. omnia gr. et lat. ed. *Cordelerius*, S. J. 2 fol. Par. 1634. — *Migne*, S. gr. tom. III et IV.

CYRIL OF ALEXANDRIA, d. 444. — Opp. omnia gr. et lat. ed. *Aubertus*, 6 fol. Par. 1638 — *Migne*, S. gr. tom. LXVIII–LXXVII.

EUCHERIUS, B., d. about 449. — *Migne*, S. lat. tom. L, coll. 686–1212. — *Wotke*, Eucherii opp. omnia, pars. I. Vindob. 1894.

HILARY OF ARLES, d. 449. — Opp. omnia ed. *Salinas*, Rom. 1731. — *Migne*, S. lat. tom. L, coll. 1214–1292.

VINCENT OF LERINS, d. about 450. — *Steph. Balusius*, Par. 1663. — *Migne*, S. lat. tom. L, coll. 637–686.

PETER CHRYSOLOGUS, d. about 450. — Sermones ed. *Seb. Pauli*, fol. Aug. Vind. 1753.

PROSPER OF AQUITAINE, d. about 463. — Opp. omnia ed. *Le Brun et Mangeant*, O. S. B. fol. Paris 1771; emend., Venet. 1782. 4°.

SEDULIUS, d. 455. — Opp. omnia ed. *Arevalus*, Romæ 1794. — *Huemer*, in Corp. script. eccl. lat. vol. X, Vindob. 1885.

THEODORET OF CYRUS, d. 458. — Opp. omnia gr. et lat. ed. *Sirmond*, S. J. 4 fol. Paris 1642. — *Schulze*, 5 tom. 8°. Halæ 1769–1774.

LEO, THE GREAT, P., d. 461. — Opp. omnia ed. *Ballerini*. 3 fol. Venet. 1753–1757.

SALVIAN, d. about 490. — Opp. omnia ed. *Steph. Balusius*, 4°. Venet. 1774. — *Pauly*, in Corp. script. eccl. lat. vol. VIII, Vindob. 1883.

## VI. ECCLESIASTICAL WRITERS OF THE SIXTH AND SEVENTH CENTURIES.

ENNODIUS, d. 521. — Ed. *Sirmond* 8°. Par. 1611. — *Hartel*, in Corp. script. eccl. lat. vol. VI. Vindob.

1882. — *Vogel*, in Mon. Germ. hist. auctor. antiquissim. tom. VII. Berol. 1885.

BOETHIUS, d. 525. — *Migne*, S. lat. tom. LXIII–LXIV.—*Peiper*, Boethii Philosophiæ consolationis libri V, ejusdemque opuscula sacra. Lips. 1881.

FULGENTIUS, d. 533. — Ed. *Mangeant*, 4⁰. Paris 1684. — *Migne*, S. lat. tom. LXV, coll. 103–1020.

CÆSARIUS OF ARLES, d. 542. — Still incomplete. — *Migne*, S. lat. tom. LXVII, coll. 997–1166.

BENEDICT, FOUNDER OF THE BENEDICTINE ORDER, d. 543. —*Migne*, S. lat. tom. LXVI, coll. 125–941. — Regula ed. *Edm. Schmidt*, O. S. B. Ratisb. 1892.

CASSIODORIUS, d. 570. — Opp. omnia ed. *Duvallius*, 2 tom. Par. 1600. — *Garet*, O. S. B. 2 fol. Venet. 1729.

GREGORY OF TOURS, d. 594. — Opp. omnia ed. *Th. Ruinart*, O. S. B. fol. Par. 1699.

VENANTIUS FORTUNATUS, d. about 602. — Ed. *Luchi*, O. S. B. 2 tom. 4°. Romæ 1787. — *Leo* et *Krusch*, Opp. Venant. 4°. Berol. 1881–1885.

GREGORY, THE GREAT, P., d. 604. — Opp. omnia ed. *Gallicioli*, 17 vols. 4°. Venet. 1768–1776. — *Ewald Hartmann*, Gregorii I. Papæ Registrum epistolarum libri I–IX. 2 tom. Berol. 1891–1893.

JOHN CLIMACUS, d. 600. — Opp. omnia gr. et lat. ed. *Raderus*, S. J. fol. Par. 1633.

ISIDORE OF SEVILLE, d. 636. — Opp. omnia ed. *Arevalus*, S. J. 7 vols. 4°. Romæ 1797–1803.

SOPHRONIUS, d. 638. — After *Mai*, *Migne*, S. gr. tom. LXXXVI, coll. 3116–4014.

MAXIMUS, THE CONFESSOR, d. 662. — *Migne*, S. gr. tom. XC–XCI.

ANASTASIUS SINAITA, d. about 700. — *Gretser*, gr. et lat. 4°. Ingolst. 1606 et 1617.

JOHN DAMASCENE, d. before 754. — Opp. omnia gr. et lat. ed. *Le Quien*, 2 fol. Venet. 1748.

N. B. Further particulars as to the editions of ecclesiastical writers and references to the appertaining literature, are to be found in the " Répertoire des sources historiques du moyen-âge, par *Ulysse Chevalier*, Paris 1877-1886, and in the " Patrologie " of Dr. Bardenhewer, Freiburg, 1894.

# ALPHABETICAL INDEX.

(348)